COLLINS

GREEK

PHRASE BOOK

D1578810

■ HarperCollins*Publishers*

first published in this edition 1995

© HarperCollins Publishers 1995

ISBN 0 00 470866-0

A catalogue record for this book is available from the British Library

Typeset by Morton Word Processing Ltd, Scarborough
Printed in Great Britain by
HarperCollins Manufacturing, Glasgow

Introduction

Your **Collins Phrase Book** is designed to give you instant access to all the words and phrases you will want while travelling abroad on business or for pleasure.

Unlike other phrase books it is arranged in A-Z order to take you straight to the word you want without having to search through different topics. And its simple, easy-to-use pronunciation guide to every word and phrase will ensure you communicate with confidence.

At the bottom of each page there is a list of *ABSOLUTE ESSENTIALS* – the key phrases and expressions you will need in any situation. And between the two sides of your **Phrase Book** you will find further explanations of pronunciation, charts showing how to convert from metric to imperial measures and easy reference lists of *Car Parts, Colours, Countries, Drinks, Fish and Seafood, Fruit and Nuts, Meats, Shops,* and *Vegetables*. These pages have a grey border to help you find them easily and to show you where one side of the **Phrase Book** ends and the other begins.

And finally, in the comprehensive glossary at the end of your **Phrase Book** you will find over 4,000 foreign-language words and phrases clearly translated. So in one complete package you have all the benefits of a dictionary with the simplicity of a phrase book. We hope you will enjoy using it.

Abbreviations used in the text

adj	adjective
adv	adverb
Anat	anatomical
cm	centimetre(s)
conj	conjunction
equiv	equivalent
etc	etcetera
f	feminine noun
fpl	feminine plural noun
g	gram(s)
kg	kilogram(s)
km	kilometre(s)
l	litre(s)
m	masculine noun; metre(s)
m/f	masculine or feminine noun
mpl	masculine plural noun
n	noun
pl	plural noun
prep	preposition
®	registered trade mark
sing	singular
vb	verb

ENGLISH-GREEK

ENGLISH–GREEK

a	ένας	"enas"
	μία	"meea"
	ένα	"ena"
▷ a man	ένας άντρας	"enas andras"
▷ a woman	μία γυναίκα	"meea yeeneka"
abbey	το μοναστήρι	"to mona-steeree"
about:		
▷ a book about Athens	ένα βιβλίο για την Αθήνα	"ena veevlee-o ya teen Atheena"
▷ at about ten o'clock	περίπου στις δέκα	"pereepoo stees dheka"
above	πάνω	"pano"
accident	το δυστύχημα	"to dheestee-kheema"
▷ I've had an accident	είχα ένα ατύχημα	"eekha ena atee-kheema"
▷ there's been an accident	έχει γίνει ατύχημα	"ekhee yeenee atee-kheema"
accommodation	η στέγη	"ee ste-yee"
▷ I need three nights' acccommodation	χρειάζομαι στέγη για τρεις μέρες	"khreeazo-me steyee ya trees me-res"
ache	ο πόνος	"o ponos"
▷ my head aches	πονάει το κεφάλι μου	"ponaee to kefali moo"
▷ I've got a stomach ache	με πονάει το στομάχι μου	"me ponaee to stomakhee moo"
activities	οι δραστηριότητες	"ee dhrasteeree-otee-tes"
▷ do you have activities for children?	έχετε δραστηρι-ότητες για παιδιά;	"ekhe-te dhrasteeree-otee-tes ya pe-dheea"
▷ what indoor/outdoor activities are there?	τι δραστηριότητες κλειστού/ανοιχτού χώρου υπάρχουν;	"tee dhrasteeree-otee-tes kleestoo/aneekhtoo khoroo eeparkhoon"
adaptor	ο μετασχηματιστής	"o meta-skheema-teestees"
address	η διεύθυνση	"ee dhee-ef-theensee"

▷ **my address is ...**	η διεύθυνσή μου είναι ...	"ee dhee-**ef**-theen**see** moo **ee**-ne"
▷ **take me to this address**	σ'αυτή τη διεύθυνση	"s**aftee** tee dhee-**ef**-theensee"
▷ **will you write down the address, please?**	μπορείτε να μου γράψετε την διεύθυνση, παρακαλώ;	"bor**ee**-te na moo **ghra**-pse-te teen dhee-**ef**-theensee para-ka**lo**"
adhesive tape	η συγκολλητική ταινία	"ee seengo-leetee**kee** tenee-a"
▷ **I need some adhesive tape**	θέλω λίγο σελοτέιπ	"**the**-lo l**ee**gho selo-**te**-eep"
admission charge	η είσοδος	"ee **ee**so-dhos"
adult	ο ενήλικας	"o e**nee**-leekas"
advance:		
▷ **in advance**	προκαταβολικώς	"prokata-volee**kos**"
▷ **do I pay in advance?**	πληρώνω προκαταβολικά;	"pleer**o**no prokata-vol**ee**ka"
▷ **do I need to book in advance?**	χρειάζεται να κάνω κράτηση προκαταβολικά;	"khree**a**-ze-te na **ka**no **kra**teesee prokata-vol**ee**ka"
aerobics	αερόμπικ	"aer**o**beek"
after	αργότερα	"ar**gho**-tera"
afternoon	το απόγευμα	"a**po**-yevma"
aftershave	το αφτερσέιβ	"after-**se**-eev"
again	πάλι	"p**alee**"
▷ **can you try again?**	μπορείτε να ξαναδοκιμάσετε;	"bor**ee**-te na ksa-na-dhokee**ma**-se-te"
agent	ο πράκτορας	"o **prak**toras"
ago:		
▷ **long ago**	πολύ πριν	"pol**ee** preen"

▷ **a week ago**	πριν μία βδομάδα	"preen **mee**a vdho-**ma**dha"
AIDS	έιτζ	"aids"
air conditioning	ο κλιματισμός	"o kleema-tees**mos**"
▷ **the air conditioning is not working**	ο κλιματισμός δεν δουλεύει	"o kleema-tees**mos** den dhou-**le**vee"
air hostess	η αεροσυνοδός	"ee aero-seeno**dhos**"
airline	η αεροπορική εταιρία	"aero-poree**kee** e-teree-a"
air mail:		
▷ **by air mail**	αεροπορικώς	"aero-poree**kos**"
air mattress	το στρώμα για τη θάλασσα	"to **stro**ma ya tee **tha**lasa"
airport	το αεροδρόμιο	"to aero-**dhro**mee-o"
▷ **to the airport, please**	στο αεροδρόμιο, παρακαλώ	"sto aero-**dhro**mee-o para-ka**lo**"
aisle	ο διάδρομος	"o dhee-**a**dhromos"
▷ **I'd like an aisle seat**	θα ήθελα θέση στο διάδρομο	"tha **ee**thela **the**see sto dhee-**a**dhromo"
alarm call	η αφύπνιση	"ee a**fee**pneesee"
▷ **an alarm call at 7 am, please**	με ξυπνάτε στις 7 το πρωί, παρακαλώ	"me kseep**na**-te stees ef-**ta** to pro**ee** para-ka**lo**"
alarm clock	το ξυπνητήρι	"to xeepnee-**tee**ree"
alcohol	το οινόπνευμα	"to ee**no**-pnevma"
alcoholic	οινοπνευματώδης	"eeno-pnevma-**to**dhees"
all	όλος	"**o**los"
	όλη	"**o**lee"
	όλο	"**o**lo"
(*plural*)	όλοι	"**o**lee"
	όλες	"**o**les"
	όλα	"**o**la"

ABSOLUTE ESSENTIALS

I don't understand	δεν καταλαβαίνω	"dhen kata-la**ve**no"
I don't speak Greek	δεν μιλάω ελληνικά	"dhen meela-o elee-nee**ka**"
do you speak English?	μιλάτε αγγλικά;	"meela-te anglee-**ka**"
more slowly please	πιο σιγά παρακαλώ	"peeo see**gha** para-ka**lo**"

▷ **all the milk**	όλο το γάλα	"**o**lo to **gha**la"
▷ **all (the) boys**	όλα τα αγόρια	"**o**la ta a**gho**ree-a"
▷ **all (the) girls**	όλα τα κορίτσια	"**o**la ta ko**ree**tsee-a"
allergic to	αλλεργικός σε	"aler-yee**kos** se"
▷ **I'm allergic to penicillin**	είμαι αλλεργικός στην πενικιλλίνη	"**ee**-me aler-yee**kos** steen peneekee-**lee**nee"
allowance	επιτρεπόμενη ποσότητα	"epee-tre**po**-menee poso-**tee**ta"
▷ **I have the usual allowances of alcohol/tobacco**	έχω ότι επιτρέπει ο κανονισμός για οινοπνευματώδη/ καπνό	"**ekho o**tee epee-**tre**pee o kanonees**mos** ya eenopnevma-**to**dhee/ kap**no**"
all right	εντάξει	"en**tak**see"
▷ **are you all right?**	είστε εντάξει;	"**ees**-te en**tak**see"
almond	το αμύγδαλο	"to a**meegh**-dhalo"
almost	σχεδόν	"skhe**dhon**"
also	επίσης	"e**pee**sees"
always	πάντα	"**pan**da"
am:		
▷ **I am**	είμαι	"**ee**-me"
ambulance	το ασθενοφόρο	"to astheno-**fo**ro"
▷ **call an ambulance**	καλέστε ένα ασθενοφόρο	"ka**les**-te **e**na astheno-**fo**ro"
America	η Αμερική	"ee ameree-**kee** "
American *adj*	αμερικανικός	"ameree-ka**nee**kos"
▷ **I'm American**	είμαι Αμερικανός/ Αμερικανίδα	"**ee**-me amereeka-**nos**/ ameree-ka**nee**dha"
anaesthetic	το αναισθητικό	"to anes-theetee**ko**"
and	και	"ke"
another	άλλος	"**a**los"

ABSOLUTE ESSENTIALS		
I would like ...	θα ήθελα ...	"tha **ee**thela"
I need ...	χρειάζομαι ...	"khree-**a**zo-me"
where is ...?	πού είναι ...;	"poo **ee**-ne"
we're looking for ...	ψάχνουμε ...	"**psa**khnoo-me"

▷ **another glass of beer**	ακόμα ένα ποτήρι μπύρα	"**akoma ena** po**teeree beera**"
antibiotics	τα αντιβιοτικά	"ta andeevee-oteeka"
antifreeze	το αντιπηκτικό υγρό	"to andee-peekteeko eeghro"
antihistamine	το αντιισταμινικό	"to antee-eestameeneeko"
antiseptic	το αντισηπτικό	"to andeeseep-teeko"
any	καθόλου	"katholoo"
▷ **I haven't any**	δεν έχω καθόλου	"dhen ekho katholoo"
anyway	οπωσδήποτε	"oposdheepo-te"
anywhere	οπουδήποτε	"opoodheepo-te"
apartment	το διαμέρισμα	"to dheea-mereesma"
▷ **we've booked an apartment in the name of ...**	έχουμε κλείσει ένα διαμέρισμα στο όνομα ...	"ekhoo-me kleesee ena dhea-emereesma sto onoma"
aperitif	το απεριτίφ	"to aperitif"
▷ **we'd like an aperitif**	θα θέλαμε ένα απεριτίφ	"tha thela-me ena aperee-teef"
apple	το μήλο	"to meelo"
appointment	το ραντεβού	"to ran-devoo"
▷ **I'd like to make an appointment**	θα ήθελα να κλείσω ραντεβού	"tha eethela na kleeso ran-devoo"
▷ **can I have an appointment?**	μου κλείνετε ραντεβού;	"moo klee-ne-te ran-devoo"
▷ **I have an appointment with ...**	έχω ραντεβού με ...	"ekho ran-devoo me"
apricot	το βερύκοκκο	"to veree-koko"
April	Απρίλιος	"a-preeleeos"

ABSOLUTE ESSENTIALS

do you have ...?	έχετε ...;	"ekhe-te"
is there ...?	υπάρχει ...;	"ee-parkhee"
are there ...?	υπάρχουν ...;	"ee-parkhoon"
how much is ...?	πόσο κάνει ...;	"poso kanee"

are:

▷ **you are** (*informal singular*)	είσαι	"**ee**-se"
▷ **we are**	είμαστε	"**ee**mas-te"
▷ **you are** (*plural or formal singular*)	είστε	"**ees**-te"
▷ **they are**	είναι	"**ee**-ne"
arm	το μπράτσο	"to **brat**so"
armbands	τα μπρατσάκια	"ta brat**sa**-keea"
arrivals (*at airport*)	οι αφίξεις	"ee a**feek**sees"
to **arrive**	φτάνω	"**ftano**"
▷ **what time does it arrive?**	τι ώρα φτάνει;	"tee **o**-ra **fta**nee"
▷ **we arrived early/late**	φτάσαμε νωρίς/αργά	"**fta**sa-me no**rees**/ar**gha**"
art gallery	η πινακοθήκη	"ee peenako-**thee**kee"
artichoke	η αγκινάρα	"ee agee**na**ra"
ashtray	το τασάκι	"to ta-**sa**kee"
▷ **may I have an ashtray?**	μπορώ να έχω ένα τασάκι;	"bo-**ro** na ekho **e**na ta-**sa**kee"
asparagus	το σπαράγγι	"to spa-**ra**ngee"
aspirin	η ασπιρίνη	"ee aspee-**ree**nee"
asthma	το άσθμα	"to **asth**ma"
▷ **I suffer from asthma**	υποφέρω από άσθμα	"eepo**fe**ro a**po asth**ma"
at	σε	"se"
▷ **at home**	στο σπίτι	"sto **spee**tee"
Athens	η Αθήνα	"ee A**thee**na"
aubergine	η μελιτζάνα	"ee meleed-**za**na"
August	Αύγουστος	"**av**-ghoostos"
Australia	η Αυστραλία	"ee af-stra**lee**-a "
Australian *adj*	αυστραλέζικος	"afstra-**le**zeekos"

▷ **I'm Australian**	είμαι Αυστραλός/ Αυστραλίδα	"**ee**-me af-stra**los**/af-stra**lee**dha"
Austria	η Αυστρία	"ee af**stree**a "
Austrian *adj*	αυστριακός	"afstria**kos** "
automatic	αυτόματος	"af**to**-matos"
▷ **is it an automatic (car)?**	είναι αυτόματο (αυτοκίνητο);	"**ee**-ne afto-mato (afto-**kee**neeto)"
autumn	το φθινόπωρο	"to ftheeno-poro"
avocado	το αβοκάντο	"to avo-kando"
baby	το μωρό	"to mo**ro**"
baby food	οι βρεφικές τροφές	"ee vrefee-**kes** tro-**fes**"
baby-sitter	η μπειμπισίτερ	"ee baby-sitter"
baby-sitting:		
▷ **is there a baby-sitting service?**	υπάρχει υπηρεσία μπέιμπυ-σίτινγκ;	"ee**par**-khee epee-re**see**a baby-sitting"
back¹ *n (of a person)*	η πλάτη	"ee pla**tee**"
▷ **I've got a bad back**	με πονάει η μέση μου	"me po**nae**e ee **me**see moo"
▷ **I've hurt my back**	έχω χτυπήσει την πλάτη μου	"**e**kho khtee**pee**see teen **pla**tee moo"
back² *adv:*		
▷ **we must be back at the hotel before six o'clock**	πρέπει να γυρίσουμε στο ξενοδοχείο πριν τις έξι	"**pre**pee na ye**eroo**soo-me sto ksenodho**khee**o preen tees **ek**see"
backpack	το σακίδιο	"to sa**kee**dhe-o"
bacon	το μπαίηκον	"to **be**-eekon"
bad (of food)	χαλασμένος	"khalas-**me**nos"
(of weather)	κακός	"ka**kos**"
bag (small)	η τσάντα	"**ee tsan**da"
(suitcase)	η βαλίτσα	"ee va**leet**-sa"

ABSOLUTE ESSENTIALS

I don't understand	δεν καταλαβαίνω	"dhen kata-la**ve**no"
I don't speak Greek	δεν μιλάω ελληνικά	"dhen meela-o elee-nee**ka**"
do you speak English?	μιλάτε αγγλικά;	"meela-te anglee-**ka**"
more slowly please	πιο σιγά παρακαλώ	"**pee**o seegha para-ka**lo**"

baggage:

▷ **baggage allowance**	επιτρεπόμενο βάρος αποσκευών	"epee-trepo-meno **va**-ros apo-ske**von**"
▷ **what is the baggage allowance?**	πόσο βάρος αποσκευών επιτρέπεται;	"**po**so **va**-ros apo-ske**von** epeetre**pe**-te"
▷ **baggage reclaim**	παραλαβή αποσκευών	"pa-ra-la**vee** apo-ske**von**"
baker's	ο φούρνος	"o **foor**nos"
balcony	το μπαλκόνι;	"to bal**ko**nee"
▷ **do you have a room with a balcony?**	έχετε δωμάτιο με μπαλκόνι;	"**ekhe**-te dho-**ma**teeo me bal**ko**-nee"
ball	η μπάλα	"ee **ba**la"
banana	η μπανάνα	"ee ba**na**na"
band (*musical*)	η ορχήστρα	"ee or-**khee**stra"
bandage	ο επίδεσμος	"o e**pee**dhesmos"
bank	η τράπεζα	"ee **tra**-peza"
▷ **is there a bank nearby?**	υπάρχει τράπεζα εδώ κοντά;	"ee**par**khee **tra**-peza e**dho** kon**da**"
bar	το μπαρ	"to bar"
barber	ο κουρέας	"o koo**re**-as"
basket	το καλάθι	"to ka**la**thee"
bath (*tub*)	η μπανιέρα	"ee ban**ee**-era"
▷ **to take a bath**	κάνω μπάνιο	"**ka**no ba**nee**-o"
bathing cap	ο σκούφος του μπάνιου	"o **skoo**fos too ba**nee**-oo"
bathroom	το μπάνιο	"to **ba**nee-o"
battery	η μπαταρία	"ee bata**ree**-a"

to be:

I am	είμαι	"**ee**-me"
you are (*informal singular*)	είσαι	"**ee**-se"
he/she/it is	είναι	"**ee**-ne"
we are	είμαστε	"**ee**mas-te"
you are (*plural or formal singular*)	είστε	"**ees**-te"
they are	είναι	"**ee**-ne"

beach	η πλαζ	"ee plaz"
bean (*haricot*)	το φασόλι	"to fa**so**lee"
(*broad*)	το κουκκί	"to koo**kee**"
(*green*)	το φασολάκι	"to faso-la**kee**"
beautiful	όμορφος	"**omorfos**"
bed	το κρεβάτι	"to kre-**vatee**"
bedding	τα σεντόνια	"ta sen**do**neea"
▷ **is there any spare bedding?**	έχετε επιπλέον σεντόνια;	"**ekhe**-te epee**ple**on sen**do**neea"
bedroom	η κρεβατοκάμαρα	"ee krevato-**kamara**"
beef	το βοδινό	"to vodhee-**no**"
beer	η μπύρα	"ee **beera**"
▷ **a draught beer, please**	μία βαρελίσια μπύρα, παρακαλώ	"**mee**a va-re**lee**seea **beera** para-ka**lo**"
beetroot	το παντζάρι	"to pand-**zaree**"
before (*time*)	πριν	"preen"
(*place*)	μπροστά από	"bro**sta apo**"
to begin	αρχίζω	"ar-**khee**zo"
behind	πίσω	"**pee**so"
below	κάτω από	"**kato apo**"

ABSOLUTE ESSENTIALS

do you have ...?	έχετε ...;	"**ekhe**-te"
is there ...?	υπάρχει ...;	"ee-**parkhee**"
are there ...?	υπάρχουν ...;	"ee-**parkhoon**"
how much is ...?	πόσο κάνει ...;	"**poso kanee**"

belt	η ζώνη	"ee **zo**nee"
Berlin	το Βερολίνο	"to vero**lee**no"
beside	δίπλα σε	"**dhee**pla se"
best	ο καλύτερος	"ka**lee**-teros"
better (than)	καλύτερος (από)	"ka**lee**-teros (a**po**)"
between	μεταξύ	"metak-**see**"
bicycle	το ποδήλατο	"to pod**hee**la-to"
big	μεγάλος	"me**gha**los"
▷ **it's too big**	είναι πολύ μεγάλο	"**ee**-ne po**lee** me**gha**lo"
bigger	μεγαλύτερος	"megha-**lee**teros"
▷ **do you have a bigger one?**	έχετε ένα μεγαλύτερο;	"**ekhe**-te **e**na megha-**lee**tero"
bikini	το μπικίνι	"to bee**kee**nee"
bill	ο λογαριασμός	"o logharee-as**mos**"
▷ **put it on my bill**	βάλτε το στο λογαριασμό μου	"**val**-te to sto logharee-as**mo** moo"
▷ **the bill, please**	το λογαριασμό, παρακαλώ	"to logharee-as**mo** para-ka**lo**"
▷ **I'd like an itemized bill**	θα ήθελα λεπτομερή λογαριασμό	"tha **ee**thela lepto-me**ree** logharee-as**mo**"
bin	το καλάθι των αχρήστων	"to ka**la**thee ton akh**ree**-ston"
binoculars	τα κυάλια	"ta kee-**a**lee-a"
bird	το πουλί	"to poo**lee**"
birthday	τα γενέθλια	"ta ye**neth**lee-a"
▷ **Happy Birthday!**	να τα εκατοστήσεις!	"na ta ekato**stee**-sees"
birthday card	η κάρτα γενεθλίων	"ee **kar**ta yeneth**lee**-on"
bit:		
▷ **a bit of**	ένα κομμάτι	"**e**na ko**ma**tee"
to **bite** (*insect*)	τσιμπάω	"tsee**ba**o"

ABSOLUTE ESSENTIALS		
yes (please)	ναι (παρακαλώ)	"ne (para-ka**lo**)"
no (thank you)	όχι (ευχαριστώ)	"**okhee** (efkharee**sto**)"
hello	γεια σας	"ya sas"
goodbye	αντίο	"an**dee**-o"

bitten:

▷ **I have been bitten**   με δάγκωσε   "**me dhan**gose"

bitter   πικρός   "pee**kros**"

black   μαύρος   "**mav**ros"

blackcurrant   το μαύρο φραγκοστάφυλο   "to **ma**-vro frango-**staf**eelo"

blanket   η κουβέρτα   "ee koo-**ver**ta"

bleach   το λευκαντικό   "to lefkan-dee**ko**"

blister   η φουσκάλα   "ee foos**ka**la"

blocked (pipe)   βουλωμένος   "voolo-**me**nos"
(nose)   κλειστή   "klees**tee**"

blood group   η ομάδα αίματος   "ee o**ma**dha **e**matos"
▷ **my blood group is ...**   είμαι ομάδα αίματος...   "**ee**-me o**ma**dha **e**matos"

blouse   η μπλούζα   "ee **bloo**za"

blow-dry   στέγνωμα   "**ste**-ghnoma"
▷ **a cut and blow-dry, please**   κούρεμα και στέγνωμα, παρακαλώ   "**koo**-rema ke **ste**-ghnoma para-ka**lo**"

blue   μπλε   "ble"

boarding card   η κάρτα επιβιβάσεως   "ee **kar**ta epee-veeva-**se**os"

boarding house   η πανσιόν   "ee pansee-**on**"

boat (small)   η βάρκα   "ee **var**ka"
(ship)   το πλοίο   "to **plee**-o"

boat trip   η βαρκάδα   "ee var**ka**dha"
▷ **are there any boat trips on the river/ lake?**   γίνονται βαρκάδες στο ποτάμι/λίμνη;   "**yee**non-de var**ka**-dhes sto po**ta**mee/**leem**nee"

to **boil**   βράζω   "**vra**zo"

ABSOLUTE ESSENTIALS

I don't understand	δεν καταλαβαίνω	"dhen kata-la**ve**no"
I don't speak Greek	δεν μιλάω ελληνικά	"dhen meela-o elee-nee**ka**"
do you speak English?	μιλάτε αγγλικά;	"meela-te anglee-**ka**"
more slowly please	πιο σιγά παρακαλώ	"**peeo** see**gha** para-ka**lo**"

book¹ *n*	το βιβλίο	"to veev**lee**-o"
▷ **book of tickets**	δεσμίδα εισιτηρίων	"dhes**mee**dha eeseetee**ree**-on"
to **book**² *vb (room, tickets)*	κλείνω	"**klee**no"
▷ **the table is booked for eight o'clock this evening**	το τραπέζι είναι κλεισμένο για τις οχτώ το βράδυ	"to tra-**pe**zee **ee**-ne klees**me**no ya tees okh**to** to **vra**-dhee"
▷ **can you book me into a hotel?**	μπορείτε να μου κλείσετε δωμάτιο σε ένα ξενοδοχείο;	"bo**ree**-te na moo klee-se-te dhoma-**tee**o se **e**na xeno-dho**khee**-o"
▷ **should I book in advance?**	πρέπει να κάνω κράτηση προκαταβολικά;	"**pre**pee na **ka**no **kra**teesee prokata-volee**ka**"
booking:		
▷ **to make a booking**	κλείνω θέση	"**klee**no **the**see"
▷ **can I change my booking?**	μπορώ να αλλάξω το εισιτήριό μου;	"bo**ro** na a**lak**so to eesee**tee**ree-o moo"
▷ **I confirmed my booking by letter**	έκανα την κράτηση γραπτώς	"**e**kana teen **kra**tee-see ghra-**ptos**"
booking office *(railways, airlines)*	το εκδοτήριο	"to ekdho**tee**ree-o"
(theatre)	το ταμείο	"to ta**mee**-o"
bookshop	το βιβλιοπωλείο	"to veevlee-opo**lee**-o"
boot	το πορτ-μπαγκάζ	"to port-ba**gaz**"
boots	οι μπότες	"ee **bo**tes"
border *(frontier)*	τα σύνορα	"ta **seen**-ora"
both	και οι δυο	"ke ee **dhee**-o"
bottle	το μπουκάλι	"to boo-**kalee**"

▷ we'd like a bottle of mineral water	θα θέλαμε ένα μπουκάλι επιτραπέζιο νερό	"tha **thela**-me **e**na boo-**ka**lee epeetra**pe**zee-o **ne**ro"
▷ a bottle of gas	μία φιάλη γκαζιού	"**mee**a fee**a**lee gazee**oo**"
bottle opener	το ανοιχτήρι	"to aneekh**tee**ree"
box *(container)*	το κιβώτιο	"to kee**vo**tee-o"
(cardboard)	το κουτί	"to koo**tee**"
box office	το ταμείο	"to ta**mee**-o"
boy	το αγόρι	"to a**gho**-ree"
boyfriend	ο φίλος	"o **fee**los"
bra	το σουτιέν	"to sootee-**en**"
bracelet	το βραχιόλι	"to vrakhee-**o**lee"
brake fluid	το υγρό των φρένων	"to **ee**ghro ton **fre**non"
brakes	τα φρένα	"ta **fre**na"
brandy	το κονιάκ	"to konee-**ak**"
▷ I'll have a brandy	θα πάρω ένα κονιάκ	"tha **pa**-ro **e**na konee-**ak**"
bread	το ψωμί	"to pso**mee**"
▷ could we have some more bread?	μπορούμε να έχουμε λίγο ψωμί ακόμα;	"bo**roo**-me na **e**khoo-me **lee**gho pso**mee** a**ko**ma"
breakable	εύθραυστος	"**ef**-thraf-stos"
breakdown	η βλάβη	"ee **vla**voo"
breakdown van	ο γερανός	"o yera-**nos**"
▷ can you send a breakdown van?	μπορείτε να στείλετε ένα γερανό;	"bo**ree**-te na **stee**-le-te **e**na yera-**no**"
breakfast	το πρωινό	"to pro-ee**no**"
▷ what time is breakfast?	τι ώρα είναι το πρωινό;	"tee **o**-ra **ee**-ne to pro-ee**no**"
▷ can we have breakfast in our room?	μπορούμε να έχουμε πρωινό στο δωμάτιό μας;	"bo**roo**-me na **e**khoo-me pro-ee**no** sto dhoma**tee**-o mas"

breast	το στήθος	"to **steet**hos"
to **breathe**	αναπνέω	"anap-**neo**"
▷ he can't breathe	δεν μπορεί να αναπνεύσει	"dhen bo**ree** na anap**nef**see"
briefcase	ο χαρτοφύλακας	"o kharto**feel**akas"
to **bring**	φέρνω	"**fer**no"
Britain	η Βρετανία	"ee vretan**ee**-a"
▷ have you ever been to Britain?	έχετε πάει στη Βρετανία;	"**e**-khe-te paee stee vretan**ee**-a"
British *adj*	βρετανικός	"vretanee**kos**"
▷ I am British	είμαι Βρετανός/ Βρετανίδα	"**ee**-me vreta-**nos**/ vreta**need**ha"
broccoli	το μπρόκολο	"to **bro**kolo"
brochure	το φυλλάδιο	"to feel**adh**ee-o"
broken	σπασμένος	"spas-**men**os"
▷ I have broken the window	έσπασα το παράθυρο	"**es**pasa to para**thee**ro"
▷ the lock is broken	έχει σπάσει η κλειδαριά	"ekhee **spa**see ee klee-dhar**ee**-a"
broken down	χαλασμένος	"khalas-**men**os"
▷ my car has broken down	το αυτοκίνητό μου έχει πάθει βλάβη	"to afto-**kee**neeto moo ekhee **pa**thee **vla**-vee"
brooch	η καρφίτσα	"ee kar**feet**-sa"
brother	ο αδελφός	"o adhel-**fos**"
brown	καφέ	"kafe"
brush	η βούρτσα	"ee **voort**-sa"
Brussels	οι Βρυξέλλες	"ee vreek**se**-les"
bucket	ο κουβάς	"o koo**vas**"
buffet	ο μπουφές	"o boo-**fes**"

ABSOLUTE ESSENTIALS

yes (please)	ναι (παρακαλώ)	"ne (para-ka**lo**)"
no (thank you)	όχι (ευχαριστώ)	"**okhee** (efkhar**eesto**)"
hello	γεια σας	"ya sas"
goodbye	αντίο	"an**dee**-o"

buffet car	το βαγόνι εστιατόριο	"to va**gho**nee e-steeato**ree**-oo"
bulb (*light*)	η λάμπα	"ee **lam**pa"
bun	το ψωμάκι	"to pso**ma**-kee"
bureau de change (*bank*)	ξένο συνάλλαγμα	"**kse**no see**na**laghma"
to **burst**	σκάζω	"**ska**-zo"
▷ **a burst tyre**	σκασμένο λάστιχο	" skas-**me**no **la**-steekho"
bus	το λεωφορείο	"to leo-fo**ree**-o"
▷ **where do I get the bus to town?**	από πού μπορώ να πάρω το λεωφορείο για την πόλη;	"**apo** poo bo-**ro** na **pa**-ro to leo-fo**ree**-o ya teen **po**lee"
▷ **does this bus go to ...?**	πηγαίνει αυτό το λεωφορείο στο ...;	"pee-**yenee** afto to leo-fo**ree**-o sto"
▷ **where do I get a bus for the cathedral?**	από πού παίρνω το λεωφορείο για τη μητρόπολη;	"**apo** poo **perno** to leo-fo**ree**-o ya tee mee**tro**-polee"
▷ **which bus do I take for the museum?**	ποιο λεωφορείο πρέπει να πάρω για το μουσείο;	"**peeo** leo-fo**ree**-o **prepee** na **paro** ya to moo**seeo**"
▷ **how frequent are the buses to town?**	πόσο συχνά έχει λεωφορείο για την πόλη;	"**poso** see**khna e**khee leo-fo**ree**-o ya teen **po**lee"
▷ **what time is the last bus?**	τι ώρα είναι το τελευταίο λεωφορείο;	"tee **o**-ra **ee**-no to telef-**te**-o leo-fo**ree**-o"
▷ **what time does the bus leave?**	τι ώρα φεύγει το λεωφορείο;	"tee **o**-ra **fev**yee to leo-fo**ree**-o"
▷ **what time does the bus arrive?**	τι ώρα φτάνει το λεωφορείο;	"tee **o**-ra **fta**nee to leo-fo**ree**-o"
business	η δουλειά	"ee dhoolee-**a**"
▷ **I am here on business**	είμαι εδώ για δουλειές	"**ee**-me e**dho** ya dhoolee-**es**"

ABSOLUTE ESSENTIALS

I don't understand	δεν καταλαβαίνω	"dhen kata-la**veno**"
I don't speak Greek	δεν μιλάω ελληνικά	"dhen meela-o elee-**neeka**"
do you speak English?	μιλάτε αγγλικά;	"meela-te anglee-**ka**"
more slowly please	πιο σιγά παρακαλώ	"**peeo** seegha para-**kalo**"

▷ a business trip	επαγγελματικό ταξίδι	"e-pan-gelmateeko takseedhee"
bus station	ο σταθμός του λεωφορείου	"o stath-mos too leo-foree-oo"
bus stop	η στάση του λεωφορείου	"ee sta-see too leo-foree-oo"
bus tour	η εκδρομή με λεωφορείο	"ee ek-dhromee me leo-foree-o"
busy	απασχολημένος	"apas-kholee-menos"
▷ the line is busy	η γραμμή είναι κατηλειμμένη	"ee ghra-mee ee-ne kateelee-menee"
but	αλλά	"ala"
butcher's	το κρεοπωλείο	"to kreo-polee-o"
butter	το βούτυρο	"to voo-teero"
button	το κουμπί	"to koombee"
to **buy**	αγοράζω	"agho-razo"
▷ where do we buy our tickets?	πού αγοράζουμε εισιτήρια;	"poo aghora-zoo-me eeseeteeree-a"
▷ where can I buy some postcards?	πού μπορώ να αγοράσω καρτ-ποστάλ;	"poo bo-ro na aghoraso kart-postal"
by (beside)	κοντά σε	"konda se"
(time)	μέχρι	"mekhree"
bypass	η παρακαμπτήριος	"ee parakamteeree-os"
cabaret	το καμπαρέ	"to kaba-re"
▷ where can we go to see a cabaret?	πού μπορούμε να δούμε καμπαρέ;	"poo boroo-me na dhoo-me kaba-re"
cabbage	το λάχανο	"to lakhano"
cabin (on ship)	η καμπίνα	"ee kabee-na"
cable car	το τελεφερίκ	"to tele-fe-reek"

ABSOLUTE ESSENTIALS

I would like ...	θα ήθελα ...	"tha eethela"
I need ...	χρειάζομαι ...	"khree-azo-me"
where is ...?	πού είναι ...;	"poo ee-ne"
we're looking for ...	ψάχνουμε ...	"psakhnoo-me"

café	το καφενείο	"to ka-fe**nee**-o"
cake	το γλύκισμα	"to **ghlee**-keesma"
calculator	το κομπιουτεράκι	"to kombee-oote**ra**kee"
call¹ n (telephone)	το τηλεφώνημα	"to teele-**fo**neema"
▷ **I'd like to make a call**	θα ήθελα να κάνω ένα τηλεφώνημα	"tha **ee**-thela na kano ena teele-**fo**neema"
▷ **can I make an international call?**	μπορώ να τηλεφωνήσω στο εξωτερικό;	"bo-**ro** na teele-fo**nee**so sto ekso-te**ree**ko"
▷ **long-distance call**	υπεραστικό τηλεφώνημα	"eepe-ra**stee**ko teele-**fo**neema"
to **call²** vb	φωνάζω	"fo-**na**zo"
▷ **may I call you tomorrow?** (phone call)	μπορώ να σας τηλεφωνήσω αύριο;	"bo-**ro** na sas teele-fo**nee**so **av**ree-o"
calm	ήσυχος	"**ee**see-khos"
▷ **keep calm!**	ψυχραιμία!	"pseekhre-**mee**a"
camcorder	η βιντεοκάμερα	"ee veede-o-**ka**-mera"
camera	η φωτογραφική μηχανή	"ee foto-ghrafee**kee** meekha-**nee**"
to **camp**	κατασκηνώνω	"kata-skee**no**no"
▷ **may we camp here?**	μπορούμε να κατασκηνώσουμε εδώ;	"bo**roo**-me na kata-skee**no**-soo-me o**dho**"
camp site	ο χώρος κατασκηνώσεως	"o **kho**-ros ka-taskeeno-se-os"
	το κάμπινγκ	"to camping"
▷ **we're looking for a camp site**	ψάχνουμε για κάποιο κάμπινγκ	"**psakh**-noo-me ya **ka**pee-o camping"
can¹ n (of food)	η κονσέρβα	"ee kon-**serva**"
(for oil)	ο τενεκές	"o te-ne-**kes**"

can² *vb:*

I can	μπορώ	"bo-**ro**"
you can (*informal singular*)	μπορείς	"bo**rees**"
he/she/it can	μπορεί	"bo**ree**"
we can	μπορούμε	"bo**roo**-me"
you can (*plural or formal singular*)	μπορείτε	"bo**ree**-te"
they can	μπορούν	"bo**roon**"

▷ we can't come	δεν μπορούμε να έρθουμε	"dhen bo**roo**-me na **er**thoo-me"
Canada	ο Καναδάς	"o kana-**dhas**"
Canadian *adj*	καναδικός	"kana-dhee**kos**/ kana-**dheza**"
▷ I'm Canadian	είμαι καναδικός/ καναδέζα	"**ee**-me kana-**dhos**"
canal	το κανάλι	"to ka**nalee**"
to **cancel**	ακυρώνω	"akee-**rono**"
▷ I want to cancel my booking	θέλω να ακυρώσω την κράτησή μου	"**the**-lo na akee**roso** teen **kra**-tee**see** moo"
cancellation	η ακύρωση	"ee akee-rosee"
▷ are there any cancellations?	υπάρχουν καθόλου ακυρώσεις;	"ee**par**khoon ka-**tho**loo akee-**rosees**"
canoe	το κανό	"to ka-**no**"
▷ to go canoeing	κάνω κανό	"**ka**-no ka-**no**"
can-opener	το ανοιχτήρι	"to aneekh-**tee**ree"
car	το αυτοκίνητο	"to afto-**kee**neeto"
▷ I want to hire a car	θέλω να νοικιάσω ένα αυτοκίνητο	"**the**-lo na neekee-**a**so ena afto-**kee**neeto"
▷ my car has been broken into	μου διέρρηξαν το αυτοκίνητο	"moo dhee-**ereek**-san to afto-**kee**neeto"

ABSOLUTE ESSENTIALS		
yes (please)	ναι (παρακαλώ)	"ne (para-ka**lo**)"
no (thank you)	όχι (ευχαριστώ)	"**okhee** (efkharee**esto**)"
hello	γεια σας	"ya sas"
goodbye	αντίο	"andee-o"

▷ **my car has broken down**	το αυτοκίνητό μου έπαθε βλάβη	"to afto-**kee**neeto moo epa-the **vla**-vee"
carafe	η καράφα	"ee ka-**ra**fa"
▷ **a carafe of house wine, please**	μία καράφα κρασί χύμα, παρακαλώ	"**mee**a ka-**ra**fa krasee **khee**ma para-ka**lo**"
caravan	το τροχόσπιτο	"to trokho-**spee**to"
▷ **can we park our caravan there?**	μπορούμε να παρκάρουμε το τροχόσπιτό μας εδώ;	"bor**oo**-me na par**ka**-roo-me to trok**ho**-spee**to** mas e**dho**"
carburettor	το καρμπυρατέρ	"to karbeera-**ter**"
card	η κάρτα	"ee **kar**ta"
▷ **birthday card**	κάρτα γενεθλίων	"**kar**ta yene-**thlee**on"
▷ **playing cards**	τράπουλα	"**tra**-poola"
cardigan	το πλεκτό	"to plek**to**"
careful	προσεκτικός	"prosek-tee**khos**"
▷ **be careful!**	πρόσεχε!	"**pro**-se-khe"
car ferry	το φερυμπώτ	"to feree**bot**"
car number	ο αριθμός αυτοκινήτου	"o a-reeth**mos** afto-kee**nee**too"
car park	το πάρκινγκ	"to **par**king"
▷ **is there a car park near here?**	υπάρχει πάρκινγκ εδώ κοντά;	"ee-**par**khee **par**king e**dho** kon**da**"
carpet (*fitted*)	το χαλί η μοκέτα	"to kha**lee**" "ee mo-**ke**ta"
carriage (*railway*) (*transport of goods*)	το βαγόνι τα μεταφορικά	"to va**gho**nee" "ta meta-foree**ka**"
carrier bag	η σακούλα	"ee sa**koo**la"
▷ **can I have a carrier bag, please?**	μου δίνετε μια σακούλα, παρακαλώ;	"moo **dhee**-ne-te **mee**a sa**koo**la para-ka**lo**"

carrot	το καρότο	"to karoto"
to carry	κουβαλώ	"koo-valo"
car wash	το πλυντήριο αυτοκινήτων	"to pleenteereeo afto-keeneeton"
▷ how do I use the car wash?	πώς δουλεύει το πλυντήριο αυτοκινήτων;	"pos dhoolevee to pleenteereeo afto-keeneeton"
case	η βαλίτσα	"ee valeetsa"
cash[1] n	τα μετρητά	"ta metree-ta"
▷ I haven't any cash	δεν έχω μετρητά	"dhen ekho metree-ta"
▷ can I get cash with my credit card?	μπορώ να πάρω μετρητά με την πιστωτική μου κάρτα;	"bo-ro na pa-ro metree-ta me teen peesto-tee-kee moo karta"
to cash[2] vb:		
▷ can I cash a cheque?	μπορώ να εξαργυρώσω ένα τσεκ;	"bo-ro na eksar-yeero-so ena tsek"
cash desk	το ταμείο	"to tamee-o"
cash dispenser	η αυτόματη ταμειακή μηχανή	"ee afto-matee tameea-kee meekhanee"
cashier	ο/η ταμίας	"o/ee tamee-as"
casino	το καζίνο	"to kazeeno"
cassette	η κασέτα	"ee ka-seta"
cassette player	το κασετόφωνο	"to kaseto-fono"
castle	το κάστρο	"to kastro"
▷ is the castle open to the public?	είναι το κάστρο ανοιχτό στο κοινό;	"ee-ne to kastro aneekh-to sto kee-no"
to catch	πιάνω	"pee-ano"
▷ where do we catch the ferry to ...?	από πού παίρνουμε το φέρρυ για ...;	"apo poo pernoo-me to ferry ya"

ABSOLUTE ESSENTIALS

I would like ...	θα ήθελα ...	"tha eethela"
I need ...	χρειάζομαι ...	"khree-azo-me"
where is ...?	πού είναι ...;	"poo ee-ne"
we're looking for ...	ψάχνουμε ...	"psakhnoo-me"

Catholic	Καθολικός	"katho-lee**kos**"
	Καθολική	"katho- lee**kee**"
cauliflower	το κουνουπίδι	"to koonoo-**pee**dhee"
cave	η σπηλιά	"ee speelee-**a**"
caviar	το χαβιάρι	"to khavee-**aree**"
CD (*disc*)	το CD	"to CD"
celery	το σέλινο	"to **se**leeno"
cemetery	το νεκροταφείο	"to nekro-ta**fee**-o"
centimetre	ο πόντος	"o **pon**dos"
central	κεντρικός	"kendree-**kos**"
central station	ο κεντρικός σταθμός	"o kendree-**kos** stath**mos**"
▷ **where is the central station?**	πού είναι ο κεντρικός σταθμός;	"poo **ee**-ne o kendree-**kos** stath**mos**"
centre	το κέντρο	"to **ken**dro"
▷ **how far are we from the town centre?**	πόσο μακριά είμαστε από το κέντρο της πόλης;	"**po**so makree**a ee**-mas-te a**po** to **ken**dro tees **po**lees"
cereal (*for breakfast*)	τα δημητριακά	"ta dheemee-tree-a**ka**"
certain	βέβαιος	"**ve**-ve-os"
certificate	το πιστοποιητικό	"to peestopee-ee**tee**ko"
▷ **insurance certificate**	πιστοποιητικό ασφάλισης	"peestopee-ee**tee**ko as-**fa**lee-sees"
chain	η αλυσίδα	"ee alee-**see**dha"
▷ **do I need snow chains?**	χρειάζονται αλυσίδες για το χιόνι;	"khree**a**-zonde alee-**see**dhes ya to khee**o**nee"
chair	η καρέκλα	"ee ka**re**kla"
chalet	το σαλέ	"to sa-**le**"
champagne	η σαμπάνια	"ee sam**ba**nee-a"

ABSOLUTE ESSENTIALS

do you have ...?	έχετε ...;	"**ekhe**-te"
is there ...?	υπάρχει ...;	"ee-**parkhee**"
are there ...?	υπάρχουν ...;	"ee-**parkhoon**"
how much is ...?	πόσο κάνει ...;	"**po**so **ka**nee"

| **change**[1] n | η αλλαγή | "ee ala-**yee**" |
| (money) | τα ρέστα | "ta **resta**" |

▷ do you have change? έχετε καθόλου ψιλά; "**ekhe**-te **katholoo pseela**"

▷ sorry, I don't have any change συγγνώμη, δεν έχω καθόλου ψιλά "**seeghno**mee dhen **ekho katholoo pseela**"

▷ keep the change κρατήστε τα ρέστα "kratee-ste ta **resta**"

| to **change**[2] vb | αλλάζω | "a**lazo**" |

▷ where can I change some money? πού μπορώ να αλλάξω χρήματα; "poo bo-**ro** na a**lakso khree**-mata"

▷ can you change a 1,000 drachma note? μπορείτε να χαλάσετε ένα χιλιάρικο; "bo**ree**-te na khala-se-te ena kheelee-**areeko**"

▷ I'd like to change these traveller's cheques θα ήθελα να αλλάξω αυτά τα ταξιδιωτικά τσεκ "tha **ee**-thela na a**lakso** afta ta tak-seedhee-oteeka tsek"

▷ I want to change some pounds into drachmas θέλω να αλλάξω μερικές λίρες σε δραχμές "**the**-lo na a**lakso** meree-**kes lee**res se dhrakh**mes**"

▷ where can I change the baby? πού μπορώ να αλλάξω το μωρό; "poo bo-**ro** na a**lakso** to mo**ro**"

▷ where do we change? (clothes) πού αλλάζουμε; "poo a**lazoo**-me"

▷ where do I change? (bus etc) πού αλλάζω; "poo a**lazo**"

▷ can I change my booking? μπορώ να αλλάξω την κράτησή μου; "bo-**ro na** a**lakso** teen **kratee-see** moo"

| **changing room** (beach, sports) | τα αποδυτήρια | "ta apodhee-**teeree**-a" |

| **chapel** | το παρεκκλήσι | "to parek-**leesee**" |

| **charge**[1] n | η χρέωση | "ee **khre**-osee" |

▷ is there a charge per kilometre? υπάρχει χρέωση ανά χιλιόμετρο; "ee**par**-khee **khre**-osee ana kheelee-**o**metro"

▷ **I want to reverse the charges**	θέλω να είναι πληρωτέο από τον παραλήπτη	"**the**-lo na **ee**-ne pleero**te**o ap**o** ton para-**lee**ptee"
to **charge**[2] *vb*	χρεώνω	"khre-**o**no"
▷ **how much do you charge?**	πόσο χρεώνετε;	"**po**so khre**o**-ne-te"
▷ **please charge it to my room**	χρεώστε το στο λογαριασμό μου, παρακαλώ	"khre**os**-te to sto logharee-a**smo** moo para-ka**lo**"
cheap	φτηνός	"ftee**nos**"
cheaper	φτηνότερος	"ftee**no**-teros"
▷ **have you anything cheaper?**	έχετε κάτι φτηνότερο;	"**ekhe**-te **ka**-tee ftee**no**tero"
to **check**	ελέγχω	"e**len**-kho"
to **check in**	ο έλεγχος εισιτηρίων	"o e**len**-khos eesee-tee**ree**-on"
▷ **I'd like to check in, please**	θα ήθελα να κάνω τσεκ ιν, παρακαλώ	"tha **ee**-thela na **ka**no check in para-ka**lo**"
▷ **where do I check in for the flight to Rhodes?**	πού είναι ο έλεγχος εισιτηρίων για την πτήση για Ρόδο;	"**poo ee**-ne o e**len**-khos eesee-tee**ree**-on ya teen p**tee**see ya **ro**dho"
▷ **where do I check in my luggage?**	πού κάνω έλεγχο αποσκευών;	"**poo ka**no e**len**-kho apo-ske**von**"
▷ **when do I have to check in?**	πότε πρέπει να κάνω τσεκ ιν;	"**po**-te **pre**pee na **ka**no check in"
check-in desk	ο έλεγχος εισιτηρίων	"o e**len**-khos eesee-tee**ree**-on"
cheerio	γεια	"ya"
cheers! *(your health)*	στην υγειά σας	"steen ee-**ya**-sas"
cheese	το τυρί	"to tee**ree**"
chemist's	το φαρμακείο	"to farma**kee**-o"

ABSOLUTE ESSENTIALS

I don't understand	δεν καταλαβαίνω	"dhen kata-la**ve**no"
I don't speak Greek	δεν μιλάω ελληνικά	"dhen meela-o elee-nee**ka**"
do you speak English?	μιλάτε αγγλικά;	"meela-te anglee-**ka**"
more slowly please	πιο σιγά παρακαλώ	"**pee**o seegha para-ka**lo**"

▷ **where is the nearest chemist's?**	πού έχει φαρμακείο εδώ κοντά;	"poo **e**khee farmak**ee**-o **e**dho kond**a**"
cheque	η επιταγή	"ee epee-ta**yee**"
▷ **can I pay by cheque?**	μπορώ να πληρώσω με επιταγή;	"bo-**ro** na plee-**ro**so me epee-ta**yee**"
▷ **I want to cash a cheque, please**	θέλω να εξαργυρώσω μία επιταγή, παρακαλώ	"**the**-lo na eksar-yee**ro**so **mee**a epee-ta**yee** para-ka**lo**"
cheque book	το βιβλιαράκι επιταγών	"to veevlee-**a**rakee epee-ta**ghon**"
▷ **I've lost my cheque book**	έχασα το βιβλιαράκι των επιταγών μου	"**e**-khasa to veevlee-**a**rakee ton epee-ta**ghon** moo"
cherry	το κεράσι	"to ke**ra**see"
chest	το στήθος	"to **stee**thos"
▷ **I have a pain in my chest**	πονάω στο στήθος	"po**na**-o sto **stee**thos"
chestnut	το κάστανο	"to **ka**stano"
chewing gum	η τσίχλα	"ee **tseekh**-la"
chicken	το κοτόπουλο	"to ko**to**-poolo"
chickenpox	η ανεμοβλογιά	"ee anemovloy**ee**a"
child	το παιδί	"to pe**dhee**"
child minder	η νταντά	"ee da**da**"
children	τα παιδιά	"ta pedhee-**a**"
▷ **is there a children's pool?**	υπάρχει πισίνα για παιδιά;	"ee**par**-khee pee-**see**na ya pedhee-**a**"
chilled:		
▷ **is the wine chilled?**	είναι κρύο το κρασί;	"**ee**-ne **kree**-o to kra**see**"
chilli	η καυτερή πιπεριά	"ee kafte**ree** peeperee-**a**"
chips	οι πατάτες τηγανητές	"ee pa**ta**-tes teeghanee-**tes**"

ABSOLUTE ESSENTIALS

I would like ...	θα ήθελα ...	"tha **ee**thela"
I need ...	χρειάζομαι ...	"khree-**a**zo-me"
where is ...?	πού είναι ...;	"poo **ee**-ne"
we're looking for ...	ψάχνουμε ...	"**psa**khnoo-me"

chocolate	η σοκολάτα	"ee soko-**lata**"
▷ **I'd like a bar of chocolate, please**	θα ήθελα μία σοκολάτα, παρακαλώ	"tha **ee**-thela **mee**a soko-**lata** para-ka**lo**"
chocolates	τα σοκολατάκια	"ta soko-**latakeea**"
chop	η μπριζόλα	"ee bree**zola**"
▷ **a pork/lamb chop**	μία χοιρινή/αρνίσια μπριζόλα	"**mee**a kheeree-**nee**/ar-**nee**seea bree**zola**"
Christmas	τα Χριστούγεννα	"ta khree**stoo**-yena"
▷ **Merry Christmas!**	Καλά Χριστούγεννα!	"ka**la** khree**stoo**-yena"
church	η εκκλησία	"ee eklee**see**-a"
▷ **where is the nearest church?**	πού είναι η πιο κοντινή εκκλησία;	"poo **ee**-ne ee pee**o** kondee-**nee** eklee**see**-a"
▷ **where is there a Protestant/Catholic church?**	πού υπάρχει εκκλησία διαμαρτυρομένων/ καθολικών	"poo ee**par**-khee eklee**see**-a dhee-amarteero-**me**non/ katho-lee**kon**"
cider	ο μηλίτης	"o mee**lee**tees"
cigar	το πούρο	"to **poo**ro"
cigarette	το τσιγάρο	"to tsee-**gha**ro"
▷ **a packet of cigarettes, please**	ένα κουτί τσιγάρα, παρακαλώ	"**ena** koo**tee** tsee-**gha**ra para-ka**lo**"
cigarette papers	το τσιγαρόχαρτο	"to tsee-gha**ro**-kharto"
cinema	ο κινηματογράφος	"o keeneema-to**ghra**fos"
▷ **which film is on at the cinema?**	ποια ταινία παίζει ο κινηματογράφος;	"**pee**a te**nee**-a **pe**zee o keeneema-to**ghra**fos"
circus	το τσίρκο	"to **tseer**ko"
city	η πόλη	"ee **po**lee"
clean¹ *adj*	καθαρός	"katha-**ros**"
▷ **the room isn't clean**	το δωμάτιο δεν είναι καθαρό	"to dho**ma**-teeo dhen **ee**-ne katha-**ro**"

cleaner

6

English	Greek	Pronunciation
▷ could I have a clean spoon/fork please?	μπορώ να έχω ένα καθαρό κουτάλι/πηρούνι, παρακαλώ;	"bo-**ro** na **e**kho **e**na katha-**ro** koo**ta**lee/peeroonee para-ka**lo**"
to **clean**² vb	καθαρίζω	"katha-**ree**zo"
▷ where can I get this skirt cleaned?	πού μπορούν να μου καθαρίσουν αυτή τη φούστα;	"poo bo**roon** na moo katha-**ree**soon af**tee** tee **foo**sta"
cleaner	η καθαρίστρια	"ee katha-**ree**stree-a"
▷ which day does the cleaner come?	ποια μέρα έρχεται η καθαρίστρια;	"pee**a me**ra **er**-khe-te ee katha-**ree**stree-a"
cleansing cream	η κρέμα καθαρισμού	"ee **kre**ma katha-rees**moo**"
client	ο πελάτης	"o pe**la**-tees"
	η πελάτισσα	"ee pe**la**-teesa"
cliff	η πλαγιά	"ee playee-**a**"
climbing	η ορειβασία	"ee oree-va**see**-a"
climbing boots	οι μπότες ορειβασίας	"ee **bo**-tes oree-va**see**-as"
cloakroom	η γκαρνταρόμπα	"ee garda-**ro**ba"
clock	το ρολόι	"to ro**lo**-ee"
close¹ adj (near)	κοντινός	"kondee-**nos**"
(weather)	αποπνιχτικός	"apopnee-khtee**kos**"
to **close**² vb	κλείνω	"**klee**no"
▷ what time do the shops close?	τι ώρα κλείνουν τα μαγαζιά;	"tee **o**-ra **klee**noon ta maghazee-**a**"
▷ the door will not close	η πόρτα δεν κλείνει	"ee **por**ta dhen k**lee**nee"
closed	κλειστός	"klees**tos**"
cloth	το ύφασμα	"to **ee**fasma"
clothes	τα ρούχα	"ta **roo**kha"
clothes pegs	το μανταλάκι	"to manda-**la**khee"

ABSOLUTE ESSENTIALS

yes (please)	ναι (παρακαλώ)	"ne (para-ka**lo**)"
no (thank you)	όχι (ευχαριστώ)	"**o**khee (efkharees**to**)"
hello	γεια σας	"ya sas"
goodbye	αντίο	"an**dee**-o"

cloudy	συννεφιασμένος	"seenefeea-smenos"
cloves	το γαρύφαλλο	"to gharee-falo"
club	η λέσχη	"ee leskhee"
(for golf)	το μπαστούνι του γκολφ	"to bastoonee too golf"
(night club)	το νυχτερινό κέντρο	"to neekhte-reeno kendro"
coach (railway)	το βαγόνι	"to vaghonee"
(bus)	το πούλμαν	"to poolman"
(instructor)	ο προπονητής	"o propo-neetees"
▷ when does the coach leave in the morning?	πότε φεύγει το πούλμαν το πρωί;	"po-te fevyee to poolman to proee"
coach station	ο σταθμός λεωφορείων	"o stathmos leo- foree-on"
coach trip	το ταξίδι με πούλμαν	"to tak-seedhee me poolman"
coast	οι ακτές	"ee ak-tes"
coastguard	η ακτοφυλακή	"ee akto-feelakee"
coat	το παλτό	"to palto"
coat hanger	η κρεμάστρα	"ee krema-stra"
cockroach	η κατσαρίδα	"ee katsareedha"
cocktail	το κοκτέιλ	"to kokte-eel"
cocoa	το κακάο	"to kaka-o"
coconut	η καρύδα	"ee kareedha"
coffee	ο καφές	"o ka-fes"
▷ white coffee	καφές με γάλα	"ka-fes me ghala"
▷ black coffee	σκέτος καφές	"sketos ka-fes"
coin	το νόμισμα	"to nomees-ma"
▷ what coins do I need?	τι νομίσματα χρειάζομαι;	"tee nomees-mata khree-azo-me"

ABSOLUTE ESSENTIALS

I don't understand	δεν καταλαβαίνω	"dhen kata-laveno"
I don't speak Greek	δεν μιλάω ελληνικά	"dhen meela-o elee-neeka"
do you speak English?	μιλάτε αγγλικά;	"meela-te anglee-ka"
more slowly please	πιο σιγά παρακαλώ	"peeo seegha para-kalo"

Coke®	η Κόκα Κόλα	"ee **koka kola**"
colander	το σουρωτήρι	"to sooro-**teeree**"
cold¹ *n*	το κρύο	"to **kreeo**"
▷ **I have a cold**	είμαι κρυωμένος	"**ee**-me kree-o-**me**nos"
cold² *adj*	κρύος	"**kree**os"
▷ **I'm cold**	κρυώνω	"kree-**ono**"
▷ **will it be cold tonight?**	θα κάνει κρύο απόψε;	"tha **kanee kree**-o apop-se"

Cologne:

▷ **(eau de) Cologne**	η κολώνια	"ee kolo**neea**"
colour	το χρώμα	"to **khroma**"
▷ **I don't like the colour**	δεν μου αρέσει το χρώμα	"dhen moo a-**resee** to **khro**ma"
▷ **do you have it in another colour?**	το έχετε σε άλλο χρώμα;	"to ekhe-te se **a**-lo **khro**ma"
▷ **I need a colour film for this camera**	θέλω ένα έγχρωμο φιλμ για αυτή τη μηχανή	"**the**-lo ena **en**-khromo film ya af**tee** tee meekha**nee**"
▷ **colour TV**	έγχρωμη τηλεόραση	"**en**-khromee teele-**ora**see"
comb	η χτένα	"ee **khte**na"
to **come**	έρχομαι	"**erkho**-me"
▷ **come in!**	ελάτε μέσα!	"ela-te **me**-sa"
to **come back**	γυρίζω	"yee-**reezo**"
comfortable	αναπαυτικός	"anapaf-tee**kos**"
commission	η προμήθεια;	"ee pro**mee**-theea"
▷ **how much commission do you charge?**	πόση προμήθεια κρατάτε	"**posee** pro**mee**-theea krata-te"
compact disc player	η συσκευή CD	"ee seeske**vee** CD"

company (*firm*)	η εταιρεία	"ee etereea"
compartment (*train*)	το βαγόνι	"to vaghonee"
▷ **I would like a seat in a non-smoking compartment**	θα ήθελα μία θέση σε βαγόνι μη καπνιστών	"tha ee-thela meea thesee se vaghonee mee kapnee-ston"
to **complain**	παραπονιέμαι	"para-ponee-e-me"
▷ **I want to complain about the service** (*in shop etc*)	θέλω να διαμαρτυρηθώ για την εξυπηρέτηση	"the-lo na dee-amartee-reetho ya teen eksee-peeretee-see"
comprehensive insurance cover	η πλήρης ασφαλιστική κάλυψη	"ee pleerees asfalee-stee-kee kalee-psee"
▷ **how much extra is comprehensive insurance cover?**	πόσο επιπλέον κοστίζει μία πλήρης ασφαλιστική κάλυψη;	"poso epee-ple-on kostee-zee meea pleerees asfalee-stee-kee kalee-psee"
compulsory	υποχρεωτικός	"eepokhre-oteekos"
computer	ο υπολογιστής	"o eepolo-gheestees"
concert	η συναυλία	"ee seenavlee-a"
condensed milk	το συμπυκνωμένο γάλα	"to seembeekno-meno ghala"
condition	η κατάσταση	"ee kata-slasee"
conditioner	το κοντίσιονερ	"to kondeesee-oner"
condom	το προφυλακτικό	"to pro-feelakteeko"
▷ **a packet of condoms**	ένα κουτί προφυλακτικά	"ena kootee pro-feelakteeka"
conductor (*in bus*)	ο εισπράκτορας	"o ees- praktoras"
conference	το συνέδριο	"to seenedhree-o"
confession (*religious*)	η εξομολόγηση	"ee eksomolo-yeesee"
to **confirm**	επιβεβαιώνω	"epee-veve-ono"

congratulations!	συγχαρητήρια!	"seenkharee-**tee**ree-a"
connection (*trains etc*)	η ανταπόκριση	"ee anda-**po**kreesee"
▷ **I missed my connection**	έχασα την ανταπόκριση	"**e**khasa teen anda-**po**kreesee"
constipated:		
▷ **to be constipated**	έχω δυσκοιλιότητα	"**e**kho dheeskelee-**o**teeta"
consulate	το προξενείο	"to proksenee-o"
▷ **where is the British/ American consulate?**	πού είναι το βρετανικό/ αμερικανικό προξενείο;	"poo **ee**-ne to vretanee**ko**/ameree-kanee**ko** proksenee-o"
to **contact**	επικοινωνώ	"epeekee-no**no**"
▷ **where can I contact you?**	πού μπορώ να σας βρω;	"poo bo-**ro** na sas vro"
contact lenses	οι φακοί επαφής	"ee fa**kee** epa- **fees**"
▷ **hard contact lenses**	σκληροί φακοί επαφής	"sklee**ree** fa**kee** epa-**fees**"
▷ **soft contact lenses**	μαλακοί φακοί επαφής	"mala**kee** fa**kee** epa-**fees**"
contact lens cleaner	το υγρό καθαρισμού φακών επαφής	"to eeghro katha-rees**moo** fak**on** epa-**fees**"
continental breakfast	το ευρωπαϊκό πρόγευμα	"to evropa-ee**ko** pro-yevma"
contraceptives	τα αντισυλληπτικά	"ta andeesee- leeptee**ka**"
controls	οι διακόπτες	"ee dheea-**kop**tes"
▷ **how do I operate the controls?**	πώς λειτουργούν τα κουμπιά;	"pos leetoor-**ghoon** ta koombee-**a**"
to **cook**	μαγειρεύω	"mayee-**re**vo"
cooker	η κουζίνα	"ee koo-**zee**na"

▷ **how does the cooker work?**	πώς δουλεύει η κουζίνα;	"pos dhoo-**levee** ee koo-**zeena**"
cool	δροσερός	"dhro-**seros**"
copy[1] *n*	το αντίγραφο	"to andee-ghrafo"
to **copy**[2] *vb*	αντιγράφω	"andee-**ghrafo**"
▷ **I want to copy this document**	θέλω να αντιγράψω αυτό το έγγραφο	"**the**-lo na antee-**ghrapso** **afto** to **en**-grafo"
corkscrew	το τιρμπουσόν	"to teer-boo**son**"
corn (*sweet corn*)	το καλαμπόκι	"to kala-**bokee**"
▷ **corn on the cob**	ψητό καλαμπόκι	"psee**to** kala-**bokee**"
corner	η γωνία	"ee ghonee-a"
▷ **it's round the corner**	είναι στη γωνία	"**ee**-ne stee ghonee-a"
cornflakes	τα κορνφλέικς	"ta cornflakes"
cortisone	η κορτιζόνη	"ee korteezonee"
cosmetics	τα καλλυντικά	"ta kaleen-deeka"
to **cost**	στοιχίζω	"stee-**kheez**o"
▷ **how much does it cost to get in?**	πόσο κάνει η είσοδος;	"**poso kanee** ee eeso-dhos"
▷ **how much does that cost?**	πόσο κάνει αυτό;	"**poso kanee** afto"
cot	η κούνια μωρού	"ee **koo**neea moroo"
▷ **do you have a cot for the baby?**	έχετε κούνια για μωρό;	"ekhe-te **koo**neea ya moro"
cotton	το βαμβάκι	"to vam**vak**ee"
cotton wool	το βαμβάκι	"to vam**vak**ee"
couchette	η κουκέτα	"ee koo-**keta**"
▷ **I want to reserve a couchette**	θέλω να κλείσω μία κουκέτα	"**the**-lo na **klee**so **mee**a kooketa"
cough	ο βήχας	"o **vee**khas"
▷ **I have a cough**	έχω βήχα	"**ekho vee**kha"

▷ **do you have any cough mixture?**	έχετε σιρόπι για το βήχα;	"**ekhe**-te see**ro**pee ya to **veek**ha"
country (*nation*) (*not town*)	η χώρα η εξοχή	"ee **kho**ra" "ee ek-so**khee**"
couple	το ζευγάρι	"to zev-**gha**ree"
courgette	το κολοκυθάκι	"to kolokee-**tha**kee"
courier (*for tourists*)	ο/η συνοδός	"o/ee seen-o**dhos**"
▷ **I want to send this by courier**	θέλω να στείλω αυτό κούριερ	"**the**-lo na **stee**lo afto courier"
course (*meal*)	το πιάτο	"to pee-**a**to"
cover charge	το κουβέρ	"to koo**ver**"
crab	το καβούρι	"to ka-**voo**ree"
cramp	η κράμπα	"ee **kram**ba"
▷ **I've got cramp (in my leg)**	με έπιασε κράμπα (στο πόδι μου)	"me **e**pee-a-se **kram**ba (sto **po**dhee moo)"
to **crash**	τρακάρω	"traka-**ro**"
▷ **I've crashed my car**	τράκαρα το αυτοκίνητό μου	"**tra**ka-ra to afto-**kee**neeto moo"
crash helmet	το προστατευτικό κράνος	"to prosta-tef**tee**ko **kra**nos"
cream	η κρέμα	"ee **kre**ma"
credit card	η πιστωτική κάρτα	"ee peesto-tee**kee kar**ta"
▷ **can I pay by credit card?**	μπορώ να πληρώσω με πιστωτική κάρτα;	"bo-**ro** na plee-**ro**so me peesto-tee**kee kar**ta"
▷ **I've lost my credit card**	έχασα την πιστωτική κάρτα μου	"**ekha**sa teen peesto-tee**kee kar**ta moo"
crisps	τα πατατάκια	"ta pata**ta**-keea"
croissant	το κρουασάν	"to kroo-a**san**"
croquette	η κροκέτα	"ee kro-**ke**ta"

to **cross**	περνώ απέναντι	"perno apenandee"
▷ we have a crossed line	κάποιος μπήκε στη γραμμή	"kapeeos beeke stee ghramee"
crossing	το πέρασμα	"to perasma"
▷ how long does the crossing take?	πόση ώρα χρειάζεται για να πάμε απέναντι;	"posee o-ra khreea-ze-te ya na pa-me apenandee"
crossroads	το σταυροδρόμι	"to stavro-dhromee"
crowded	γεμάτος	"yematos"
cruise	η κρουαζιέρα	"ee kroo-azee-era"
cucumber	το αγγούρι	"to agooree"
cup	το φλυτζάνι	"to fleed-zanee"
▷ could we have another cup of tea/coffee, please?	μπορούμε να έχουμε άλλο ένα φλυτζάνι τσάι/καφέ, παρακαλώ;	"boroo-me na e-khoo-me a-lo ena fleed-zanee tsaee/kafe para-kalo"
cupboard	το ντουλάπι	"to doo-lapee"
currant	η σταφίδα	"ee sta-feedha"
current (electric)	το ρεύμα	"to revma"
▷ are there strong currents?	έχει δυνατά ρεύματα;	"ekhee dhee-nata revmata"
cushion	το μαξιλάρι	"to maksee-laree"
customs	το τελωνείο	"to telonee-o"
cut¹ n	το κόψιμο	"to kop-seemo"
▷ a cut and blow-dry, please	κούρεμα και στέγνωμα, παρακαλώ	"koo-rema ke stegh-noma para-kalo"
to **cut²** vb	κόβω	"kovo"
▷ he has cut himself	έχει κοπεί	"ekhee kopee"
▷ I've been cut off	μας κόψανε	"mas kopsa-ne"
cutlery	τα μαχαιροπήρουνα	"ta makhero-peeroona"

ABSOLUTE ESSENTIALS

do you have ...?	έχετε ...;	"ekhe-te"
is there ...?	υπάρχει ...;	"ee-parkhee"
are there ...?	υπάρχουν ...;	"ee-parkhoon"
how much is ...?	πόσο κάνει ...;	"poso kanee"

cycle	το ποδήλατο	"to po**dhee**-lato"
cycling	η ποδηλασία	"ee podhee-la**see**-a"
▷ we would like to go cycling	θα θέλαμε να πάμε για ποδηλασία	"tha **thela**-me na **pa**-me ya podhee-la**see**-a"
daily	ημερήσιος	"eeme**reesee**-os"
dairy products	τα γαλακτοκομικά προϊόντα	"ta ghala-ktokomee**ka** pro-ee**on**da"
damage	η ζημιά	"ee zeemee-**a**"
damp	υγρός	"eegh**ros**"
▷ my clothes are damp	τα ρούχα μου είναι υγρά	"ta **roo**kha moo **ee**-ne **eegh**ra"
dance[1] *n*	ο χορός	"o kho**ros**"
to **dance**[2] *vb*	χορεύω	"kho-**revo**"
dangerous	επικίνδυνος	"epee-**keen**dheenos"
dark (*colour*)	σκούρο	"**skoo**ro"
▷ it's dark	είναι σκοτεινά	"**ee**-ne skotee-**na**"
date (*calendar*)	η ημερομηνία	"ee eemero-mee**nee**-a"
(*fruit*)	ο χουρμάς	"o khoor-**mas**"
▷ what is the date?	τι ημερομηνία έχουμε;	"tee eemero-mee**nee**-a ek**hoo**-me"
date of birth	η ημερομηνία γεννήσεως	"ee eemero-mee**nee**-a ye**nee**se-os"
daughter	η κόρη	"ee **ko**ree"
day	η μέρα	"ee **me**ra"
day trip	η ημερήσια εκδρομή	"ee eeme-**ree**see-a ek-dhro**mee**"
dear	αγαπητός	"agha-pee**tos**"
(*expensive*)	ακριβός	"akree-**vos**"
decaffeinated	χωρίς καφεΐνη	"kho**rees** kafe- **ee**nee"
December	Δεκέμβριος	"dhe**kem**-vreeos"

deck	το κατάστρωμα	"to kata-stroma"
▷ can we go out on deck?	μπορούμε να βγούμε στο κατάστρωμα;	"boroo-me na vghoo-me sto kata-stroma"
deck chair	η σαιζλόγκ	"ee sez-long"
to declare	δηλώνω	"dhee-lono"
▷ I have nothing to declare	δεν έχω να δηλώσω τίποτα	"dhen ekho na dhee-loso tee-pota"
▷ I have a bottle of spirits to declare	έχω ένα μπουκάλι ποτό να δηλώσω	"ekho ena bookalee poto na dhee-loso"
deep	βαθύς	"vathees"
▷ how deep is the water?	πόσο βαθιά είναι τα νερά;	"poso vathee-a ee-ne ta nera"
deep freeze	η κατάψυξη	"ee katapseeksee"
to defrost (food)	ξεπαγώνω	"ksepa-ghono"
to delay	καθυστερώ	"kathee-stero"
▷ the flight has been delayed (by 6 hours)	η πτήση έχει καθυστέρηση (6 ώρες)	"ee ptee-see ekhee kathee-stereesee (eksee o-res)"
delicious	νόστιμος	"no-steemos"
dentist	ο/η οδοντογιατρός	"o/ee odhondo-yatros"
▷ I need to see a dentist (urgently)	πρέπει να δω τον οδοντογιατρό (επειγόντως)	"prepee na dho ton odhondo-yatro (epee-ghondos)"
dentures	η οδοντοστοιχία	"ee odhon-dostee-khee-a"
▷ my dentures need repairing	η οδοντοστοιχία μου θέλει επιδιόρθωση	"ee odhon-dostee-khee-a moo thelee epee-dheeorthosee"
deodorant	το αποσμητικό	"to apos-meeteeko"
department store	το πολυκατάστημα	"to poleeka-tasteema"
departure	η αναχώρηση	"ee ana-khoreesee"
departure lounge	η αίθουσα αναχωρήσεων	"ee ethoo-sa ana-khoreesee-on"

ABSOLUTE ESSENTIALS

I don't understand	δεν καταλαβαίνω	"dhen kata-laveno"
I don't speak Greek	δεν μιλάω ελληνικά	"dhen meela-o elee-neeka"
do you speak English?	μιλάτε αγγλικά;	"meela-te anglee-ka"
more slowly please	πιο σιγά παρακαλώ	"peeo seegha para-kalo"

departures	αναχωρήσεις	"ana-khoreesees"
deposit (*in a bank*)	η κατάθεση	"ee kata-thesee"
(*part payment*)	η προκαταβολή	"ee proka-tavolee"
▷ **what is the deposit?**	πόση είναι η προκαταβολή;	"po-see ee-ne ee proka-tavolee"
dessert	το επιδόρπιο	"to epee-dhorpee-o"
▷ **we'd like a dessert**	θα θέλαμε επιδόρπιο	"tha thela-me epee-dhorpee-o"
▷ **the dessert menu, please**	τον κατάλογο με τα επιδόρπια, παρακαλώ	"ton kata-lohgo me ta epee-dhorpee-a para-kalo"
details	οι λεπτομέρειες	"ee lepto-meree-es"
detergent	το απορρυπαντικό	"to aporee-pandeeko"
detour:		
▷ **to make a detour**	βγαίνω απο το δρόμο	"vyeno apo to dhromo"
to **develop** (*film*)	εμφανίζω	"emfaneezo"
diabetic	διαβητικός	"dhee-avee-teekos"
	διαβητική	"dhee- avee-teekee"
▷ **I am diabetic**	είμαι διαβητικός/διαβητική	"ee-me dhee-avee-teekos/dhee-avee-teekee"
dialling code	ο τηλεφωνικός κώδικας	"o teele-foneekos kodhee-kas"
▷ **what is the dialling code for the UK?**	ποιος είναι ο τηλεφωνικός κώδικας για τη Βρετανία;	"peeos ee-ne o teele-foneekos kodhee-kas ya tee vre-taneea"
diamond	το διαμάντι	"to dhee-amandee"
diarrhoea	η διάρροια	"ee dheearee-a"
▷ **I need something for diarrhoea**	χρειάζομαι κάτι για τη διάρροια	"khree-azo-me katee ya tee dheearee-a"
diary	το ημερολόγιο	"to eemero-loyee-o"

dictionary	το λεξικό	"to leksee-**ko**"
diet	η δίαιτα	"ee **dhee**-eta"
different	διαφορετικός	"dhee-afo-reteekos"
>I would like something different	θα ήθελα κάτι διαφορετικό	"tha **ee**thela **ka**tee dhee-afo-reteeko"
difficult	δύσκολος	"**dhees**-kolos"
dinghy	η φουσκωτή βάρκα	"ee fooskotee varka"
dining room	η τραπεζαρία	"ee trapezaree-a"
dinner	το βραδυνό	"to vradheeno"
direct	άμεσος	"a-mesos"
directory (*telephone*)	ο τηλεφωνικός κατάλογος	"o teele-foneekos kata-loghos"
directory enquiries	οι πληροφορίες καταλόγου	"ee plee-roforee-es kata-loghoo"
>what is the number for directory enquiries?	ποιος είναι ο αριθμός για τις πληροφορίες;	"peeos ee-ne o areethmos ya tees plee-roforee-es"
dirty	βρώμικος	"vromeekos"
>the washbasin is dirty	ο νιπτήρας είναι λερωμένος	"o neep-teeras ee-ne lero-menos"
disabled	ανάπηρος	"ana-peeros"
>is there a toilet for the disabled?	υπάρχει τουαλέτα για ανάπηρους;	"eepar-khee too-a-leta ya ana-peeroos"
>do you have facilities for the disabled?	έχετε διευκολύνεις για ανάπηρους;	"ekhe-te dhee-efkoleen-sees ya ana-peeroos"
disco	η ντισκοτέκ	"ee dhee-skotek"
discount	η έκπτωση	"ee ek-ptosee"
>do you offer a discount for cash?	υπάρχει έκπτωση αν η πληρωμή γίνει με μετρητά;	"eepar-khee ek-ptosee an ee pleeromee yee-nee me metree-ta"

▷ **are there discounts for students/children?**	υπάρχει έκπτωση για φοιτητές/παιδιά;	"eepar-khee **ek**-ptosee ya feetee-**tes**/pedheea"
dish	το πιάτο	"to peeato"
▷ **how do you cook this dish?**	πώς μαγειρεύετε αυτό το πιάτο;	"pos magheere-ve-te afto to peeato"
▷ **how is this dish served?**	πώς σερβίρεται αυτό το πιάτο;	"pos servee-re-te afto to peeato"
▷ **what is in this dish?**	τι έχει αυτό το πιάτο;	"tee ekhee afto to peeato"
dishtowel	το πανί για τα πιάτα	"to panee ya ta peeata"
dishwasher	το πλυντήριο πιάτων	"to pleenteeree-o pee-aton"
disinfectant	το απολυμαντικό	"to apolee-mandeeko"
distilled water	το απεσταγμένο νερό	"to apestagh-meno nero"
to **dive**	βουτάω	"voota-o"
▷ **where is the best place to dive?**	πού είναι το καλύτερο μέρος για βουτιές;	"poo ee-ne to kaleetero meros ya vootee-es"
diversion	η παράκαμψη	"ee parakampsee"
▷ **is there a diversion?**	υπάρχει παράκαμψη;	"eepar-khee parakampsee"
diving	το υποβρύχιο κολύμπι	"to eepo-vreekheeo koleem-bee"
▷ **I'd like to go diving**	θα ήθελα να πάω για υποβρύχιο κολύμπι	"tha eethela na pao ya eepo-vreekheeo koleem-bee"
divorced	χωρισμένος χωρισμένη	"khorees-menos" "khorees-menee"
dizzy	ζαλισμένος	"zalees-menos"
▷ **I feel dizzy**	έχω ζαλάδα	"ekho zaladha"

to do:

I do	κάνω	"kano"
you do (*informal singular*)	κάνεις	"kanees"
he/she/it does	κάνει	"kanee"
we do	κάνουμε	"kanoo-me"
you do (*plural or formal singular*)	κάνετε	"ka-ne-te"
they do	κάνουν	"kanoon"

doctor	ο/η γιατρός	"o/ee yatros"
▷ **can I please have an appointment with the doctor?**	μπορώ να κλείσω ένα ραντεβού με το γιατρό, παρακαλώ;	"bo-ro na kleeso ena randevoo me to yatro para-kalo"
▷ **I need a doctor**	χρειάζομαι γιατρό	"khree-azo-me yatro"
▷ **call a doctor**	καλέστε ένα γιατρό	"kales-te ena yatro"
dollar	το δολάριο	"to dholaree-o"
door	η πόρτα	"ee porta"
double	διπλός	"dheeplos"
double bed	το διπλό κρεβάτι	"to dheeplo kre-vatee"
double room	το δίκλινο δωμάτιο	"to dheekleeno dhomatee-o"
▷ **I want to reserve a double room**	θέλω να κλείσω ένα δίκλινο δωμάτιο	"the-lo na kleeso ena dheekleeno dhomatee-o"

down:

▷ **to go down**	κατεβαίνω	"kate-veno"
downstairs	κάτω	"ka-to"
drachmas	δραχμές	"drakhmes"
drain	η αποχέτευση	"ee apo-khe-te-fsee"

ABSOLUTE ESSENTIALS

I don't understand	δεν καταλαβαίνω	"dhen kata-laveno"
I don't speak Greek	δεν μιλάω ελληνικά	"dhen meela-o elee-neeka"
do you speak English?	μιλάτε αγγλικά;	"meela-te anglee-ka"
more slowly please	πιο σιγά παρακαλώ	"peeo seegha para-kalo"

▷ **the drain is blocked**	η αποχέτευση έχει βουλώσει	"ee apo-**khe**-te-fsee **ekhee** voo**lo**see"
draught (*in room*)	το ρεύμα	"to **rev**ma"
draught beer	βαρελίσια μπύρα	"vare-**lee**seea **bee**ra"
▷ **a draught beer, please**	μία βαρελίσια μπύρα, παρακαλώ	"**mee**a vare-**lee**seea **bee**ra para-ka**lo**"
dress¹ *n*	το φόρεμα	"to **fo**-rema"
to **dress**² *vb*	ντύνομαι	"**dee**no-me"
dressing (*for salad*)	το λαδόξυδο	"to la**dho**kseedho"
drink¹ *n*	το ποτό	"to po**to**"
▷ **would you like a drink?**	θέλετε ένα ποτό;	"**the**-le-te ena po**to**"
▷ **a cold/hot drink**	ένα κρύο/ζεστό ποτό	"ena **kree**-o/ze**sto** po**to**"
to **drink**² *vb*	πίνω	"**pee**no"
▷ **what would you like to drink?**	τι θέλετε να πιείτε;	"tee **the**-le-te na **pyee**-te"
drinking chocolate	η σοκολάτα ρόφημα	"ee soko-**la**ta **ro**feema"
drinking water	το πόσιμο νερό	"to **po**seemo ne**ro**"
to **drive**	οδηγώ	"odhee-**gho**"
▷ **he was driving too fast**	οδηγούσε με μεγάλη ταχύτητα	"odhee-**ghoo**-se me me**gha**lee ta**khee**-teeta"
driver	ο/η οδηγός	"o/ee odhee-**ghos**"
driving licence	η άδεια οδήγησης	"ee **adhee**-a o**dhee**-yeesees"
▷ **my driving licence number is ...**	ο αριθμός της άδειας οδήγησης είναι ...	"o areeth**mos** tees **adhee**as o**dhee**-yeesees **ee**-ne"
▷ **I don't have my driving licence on me**	δεν έχω μαζί μου την άδεια οδήγησης	"dhen **ekho** ma**zee** moo teen **adhee**-a o**dhee**-yeesees"

ABSOLUTE ESSENTIALS

I would like ...	θα ήθελα ...	"tha **ee**thela"
I need ...	χρειάζομαι ...	"khree-**azo**-me"
where is ...?	πού είναι ...;	"poo **ee**-ne"
we're looking for ...	ψάχνουμε ...	"**psakh**noo-me"

to **drown**	πνίγομαι	"**pnee**-gho-me"
▷ someone is drowning!	κάποιος πνίγεται!	"**kapee**-os **pnee**-ye-te"
drunk	μεθυσμένος	"methees-**menos**"
dry¹ *adj*	στεγνός	"stegh-**nos**"
to **dry**² *vb*	στεγνώνω	"stegh-**nono**"
▷ where can I dry my clothes?	πού μπορώ να στεγνώσω τα ρούχα μου;	"poo bo-**ro** na stegh-**noso** ta **rook**ha moo"
to **dry-clean:**		
▷ I need this dry-cleaned	αυτό χρειάζεται στεγνό καθάρισμα	"**afto** khreea-ze-te stegh-**no** katharee-sma"
dry-cleaner's	το καθαριστήριο	"to katharee-**steeree**-o"
duck	η πάπια	"ee **papee**-a"
due:		
▷ when is the train due?	πότε θα φτάσει το τραίνο;	"**po**-te tha **fta**see to **treno**"
dummy	η πιπίλα	"ee pee-**peela**"
during	κατά τη διάρκεια	"kata tee dhee-**arkee**-a"
duty-free	αφορολόγητος	"afo-ro**lo**-yeetos"
duty-free shop	το κατάστημα αφορολόγητων	"to kata-steema afo-ro**lo**-yeeton"
duvet	το πάπλωμα	"to **paplo**-ma"
dynamo	το δυναμό	"to dheena-**mo**"
each	κάθε	"**ka**-the"
▷ 100 drachmas each	100 δραχμές ο καθένας	"eka**to** drakh**mes** o ka-**thenas**"
ear	το αυτί	"to af**tee**"
earache:		
▷ I have earache	με πονάει το αυτί μου	"me pona-ee to af**tee** moo"

ABSOLUTE ESSENTIALS

do you have ...?	έχετε ...;	"**ekhe**-te"
is there ...?	υπάρχει ...;	"ee-**parkhee**"
are there ...?	υπάρχουν ...;	"ee-**parkhoon**"
how much is ...?	πόσο κάνει ...;	"**poso kanee**"

earlier	νωρίτερα	"noree-tera"
▷ **I would prefer an earlier flight**	θα προτιμούσα μία πτήση νωρίτερα	"tha protee-**moo**sa **mee**a **ptee**-see no**ree**-tera"
early	νωρίς	"no**rees**"
earrings	τα σκουλαρίκια	"ta skoola-**ree**kee-a"
east	η ανατολή	"ee ana-to**lee**"
Easter	το Πάσχα	"to **pas**kha"
easy	εύκολος	"**ef**-kolos"
to **eat**	τρώω	"**tro**-o"
▷ **I don't eat meat**	δεν τρώω κρέας	"dhen **tro**-o kreas"
▷ **would you like something to eat?**	θέλετε κάτι να φάτε;	"**the**le-te **ka**tee na **fa**-te"
▷ **have you eaten?**	έχετε φάει;	"**ekhe**-te **fa**-ee"
EC	ΕΚ	
egg	το αυγό	"to av**gho**"
▷ **fried eggs**	αυγά τηγανητά	"av**gha** teeghaneeta"
▷ **hard-boiled egg**	αυγά βραστά σφιχτά	"av**gha** vrasta sfeekh**ta**"
▷ **scrambled egg**	αυγά ομελέτα	"av**gha** omele**ta**"
▷ **boiled eggs**	αυγά βραστά	"av**gha** vra**sta**"
▷ **poached eggs**	αυγά ποσέ	"av**gha** po-**se**"
eight	οκτώ	"ok**to**"
eighteen	δεκαοκτώ	"dheka-ok**to**"
eighty	ογδόντα	"ogh-**dhon**da"
either:		
▷ **either ... or**	ή ... ή	"ee ... ee"
elastic band	το λαστιχάκι	"to lastee-**kha**kee"
electric	ηλεκτρικός	"eelek-tree**kos**"
electrician	ο ηλεκτρολόγος	"o eelektro-**lo**ghos"
electricity	ο ηλεκτρισμός	"o eelek-trees-**mos**"

ABSOLUTE ESSENTIALS		
yes (please)	ναι (παρακαλώ)	"ne (para-ka**lo**)"
no (thank you)	όχι (ευχαριστώ)	"**okhee** (efkharee**sto**)"
hello	γεια σας	"ya sas"
goodbye	αντίο	"an**dee**-o"

English	Greek	Pronunciation
▷ **is the cost of electricity included in the rental?**	το ηλεκτρικό περιλαμβάνεται στην τιμή;	"to eelektreeko pereelamvane-te steen teemee"
electricity meter	ο μετρητής του ηλεκτρικού	"o metree-tees-too eelek-treekoo"
electric razor	η ηλεκτρική ξυριστική μηχανή	"ee eelektreekee kseeree-steekee meekha-nee"
eleven	έντεκα	"en-deka"
to **embark**	επιβιβάζομαι	"e-pee-veeva-zo-me"
▷ **when do we embark?**	πότε επιβιβαζόμαστε;	"po-te e-pee-veeva-zomas-te"
embassy	η πρεσβεία	"ee presvee-a"
emergency:		
▷ **it's an emergency**	είναι επείγον	"ee-ne epee-ghon"
empty	άδειος	"adhee-os"
end	το τέλος	"to telos"
engaged (to be married)	αρραβωνιασμένος αρραβωνιασμένη	"aravonee- asmenos" "aravonee-asmenee"
(toilet)	κατειλημμένη	"kateelee-menee"
(phone)	μιλάει	"meelaee"
▷ **the line's engaged**	μιλάει το τηλέφωνο	"meelaee to teelefo-no"
engine	η μηχανή	"ee mee-khanee"
England	η Αγγλία	"ee anglee-a"
English adj	αγγλικός	"angleekos"
▷ **I'm English**	είμαι 'Αγγλος/ Αγγλίδα	"ee-me anglos/anglee-dha"
▷ **do you speak English?**	μιλάτε αγγλικά;	"meela-te anglee-ka"
▷ **do you have any English books/ newspapers?**	έχετε αγγλικά βιβλία/εφημερίδες;	"ekhe-te angleeka vee-vlee-a/efeeme-reedhes"

ABSOLUTE ESSENTIALS

I don't understand	δεν καταλαβαίνω	"dhen kata-laveno"
I don't speak Greek	δεν μιλάω ελληνικά	"dhen meela-o elee-neeka"
do you speak English?	μιλάτε αγγλικά;	"meela-te anglee-ka"
more slowly please	πιο σιγά παρακαλώ	"peeo seegha para-kalo"

to enjoy:		
▷ **to enjoy oneself**	διασκεδάζω	"dhee-aske-**dha**zo"
▷ **I enjoyed the tour**	μου άρεσε η εκδρομή	"moo **a**-re-se ee ekdhro**mee**"
▷ **I enjoy swimming**	μου αρέσει το κολύμπι	"moo a**re**see to ko**leem**bee"
▷ **enjoy your meal**	καλή όρεξη	"ka**lee o**reksee"
enough	αρκετά	"arke-**ta**"
enquiry desk	το γραφείο πληροφοριών	"to ghra**fee**-o pleero-foree-**on**"
entertainment	η διασκέδαση	"ee dhee-a**ske**dha-see"
▷ **what entertainment is there?**	τι υπάρχει για διασκέδαση;	"tee ee-**par**khee ya dhee-a**ske**dha-see"
entrance	η είσοδος	"ee **ee**sodhos"
entrance fee	η είσοδος	"ee **ee**sodhos"
entry visa	η βίζα εισόδου	"ee **vee**za ee**so**dhoo"
▷ **I have an entry visa**	έχω βίζα εισόδου	"**ekho vee**za ee**so**dhoo"
envelope	ο φάκελος	"o **fa**-kelos"
equipment	ο εξοπλισμός	"o eksoplees-**mos**"
escalator	η κυλιόμενη σκάλα	"ee keelee-**o**menee **ska**la"
especially	ειδικά	"eedhee-**ka**"
essential	απαραίτητος	"apa**re**-teetos"
Eurocheque	η ευρωεπιταγή	"ee evro-epee**ta**yee"
▷ **do you take Eurocheques?**	δέχεστε ευρωεπιταγές;	"**dhe**-khes-te evro-epee**ta**yes"
Europe	η Ευρώπη	"ee ev**ro**pee"
European *adj*	ευρωπαϊκός	"evropa-ee**kos**"
European Community	η Ευρωπαϊκή Κοινότητα	"ee evropa-ee**kee** keeno**tee**ta"

ABSOLUTE ESSENTIALS		
I would like ...	θα ήθελα ...	"tha **ee**thela"
I need ...	χρειάζομαι ...	"khree-**a**zo-me"
where is ...?	πού είναι ...;	"poo **ee**-ne"
we're looking for ...	ψάχνουμε ...	"**psa**khnoo-me"

evening	το βράδυ	"to **vra**dhee"
▷ **in the evening**	το βράδυ	"to **vra**dhee"
▷ **what is there to do in the evenings?**	πού μπορούμε να πηγαίνουμε τα βράδυα;	"poo boo**roo**-me na pee-**ye**noo-me ta **vra**dhee-a"
▷ **what are you doing this evening?**	τι κάνετε απόψε το βράδυ;	"tee **ka**-ne-te a**pop**-se to **vra**dhee"
▷ **evening meal**	βραδυνό γεύμα	"vradhee-**no yev**ma"
every	κάθε	"**ka**-the"
	καθένας	"ka-**the**nas"
	καθεμία	"ka-the**mee**a"
	καθένα	"ka-**the**na"
everyone	όλοι	"**o**lee"
everything	όλα	"**o**la"
excellent	εξαιρετικός	"ekse-retee**kos**"
▷ **the meal was excellent**	το γεύμα ήταν εξαιρετικό	"to **yev**ma **ee**tan ekse-retee**ko**"
except	εκτός από	"ek**tos** a**po**"
excess luggage	το υπέρβαρο	"to ee**per**varo"
exchange[1] *n*	η ανταλλαγή	"ee anda-la**yee**"
to **exchange**[2] *vb*	αλλάζω	"a**la**-zo"
▷ **could I exchange this, please?**	μπορώ να το αλλάξω αυτό, παρακαλώ;	"bo-**ro** na to a**la**-kso af**to** para-ka**lo**"
exchange rate	η τιμή του συναλλάγματος	"ee tee**mee** too seena**lagh**-matos"
▷ **what is the exchange rate?**	ποια είναι η τιμή του συναλλάγματος;	"pee**a ee**-ne ee tee**mee** too seena**lagh**-matos"
excursion	η εκδρομή	"ee ek-dhro**mee**"
▷ **what excursions are there?**	τι εκδρομές γίνονται;	"tee ek-dhro**mes yee**non-de"
to **excuse**	συγχωρώ	"seenkho**ro**"
▷ **excuse me!**	με συγχωρείτε!	"me seenkho-**ree**-te"

ABSOLUTE ESSENTIALS

do you have ...?	έχετε ...;	"**ekhe**-te"
is there ...?	υπάρχει ...;	"ee-**par**khee"
are there ...?	υπάρχουν ...;	"ee-**par**khoon"
how much is ...?	πόσο κάνει ...;	"**poso ka**nee"

exhaust pipe	η εξάτμιση	"ee **eksat**-meesee"
exhibition	η έκθεση	"ee **ek**-thesee"
exit	η έξοδος;	"ee **ekso**-dhos"
▷ **where is the exit?**	πού είναι η έξοδος	"poo **ee**-ne ee **ekso**-dhos"
▷ **which exit for ...?**	από ποια έξοδο για ...;	"**apo** peea **ekso**-dho ya"
expensive	ακριβός	"akree-**vos**"
▷ **I want something more expensive**	θέλω κάτι πιο ακριβό	"**the**-lo **ka**tee peeo akree-**vo**"
▷ **it's too expensive**	είναι πολύ ακριβό	"**ee**-ne po**lee** akree-**vo**"
expert	ο/η ειδικός	"o/ee eedhee-**kos**"
to **expire**	λήγω	"**lee**gho"
express (train)	η ταχεία	"ee ta**khee**-a"
extra:		
▷ **it costs extra**	στοιχίζει επιπλέον	"stee-**khee**zee epee-**ple**-on"
▷ **extra money**	περισσότερα χρήματα	"peree-**so**tera **khree**-mata"
eye	το μάτι	"to **ma**tee"
▷ **I have something in my eye**	κάτι έχει μπει στο μάτι μου	"**ka**-tee **e**khee bee sto **ma**-tee moo"
eyes	τα μάτια	"ta **ma**tee-a"
eye shadow	η σκιά για τα μάτια	"ee ski**a** ya ta **ma**teea"
face	το πρόσωπο	"to **pro**-sopo"
facilities	οι ευκολίες	"ee ef-ko**lee**-es"
▷ **do you have any facilities for the disabled?**	έχετε διευκολύνσεις για ανάπηρους;	"**e**khe-te dhee-efko**leen**-sees ya ana-**pee**roos"
▷ **do you have facilities for children?**	υπάρχουν ευκολίες για παιδιά;	"ee**par**khoon efko**lee**-es ya pedhee**a**"

▷ **are there facilities for mothers with babies?**	τι διευκολύνσεις έχετε για μητέρες με μωρά;	"tee dhee-efkoleen-sees ekhe-te ya meeteres me mora"
factor	ο δείκτης	"o dhee-ktees"
▷ **factor 8/15 suntan lotion**	αντηλιακό με δείκτη προστασίας 8/15	"andee-lee-ako me dheek-tee prosta-see-as okto/dhekapen-de"
factory	το εργοστάσιο	"to erghostaseeo"
▷ **I work in a factory**	δουλεύω σε εργοστάσιο	"dhoolevo se erghostaseeo"
to **faint**	λιποθυμώ	"leepo-thee-mo"
▷ **she has fainted**	λιποθύμησε	"leepotheemee-se"
fair[1] n (commercial)	η έκθεση	"ee ek-thesee"
(fun fair)	το λούνα παρκ	"to loona park"
fair[2] adj (hair)	ξανθός	"ksanthos"
to **fall**	πέφτω	"pefto"
family	η οικογένεια	"ee eeko-yenee-a"
famous	διάσημος	"dhee-aseemos"
fan (electric)	ο ανεμιστήρας	"o a-nemees-teeras"
(supporter)	ο θαυμαστής	"o thav-mastees"
	η θαυμάστρια	"ee thav-mastree-a"
fan belt	το λουρί του ανεμιστήρα	"to looree too a-nemees-teera"
far	μακριά	"makree-a"
▷ **how far is it to ...?**	πόσο μακριά είναι ...;	"poso makree-a ee-ne"
▷ **is it far?**	είναι μακριά;	"ee-ne makree-a"
fare (in bus, train)	το εισιτήριο	"to eesee- teeree-o"
▷ **what is the fare to the town centre?**	πόσο είναι το εισιτήριο για το κέντρο της πόλης;	"poso ee-ne to eesee-teeree-o ya to kendro tees polees"

ABSOLUTE ESSENTIALS

I don't understand	δεν καταλαβαίνω	"dhen kata-laveno"
I don't speak Greek	δεν μιλάω ελληνικά	"dhen meela-o elee-neeka"
do you speak English?	μιλάτε αγγλικά;	"meela-te anglee-ka"
more slowly please	πιο σιγά παρακαλώ	"peeo seegha para-kalo"

farm	το αγρόκτημα	"to **aghrok**-teema"
farmhouse	η αγροικία	"ee aghree-**kee**a"
fast	γρήγορα	"**ghree**-ghora"
▷ he was driving too fast	έτρεχε πολύ	"e-tre-khe po**lee**"
fast food (shop)	το φαστφουντάδικο	"to fastfood**a**dheeko"
fat¹ n	το λίπος	"to **lee**pos"
fat² adj	χοντρός	"khon**dros**"
father	ο πατέρας	"o pa-**ter**-as"
fault:		
▷ it wasn't my fault	δε φταίω εγώ	"dhe **fte**-o e**gho**"
favourite	αγαπημένος	"agha-pee**me**nos"
▷ what is your favourite drink?	ποιο ποτό προτιμάτε;	"**pee**o po**to** protee-**ma**-te"
fax	το φαξ	"to fax"
▷ can I send a fax from here?	μπορώ να στείλω φαξ από εδώ;	"bo-**ro** na **stee**lo fax a**po** e**dho**"
▷ what is the fax number?	ποιος είναι ο αριθμός του φαξ;	"**pee**os **ee**-ne o aree**thmos** too fax"
February	Φεβρουάριος	"fevroo-**aree**os"
to feed	τρέφω	"**tre**fo"
(baby)	ταΐζω	"ta-**ee**zo"
▷ where can I feed the baby?	πού μπορώ να ταΐσω το μωρό;	"poo bo-**ro** na ta-**ee**so to mo**ro**"
to feel (with hand etc)	πιάνω	"pee**a**no"
▷ I don't feel well	δεν αισθάνομαι καλά	"dhen esth**a**no-me kal**a**"
▷ I feel sick	θέλω να κάνω εμετό	"**the**-lo na **ka**no e-me-**to**"
ferry	το φερυμπώτ	"to feree**bot**"
▷ when is the next ferry?	πότε είναι το επόμενο φερυμπώτ;	"**po**-te **ee**-ne to e-**po**-meno feree**bot**"

ABSOLUTE ESSENTIALS		
I would like ...	θα ήθελα ...	"tha **ee**thela"
I need ...	χρειάζομαι ...	"khree-**a**zo-me"
where is ...?	πού είναι ...;	"poo **ee**-ne"
we're looking for ...	ψάχνουμε ...	"**psakhnoo**-me"

festival	το φεστιβάλ	"to festee**val**"
to **fetch**	φέρνω	"**fer**no"
fever	ο πυρετός	"o peere**tos**"
▷ **he has a fever**	έχει πυρετό	"**ekhee** peereto"
few:		
▷ **a few**	μερικοί	"meree-**kee**"
fiancé	ο αρραβωνιαστικός	"o aravonee-astee**kos**"
fiancée	η αρραβωνιαστικιά	"ee aravonee-astee**keea**"
field	το χωράφι	"to kho-**ra**fee"
fifteen	δεκαπέντε	"dhekapen-de"
fifty	πενήντα	"pe**neen**da"
to **fill**	γεμίζω	"ye-**mee**zo"
▷ **fill it up** (*car*)	γεμίστε το	"ye-**mees**-te to"
fillet	το φιλέτο	"to fee**le**to"
filling (*in cake etc*)	η γέμιση	"ee ye**mee**see"
(*in tooth*)	το σφράγισμα	"to **sfra**-yeesma"
▷ **a filling has come out**	μου έχει ξεκολλήσει ένα σφράγισμα	"moo ekhee kse-ko**lee**see ena **sfra**-yeesma"
▷ **could you do a temporary filling?**	μπορείτε να μου κάνετε ένα προσωρινό σφράγισμα;	"bo**ree**-te na moo **ka**-ne-te ena proso-ree**no sfra**-yeesma"
film (*for camera*)	το φιλμ	"to film"
(*in cinema*)	η ταινία	"ee te**nee**-a"
▷ **can you develop this film, please?**	μπορείτε να εμφανίσετε αυτό το φιλμ, παρακαλώ;	"bo**ree**-te na emfa-**nee**-se-te af**to** to film para-ka**lo**"
▷ **the film has jammed**	το φιλμ έχει κολλήσει	"to film **e**khee ko**lee**-see"
▷ **I need a colour/black and white film for this camera**	θέλω ένα έγχρωμο/ ασπρόμαυρο φιλμ για αυτή τη μηχανή	"**the**-lo ena **en**-khromo/ **aspro**-mavro film ya af**tee** tee meekha**nee**"

▷ which film is on at the cinema?	ποια ταινία παίζει ο κινηματογράφος;	"peea teneea pezee o keeneema-toghrafos"
filter	το φίλτρο	"to feeltro"
filter coffee	ο καφές φίλτρου	"o kafes feeltroo"
filter-tipped	με φίλτρο	"me feeltro"
fine[1] *n*	το πρόστιμο	"to prostee-mo"
▷ how much is the fine?	πόσο είναι το πρόστιμο;	"poso ee-ne to prostee-mo"
fine[2] *adj*	καλός	"kalos"
▷ is it going to be fine?	θα κάνει καλό καιρό	"tha kanee kalo kero"
to finish	τελειώνω	"telee-ono"
▷ when does the show finish?	τι ώρα τελειώνει το σόου;	"tee o-ra telee-onee to show"
▷ when will you have finished?	πότε θα τελειώσετε;	"po-te tha teleeo-se-te"
fire (*heater*)	η θερμάστρα	"ee thermas-tra"
▷ fire!	φωτιά!	"fotee-a"
fire brigade	η πυροσβεστική	"ee peeros-vesteekee"
fire extinguisher	ο πυροσβεστήρας	"o peeros-vesteeras"
first	πρώτος	"protos"
first aid	οι πρώτες βοήθειες	"ee pro-tes vo-eethee-es"
first class (*seat etc*)	πρώτη θέση	"protee thesee"
▷ a first class return to ...	πρώτη θέση με επιστροφή για ...	"protee thesee me epee-strofee ya"
first floor	ο πρώτος όροφος	"o protos orofos"
first name	το όνομα	"to onoma"
fish[1] *n*	το ψάρι	"to psaree"
to fish[2] *vb*	ψαρεύω	"psa-revo"
▷ can we fish here?	μπορούμε να ψαρέψουμε εδώ;	"boroo-me na psarep-soo-me edho"

▷ **can I go fishing?**	μπορώ να πάω για ψάρεμα;	"bo-**ro** na **pao** ya **psa**rema"
fit¹ *n*	η συγκοπή	"ee seego-**pee**"
fit² *adj (healthy)*	se fórma	"sé forma"
five	πέντε	"**pende**"
to **fix** (*arrange*)	φτιάχνω κανονίζω	"ftee-**akh**no" "kano-**nee**zo"
▷ **where can I get this fixed?**	πού μπορώ να δώσω αυτό για φτιάξιμο;	"poo bo-**ro** na **dho**-so af**to** ya ftee-**ak**seemo"
fizzy:		
▷ **a fizzy drink**	ένα ποτό με ανθρακικό	"**e**na poto me anthra-kee**ko**"
flash (*on camera*)	το φλας	"to flas"
▷ **the flash is not working**	το φλας δε δουλεύει	"to flas dhe dhoo-**le**-vee"
flask	το θερμός	"to ther**mos**"
flat (*apartment*)	το διαμέρισμα	"to dhee-a**me**reesma"
flat tyre:		
▷ **I have a flat tyre**	μ'έχει πιάσει λάστιχο	"**me**khee pee-**a**see la-**stee**kho"
flavour	η γεύση	"ee **yef**-see"
▷ **what flavours do you have?**	τι γεύσεις έχετε;	"tee **yef**-sees **e**khe-te"
flight	η πτήση	"ee **ptee**-see"
▷ **I've missed my flight**	έχασα την πτήση μου	"**e**khasa teen **ptee**-see moo"
▷ **my flight has been delayed**	η πτήση μου έχει καθυστέρηση	"ee **ptee**-see moo ekhee kathee-**ste**reesee"
▷ **are there any cheap flights?**	υπάρχουν φτηνές πτήσεις;	"ee**par**khoon ftee**nes ptee**-sees"

ABSOLUTE ESSENTIALS

I don't understand	δεν καταλαβαίνω	"dhen kata-la**ve**no"
I don't speak Greek	δεν μιλάω ελληνικά	"dhen meela-o elee-nee**ka**"
do you speak English?	μιλάτε αγγλικά;	"meela-te anglee-**ka**"
more slowly please	πιο σιγά παρακαλώ	"**pee**o seegha para-ka**lo**"

flooded:

▷ **the bathroom is flooded**	το μπάνιο πλημμύρισε	"to **ba**neeo plee-**mee**ree-se"
floor	το πάτωμα	"to **pa**-toma"
(*storey*)	ο όροφος	"o **o**rofos"
▷ **what floor is it on?**	σε ποιο όροφο είναι;	"se **pee**o **o**rofo **ee**-ne"
▷ **on the top floor**	στον τελευταίο όροφο	"ston telef**te**-o **o**rofo"
flour	το αλεύρι	"to a**lev**-ree"
▷ **plain flour**	αλεύρι άσπρο	"a**lev**-ree **a**spro"
▷ **self-raising flour**	αλεύρι που φουσκώνει μόνο του	"a**lev**-ree poo foo-**sko**nee **mo**no too"
flower	το λουλούδι	"to loo-**loo**dhee"
flu	η γρίππη	"ee **ghree**pee"
▷ **I've got flu**	έχω γρίππη	"**e**kho **ghree**pee"
to flush	τραβάω το καζανάκι	"tra**va**-o to kaza-**na**kee"
▷ **the toilet won't flush**	το καζανάκι χάλασε	"to kaza-**na**kee **kha**la-se"
fly (*insect*)	η μύγα	"ee **mee**gha"
flying:		
▷ **I hate flying**	δεν μου αρέσει να πετάω	"dhen moo a**re**see na pe**ta**-o"
fog	η ομίχλη	"ee o**mee**khlee"
to follow	ακολουθώ	"ako-loo**tho**"
food	το φαγητό	"to fa-yee**to**"
food poisoning	η τροφική δηλητηρίαση	"ee trofee-**kee** dheelee-tee**ree**-asee"
foot (*part of body*)	το πόδι	"to **po**dhee"
football (*game*)	το ποδόσφαιρο	"to po**dhos**-fero"
(*ball*)	η μπάλα ποδοσφαίρου	"ee **ba**la podhos-**fe**roo"

ABSOLUTE ESSENTIALS		
I would like ...	θα ήθελα ...	"tha **ee**thela"
I need ...	χρειάζομαι ...	"khree-**a**zo-me"
where is ...?	πού είναι ...;	"poo **ee**-ne"
we're looking for ...	ψάχνουμε ...	"**psa**khnoo-me"

▷ **let's play football**	παίζουμε ποδόσφαιρο	"**pe**zoo-me po**dhos**-fero"
for	για	"ya"
foreign	ξένος	"**kse**nos"
forest	το δάσος	"to **dha**sos"
to **forget**	ξεχνώ	"ksekh-**no**"
▷ **I've forgotten my passport/the key**	ξέχασα το διαβατήριό μου/το κλειδί	"**kse**-khasa to dhee-avatee-reeo moo/to klee**dhee**"
fork	το πηρούνι	"to pee-**roo**nee"
(*in road*)	η διακλάδωση	"ee dhee-a**kla**dhosee"
fortnight	το δεκαπενθήμερο	"to dhekapen-**thee**mero"
forty	σαράντα	"sa-**ran**da"
four	τέσσερα	"**tes**era"
fourteen	δεκατέσσερα	"dheka-**tes**era"
France	η Γαλλία	"ee gha**lee**-a"
free	ελεύθερος	"e**lef**-theros"
(*costing nothing*)	δωρεάν	"dho-re-**an**"
▷ **I am free tomorrow morning/for lunch**	είμαι ελεύθερος αύριο το πρωί/για μεσημεριανό	"**ee**-me e**lef**theros **av**reeo to pro**ee**/ya mesee-meree-a**no**"
▷ **is this seat free?**	είναι ελεύθερη αυτή η θέση;	"**ee**-ne e**lef**-there**e** aftee ee **the**see"
freezer	ο καταψύκτης	"o katap-**seek**tees"
French *adj*	γαλλικός	"ghalee**kos**"
(*language*)	γαλλικά	"ghalee**ka**"
french beans	τα φασολάκια	"ta faso-**la**kee-a"
Frenchman	ο Γάλλος	"o **gha**los"
Frenchwoman	η Γαλλίδα	"ee gha**lee**-dha"
frequent	συχνός	"seekh-**nos**"

do you have ...?	έχετε ...;	"**ekhe**-te"
is there ...?	υπάρχει ...;	"ee-**park**hee"
are there ...?	υπάρχουν ...;	"ee-**park**hoon"
how much is ...?	πόσο κάνει ...;	"**poso kanee**"

▷ how frequent are the buses?	πόσο συχνά έχει λεωφορείο;	"poso seekhna ekhee leo-foree-o"
fresh	φρέσκος	"freskos"
▷ fresh vegetables	φρέσκα λαχανικά	"freska lakha-neeka"
Friday	Παρασκευή	"para-skevee"
fridge	το ψυγείο	"to psee-yee-o"
fried	τηγανητός	"teegha-neetos"
friend	ο φίλος	"o feelos"
	η φίλη	"ee feelee"
from	από	"apo"
▷ I want to stay three nights from ... till ...	θέλω να μείνω για τρεις νύχτες από ... μέχρι...	"the-lo na meeno ya trees neekh-tes apo ... mekh-ree"
front (part)	το μπροστινό (μέρος)	"to brostee-no (meros)"
(in front)	μπροστά από	"brosta apo"
frozen (water)	παγωμένος	"pagho-menos"
(food)	κατεψυγμένος	"katep-seegh-menos"
fruit	τα φρούτα	"ta froota"
fruit juice	ο φρουτοχυμός	"o frooto-kheemos"
fruit salad	η φρουτοσαλάτα	"ee frooto-salata"
frying-pan	το τηγάνι	"to tee-ghanee"
fuel	τα καύσιμα	"ta kaf-seema"
fuel pump	η αντλία καυσίμων	"ee andlee-a kaf-seemon"
full	γεμάτος	"ye-matos"
full board	πλήρης διατροφή	"pleerees dhee-atrofee"
funny	αστείος	"astee-os"
fur	η γούνα	"ee ghoona"
fuse	η ασφάλεια	"ee asfalee-a"
▷ a fuse has blown	κάηκε η ασφάλεια	"ka-ee-ke ee asfa-leea"

ABSOLUTE ESSENTIALS

yes (please)	ναι (παρακαλώ)	"ne (para-kalo)"
no (thank you)	όχι (ευχαριστώ)	"okhee (efkhareesto)"
hello	γεια σας	"ya sas"
goodbye	αντίο	"andee-o"

gallery (*art*)	η πινακοθήκη	"ee peenako-**thee**kee"
gallon	το γαλόνι	"to gha**lo**nee"
game	το παιχνίδι	"to pekh-**nee**dhee"
▷ **a game of chess**	μια παρτίδα σκάκι	"**mee**a par**tee**-dha **ska**kee"
garage (*for repairs*)	το συνεργείο	"to seener- **yee**o"
▷ **can you tow me to a garage?**	μπορείτε να με ρυμουλκήσετε σε ένα συνεργείο;	"bo**ree**-te na me ree-mool**kee**-se-te se **e**na seener-**yee**o"
garden	ο κήπος	"o **kee**pos"
▷ **can we visit the gardens?**	μπορούμε να επισκεφτούμε τον κήπο;	"bo**roo**-me na epee-skef**too**-me ton **kee**po"
garlic	το σκόρδο	"to **skor**dho"
▷ **is there any garlic in it?**	έχει σκόρδο μέσα;	"**ekh**ee **skor**dho **me**-sa"
gas	το γκάζι	"to **ga**-zee"
▷ **I can smell gas**	μυρίζει γκάζι	"mee**ree**-zee **ga**-zee"
gas cylinder	η φιάλη γκαζιού	"ee fee-**a**lee ga-zee**oo**"
gears	οι ταχύτητες	"ee ta**khee**-teetes"
▷ **first/third gear**	πρώτη/τρίτη ταχύτητα	"**pro**tee/**tree**tee ta**khee**-teeta"
gentleman	ο κύριος	"o **kee**ree-os"
gents'	ανδρών	"an**dhron**"
▷ **where is the gents'?**	πού είναι των ανδρών;	"poo **ee**-ne ton an**dhron**"
genuine	γνήσιος	"**ghnee**see-os"
German *adj* (*language*)	γερμανικός γερμανικά	"yerma**nee**kos" "yerma**nee**ka"
German measles	η ερυθρά	"ee eree**thra**"

ABSOLUTE ESSENTIALS

I don't understand	δεν καταλαβαίνω	"dhen kata-**la**veno"
I don't speak Greek	δεν μιλάω ελληνικά	"dhen meela-o elee-nee**ka**"
do you speak English?	μιλάτε αγγλικά;	"meela-te anglee-**ka**"
more slowly please	πιο σιγά παρακαλώ	"pee**o** see**gha** para-ka**lo**"

Germany	η Γερμανία	"ee yermanee-a"
to **get**	παίρνω	"**per**no"
▷ I must get there by 8 o'clock	πρέπει να είμαι εκεί στις 8	"**pre**pee na **ee**-me e**kee** stees ok**to**"
▷ please get me a taxi	φωνάξτε μου ένα ταξί, παρακαλώ	"fo**naks**-te ena tak**see** para-ka**lo**"
to **get back**	γυρίζω;	"yee**ree**zo"
▷ when do we get back?	πότε γυρίζουμε πίσω;	"**po**-te yee-**ree**zoo-me **pee**so"
to **get into** (car etc)	μπαίνω	"**be**no"
to **get off** (from bus)	κατεβαίνω	"ka-te-**ve**no"
▷ where do I get off?	πού κατεβαίνω;	"poo ka-te-**ve**no"
▷ will you tell me where to get off?	μου λέτε πού να κατέβω;	"moo **le**-te poo na ka**te**vo"
gift	το δώρο	"to **dho**ro"
gin	το τζιν	"to tzeen"
▷ I'll have a gin and tonic	θα πάρω ένα τζιν με τόνικ	"tha **pa**-ro ena tzeen me tonic"
girl	το κορίτσι	"to ko**reet**-see"
girlfriend	η φίλη	"ee **fee**lee"
to **give**	δίνω	"**dhee**no"
to **give way**	δίνω προτεραιότητα	"**dhee**no pro-te-re-o**tee**ta"
▷ he did not give way	παραβίασε το στοπ	"para**vee**-a-se to stop"
glass (for drinking)	το ποτήρι	"to po**tee**ree"
(for windows etc)	το γυαλί	"to ya**lee**"
▷ a glass of lemonade, please	μία λεμονάδα, παρακαλώ	"**mee**a lemo-**na**dha para-ka**lo**"
▷ broken glass	σπασμένα γυαλιά	"spa**sme**na yalee-**a**"
glasses (spectacles)	τα γυαλιά	"ta yalee-**a**"

ABSOLUTE ESSENTIALS

I would like ...	θα ήθελα ...	"tha **ee**thela"
I need ...	χρειάζομαι ...	"khree-**a**zo-me"
where is ...?	πού είναι ...;	"poo **ee**-ne"
we're looking for ...	ψάχνουμε ...	"**psa**khnoo-me"

▷ can you repair my glasses?	μπορείτε να μου φτιάξετε τα γυαλιά μου;	"boree-te na moo ftee-akse-te ta yalee-a moo"
gloves	τα γάντια	"ta ghandee-a"
glue¹ n	η κόλλα	"ee kola"
to glue² vb	κολλάω	"kola-o"
to go	πηγαίνω	"peeye-no"

I go	πηγαίνω	"peeye-no"
you go (informal singular)	πηγαίνεις	"peeye-nees"
he/she/it goes	πηγαίνει	"peeye-nee"
we go	πηγαίνουμε	"peeye-noo-me"
you go (plural or formal singular)	πηγαίνετε	"peeye-ne-te"
they go	πηγαίνουν	"peeye-noon"

▷ I'm going to the beach	πηγαίνω στην παραλία	"peeye-no steen para-lee-a"
to go back	γυρίζω πίσω	"yeeree-zo peeso"
▷ I must go back now	πρέπει να γυρίσω πίσω τώρα	"prepee na yeeree-so peeso tora"
to go down	κατεβαίνω	"ka-te-veno"
goggles (for swimming)	τα προστατευτικά γυαλιά	"ta prosta-tefteeka yalee-a"
to go in	μπαίνω	"beno"
gold	ο χρυσός	"o khreesos"
(made of gold)	χρυσός	"khreesos"
gold-plated	επιχρυσωμένος	"epee-khreesome-nos"
golf	το γκολφ	"to golf"

ABSOLUTE ESSENTIALS

do you have ...?	έχετε ...;	"ekhe-te"
is there ...?	υπάρχει ...;	"ee-parkhee"
are there ...?	υπάρχουν ...;	"ee-parkhoon"
how much is ...?	πόσο κάνει ...;	"poso kanee"

English	Greek	Pronunciation
▷ where can we play golf?	πού μπορούμε να παίξουμε γκολφ;	"poo boo**roo**-me na **pek**soo-me golf"
golf course	το γήπεδο του γκολφ	"to **yee**-pedho too golf"
good	καλός	"ka**los**"
good afternoon	χαίρετε	"**khe**-re-te"
goodbye	αντίο	"an**dee**-o"
good evening	καλησπέρα	"kalee-**spe**ra"
Good Friday	η Μεγάλη Παρασκευή	"ee me-**gha**lee para-ske**vee**"
good-looking	όμορφος	"**o**-morfos"
good morning	καλημέρα	"kalee-**mera**"
good night	καληνύχτα	"kalee-**nee**khta"
to go on	προχωράω	"pro-kho**ra**-o"
▷ you go on ahead	προχώρησε μπροστά	"pro-**kho**resee mbro**sta**"
goose	η χήνα	"ee **khee**-na"
to go out	βγαίνω	"**vye**no"
gram	το γραμμάριο	"to ghra**maree**-o"
▷ 500 grams of mince meat	500 γραμμάρια κιμά	"penda**ko**seea ghra**maree**-a kee**ma**"
granddaughter	η εγγονή	"ee en-go**nee**"
grandfather	ο παππούς	"o pa**poos**"
grandmother	η γιαγιά	"ee ya-**ya**"
grandson	ο εγγονός	"o en-go**nos**"
grape	το σταφύλι	"to sta**fee**lee"
▷ a bunch of grapes	ένα τσαμπί σταφύλια	"ena tsa**bee** sta**fee**lee-a"
▷ seedless grapes	σταφύλια χωρίς κουκούτσια	"sta**fee**lee-a kho**rees** koo**koo**tsee-a"
grapefruit	το γκρέιπ-φρουτ	"to grapefruit"

ABSOLUTE ESSENTIALS

English	Greek	Pronunciation
yes (please)	ναι (παρακαλώ)	"ne (para-ka**lo**)"
no (thank you)	όχι (ευχαριστώ)	"**o**khee (efkhari**sto**)"
hello	γεια σας	"ya sas"
goodbye	αντίο	"an**dee**-o"

greasy	λιπαρός	"lee-pa**ros**"
Greece	η Ελλάδα	"ee e**ladha**"
▷ **what part of Greece are you from?**	από ποιο μέρος της Ελλάδας είστε;	"**apo** peeo **me**ros tees **ela**-dhas **ees**-te"
Greek *adj*	ελληνικός	"eleenee**kos**"
▷ **I don't speak Greek**	δεν μιλάω ελληνικά	"dhen meela-o elee-nee**ka**"
green	πράσινος	"**prasee**-nos"
grey	γκρίζος	"**gree**zos"
grilled	της σχάρας	"tees **skha**ras"
grocer's	το μπακάλικο	"to baka-leeko"
ground[1] *n*	το έδαφος	"to **edha**-fos"
ground[2] *adj* (coffee etc)	αλεσμένος	"ales-**me**nos"
ground floor	το ισόγειο	"to ee**so**-yee-o"
▷ **could I have a room on the ground floor?**	μπορώ να έχω ένα δωμάτιο στο ισόγειο;	"bo-**ro** na **e**kho ena dho**mat**ee-o sto ee**so**-yee-o"
groundsheet	ο μουσαμάς εδάφους	"o moosa**mas edha**foos"
group	η ομάδα	"ee o**madha**"
▷ **do you give discounts for groups?**	κάνετε έκπτωση σε γκρουπ;	"**kane**-te **ek**ptosee se group"
group passport	το ομαδικό διαβατήριο	"to omadhee**ko** dhee-ava**tee**reeo"
to grow	μεγαλώνω	"megha-**lo**no"
guarantee	η εγγύηση	"ee en**gee**-eesee"
▷ **a five-year guarantee**	πέντε χρόνια εγγύηση	"**pen**de **khro**nee-a en**gee**-eesee"
guard (in train)	ο υπεύθυνος τραίνου	"o ee**pef**-theenos **tre**noo"
guest	ο φιλοξενούμενος	"o feelok-se**noo**-menos"
guesthouse	ο ξενώνας	"o kse-**no**nas"

ABSOLUTE ESSENTIALS

I don't understand	δεν καταλαβαίνω	"dhen kata-la**ve**no"
I don't speak Greek	δεν μιλάω ελληνικά	"dhen meela-o elee-nee**ka**"
do you speak English?	μιλάτε αγγλικά;	"meela-te anglee-**ka**"
more slowly please	πιο σιγά παρακαλώ	"peeo seegha para-ka**lo**"

guide[1] *n*	ο/η ξεναγός	"o/ee ksena-**ghos**"
▷ **is there an English-speaking guide?**	υπάρχει ξεναγός που να μιλάει αγγλικά;	"ee**park**hee ksenaghos poo na meela-ee anglee-**ka**"
to **guide**[2] *vb*	ξεναγώ	"ksena**gho**"
guidebook	ο οδηγός	"o odhee-**ghos**"
▷ **do you have a guidebook in English?**	έχετε οδηγό στα αγγλικά;	"**ekhe**-te odhee-**gho** sta anglee-**ka**"
▷ **do you have a guidebook to the cathedral?**	έχετε βιβλίο-οδηγό για το ναό;	"**ekhe**-te veev**lee**-o-odhee**gho** ya to na-**o**"
guided tour	η περιήγηση με ξεναγό	"ee peree-**ee**yeesee me ksena-**gho**"
▷ **what time does the guided tour begin?**	τι ώρα αρχίζει η ξενάγηση	"tee **o**-ra ar**khee**zee ee ksen**a**yeesee"
gum	τα ούλα	"ta **oo**la"
▷ **my gums are bleeding/are sore**	τα ούλα μου έχουν ματώσει/με πονάνε	"ta **oo**la moo **e**khoon ma-**to**see/me pon**a**-ne"
gym	το γυμναστήριο	"to yeemna**stee**ree-o"
gym shoes	τα παπούτσια γυμναστικής	"to pa**poo**tsee-a yeemna-stee**kees**"
haemorrhoids	οι αιμορροΐδες	"ee emoro**ee**dhes"
▷ **I need something for haemorrhoids**	θέλω κάτι για αιμορροΐδες	"**the**-lo **ka**tee ya emoro**ee**dhes"
hair	τα μαλλιά	"ta mal**ea**a"
▷ **my hair is naturally curly/straight**	τα μαλλιά μου είναι φυσικά κατσαρά/ ίσια	"ta mal**ea**a moo **ee**-ne feesee**ka** katsa**ra**/ **ee**see-a"
▷ **I have greasy/dry hair**	τα μαλλιά μου είναι λιπαρά/ξηρά	"ta mal**ea**a moo **ee**-ne leepa**ra**/ksee**ra**"
hairbrush	η βούρτσα	"ee **voor**tsa"
haircut	το κούρεμα	"to **koo**-rema"

hairdresser	ο κομμωττής	"o komo-**tees**"
	η κομμώτρια	"ee komo**tree**-a"
hair dryer	το πιστολάκι	"to peesto**la**-kee"
hairgrip	το τσιμπιδάκι	"o tseembee-**dha**kee"
hair spray	το σπρέι για μαλλιά	"to **spre**-ee ya maleea"
half	το μισό	"to mee**so**"
▷ **half an hour**	μισή ώρα	"mee**see o**-ra"
▷ **half past two/three**	δύο/τρεις και μισή	"**dhee**-o/tree-s ke mee**see**"
▷ **half price**	μισή τιμή	"mee**see** tee**mee**"
▷ **a half bottle**	η μικρή μπουκάλα	"ee mee**kree** boo-**ka**la"
half board	ημιδιατροφή	"eemee-dhee-atro**fee**"
half fare	το μισό εισιτήριο	"to mee**so** eesee-**tee**ree-o"
ham	το ζαμπόν	"to zam**bon**"
hand	το χέρι	"to **khe**ree"
handbag	η τσάντα	"ee **tsan**da"
▷ **my handbag's been stolen**	μου έκλεψαν την τσάντα μου	"moo **e**-klepsan teen **tsan**da moo"
handbrake	το χειρόφρενο	"to khee**ro**freno"
handicapped	ο ανάπηρος	"o a**na**peeros"
handkerchief	το μαντήλι	"to man-**dee**lee"
handle	το χερούλι	"to khe**roo**lee"
▷ **the handle has come off**	το χερούλι έχει βγει	"to khe**roo**lee **e**khee vyee"
hand luggage	οι χειραποσκευές	"ee kheera-poske**ves**"
handmade	χειροποίητος	"kheero**pee**-eetos"
▷ **is this handmade?**	είναι χειροποίητο;	"**ee**-ne kheero**pee**-eeto"
hangover	ο πονοκέφαλος από μεθύσι	"o pono-**ke**fa-los **a**po me**thee**see"

ABSOLUTE ESSENTIALS

do you have ...?	έχετε ...;	"**ekhe**-te"
is there ...?	υπάρχει ...;	"ee-**par**khee"
are there ...?	υπάρχουν ...;	"ee-**par**khoon"
how much is ...?	πόσο κάνει ...;	"**poso ka**nee"

to **happen**	συμβαίνω	"seem-**ve**no"
▷ what happened?	τι έγινε;	"tee **e**yee-ne"
▷ when did it happen?	πότε έγινε;	"**po**-te **e**yee-ne"
happy	ευτυχισμένος	"efteekheesmenos"
▷ I'm not happy with ...	δεν είμαι ευχαριστημένος με	"dhen **ee**-me efkha- reesteeme-nos me"
harbour	το λιμάνι	"to lee-**ma**nee"
hard	σκληρός	"sklee**ros**"
hat	το καπέλο	"to ka-**pe**lo"
to **have:**		

I have	έχω	"**e**kho"
you have (*informal* *singular*)	έχεις	"**e**khees"
he/she/it has	έχει	"**e**khee"
we have	έχουμε	"**e**khoo-me"
you have (*plural or* *formal singular*)	έχετε	"**e**khe-te"
▷ they have	έχουν	"**e**khoon"

▷ **do you have ...?**	έχετε ...;	"**e**khe-te"
hay fever	το αλλεργικό συνάχι	"to aler-yee**ko** see- **na**khee"
hazelnut	το φουντούκι	"to foon-**doo**kee"
he	αυτός	"af**tos**"
head	το κεφάλι	"to ke-**fa**lee"
headache:		
▷ I have a headache	έχω πονοκέφαλο	"**e**kho pono-**ke**falo"
▷ I want something for a headache	θέλω κάτι για τον πονοκέφαλο	"**the**-lo **ka**tee ya ton pono-**ke**falo"

headlights	οι προβολείς	"ee provo**lees**"
head waiter	ο μαιτρ	"o metr"
to **hear**	ακούω	"**akoo**-o"
heart	η καρδιά	"ee kardhee-**a**"
heart attack	η καρδιακή προσβολή	"ee kardhee-a**kee** pros-vo-**lee**"
heater	η θερμάστρα	"ee ther-**ma**stra"
▷ **the heater is not working**	η θερμάστρα δεν δουλεύει	"ee therma-stra dhen dhoo-**levee**"
heating	η θέρμανση	"ee **ther**-mansee"
▷ **I can't turn the heating off/on**	δεν μπορώ να κλείσω/ανοίξω το καλοριφέρ	"dhen bo-**ro** na **klee**so/a**nee**kso to kalo-ree**fer**"
heavy	βαρύς	"va**rees**"
▷ **this is too heavy**	αυτό είναι πολύ βαρύ	"af**to** ee-ne po**lee** va**ree**"
hello	γεια σας	"ya sas"
help[1] *n*	η βοήθεια	"ee vo-**ee**thee-a"
▷ **help!**	βοήθεια!	"vo-**ee**thee-a"
▷ **fetch help quickly**	φέρτε βοήθεια γρήγορα	"**fer**-te vo-**ee**thee-a **ghree**-ghora"
to **help**[2] *vb*	βοηθώ	"vo-ee**tho**"
▷ **can you help me?**	μπορείτε να με βοηθήσετε;	"boree-te na me vo-ee**thee**-se-te"
▷ **help yourself!**	παρακαλώ πάρτε!	"para-ka**lo** **par**-te"
her *adj*	της	"tees"
▷ **it's her book!**	είναι το βιβλίο της	"**ee**-ne to veev**lee**-o tees"
here	εδώ	"ed**ho**"
▷ **here you are!**	ορίστε!	"o**reest**-e"
herring	η ρέγγα	"ee **ren**-ga"
hers	δικός της	"dhee-**kos** tees"

ABSOLUTE ESSENTIALS

I don't understand	δεν καταλαβαίνω	"dhen kata-**la**veno"
I don't speak Greek	δεν μιλάω ελληνικά	"dhen meela-o elee-neeka"
do you speak English?	μιλάτε αγγλικά;	"meela-te anglee-ka"
more slowly please	πιο σιγά παρακαλώ	"peeo seegha para-kalo"

▷ it's hers	είναι δικό της	"**ee**-ne dhee-**ko** tees"
high	ψηλός	"psee**los**"
▷ how high is it?	πόσο ψηλό είναι;	"**po**so pseelo **ee**-ne"
high blood pressure	η υψηλή πίεση	"ee eepsee**lee pee**- esee"
high chair	η ψηλή παιδική καρέκλα	"ee psee**lee** pedhee-**kee** ka-**rekla**"
highlights (*in hair*)	οι ανταύγειες	"ee an**dav**-yee-es"
hill	ο λόφος	"o **lo**fos"
(*slope*)	η πλαγιά	"ee pla**ya**"
to **hire**	νοικιάζω	"neekee-**azo**"
▷ I want to hire a car	θέλω να νοικιάσω ένα αυτοκίνητο	"**the**-lo na neekee-**aso** ena afto-**kee**neeto"
▷ can I hire a deck chair/a boat?	μπορώ να νοικιάσω μία σαιζ-λονγκ/ βάρκα;	"bo-**ro** na neekee-**aso mee**a sez-long/**va**rka"
his¹ *adj*	του	"too"
▷ it's his book	είναι το βιβλίο του	"ee-**ne** to veevlee-o too"
his² *pron*	δικός του	"dhee-**kos** too"
▷ it's his	είναι δικό του	"**ee**-ne dhee-**ko** too"
to **hit**	χτυπώ	"khtee**po**"
to **hitchhike**	κάνω ωτοστόπ	"**ka**-no oto-**stop**"
HIV-negative	μη φορέας του AIDS	"mee fo-**reas** too AIDS"
HIV-positive	φορέας του AIDS	"fo-**reas** too AIDS"
to **hold**	κρατώ	"kra**to**"
▷ could you hold this for me?	μπορείτε να μου κρατήσετε αυτό;	"bo**ree**-te na moo kra-**tee**se-te afto"
hold-up	η καθυστέρηση	"ee kathee-**stereesee**"

ABSOLUTE ESSENTIALS

I would like ...	θα ήθελα ...	"tha **ee**thela"
I need ...	χρειάζομαι ...	"khree-**azo**-me"
where is ...?	πού είναι ...;	"poo **ee**-ne"
we're looking for ...	ψάχνουμε ...	"**psa**khnoo-me"

▷ what is causing the hold-up?	τι προκαλεί την καθυστέρηση;	"tee pro-ka**lee** teen kathee-**ste**ree-see"
hole	η τρύπα	"ee **tree**pa"
holiday	οι διακοπές	"ee dhee-ako**pes**"
▷ I'm on holiday	είμαι διακοπές	"**ee**-me dhee-ako**pes**"
▷ I'm on holiday here	βρίσκομαι εδώ για διακοπές	"**vree**sko-me e**dho** ya dhee-ako**pes**"
holiday resort	το θέρετρο	"to **the**retro"
home	το σπίτι	"to **spee**tee"
▷ I'm going home tomorrow/on Tuesday	φεύγω αύριο/την Τρίτη	"**fev**-gho avreeo/teen **tree**tee"
homesick:		
▷ to be homesick	νοσταλγώ την πατρίδα μου	"nostal-**gho** teen pat**ree**-dha moo"
honey	το μέλι	"to **me**lee"
honeymoon	ο μήνας του μέλιτος	"o **mee**nas too **me**lee-tos"
to **hope** *vb*	ελπίζω	"el**pee**zo"
▷ I hope so	το ελπίζω	"to el**pee**zo"
▷ I hope not	ελπίζω όχι	"el**pee**zo **o**khee"
hors d'oeuvre	τα ορεκτικά	"ta orek-tee**ka**"
horse	το άλογο	"to **a**logho"
hose (*in car*)	ο σωλήνας	"o so**lee**-nas"
hospital	το νοσοκομείο	"to noso-ko**mee**-o"
▷ where is the nearest hospital?	πού είναι το κοντινότερο νοσοκομείο;	"poo **ee**-ne to kon-dee**no**-tero noso-ko**mee**-o"
▷ we must get him to hospital	πρέπει να τον πάμε στο νοσοκομείο	"**pre**pee na ton **pa**-me sto noso-ko**mee**-o"
hot	ζεστός	"zes**tos**"
(*spicy*)	καυτερός	"kafte**ros**"

ABSOLUTE ESSENTIALS

do you have ...?	έχετε ...;	"**ekhe**-te"
is there ...?	υπάρχει ...;	"ee-**parkhee**"
are there ...?	υπάρχουν ...;	"ee-**parkhoon**"
how much is ...?	πόσο κάνει ...;	"**poso kanee**"

▷ **I'm hot**	ζεσταίνομαι	"zes-**te**no-me"
▷ **it's hot** (*weather*)	κάνει ζέστη	"**ka**-nee **ze**stee"
hotel	το ξενοδοχείο	"to kseno-dho**khee**-o"
▷ **can you recomend a (cheap) hotel?**	μπορείτε να μας συστήσετε ένα (φτηνό) ξενοδοχείο;	"bo**ree**-te na mas see-**stee**se-te **e**na (f**tee**no) kseno-dho**khee**-o"
hour	η ώρα	"ee **o**-ra"
▷ **an hour ago**	πριν μία ώρα	"preen **mee**a **o**-ra"
▷ **in two hours' time**	σε δύο ώρες	"se **dhee**o ores"
house	το σπίτι	"to **spee**tee"
house wine	το κρασί χύμα	"to kra**see khee**ma"
how	πώς	"pos"
▷ **how much?**	πόσο;	"**po**so"
▷ **how many?**	πόσα;	"**po**sa"
▷ **how are you?**	πώς είστε;	"pos **ees**-te"
hundred	εκατό	"e-ka**to**"
hungry:		
▷ **I am hungry**	πεινάω	"peena-o"
hurry:		
▷ **I'm in a hurry**	βιάζομαι	"vee-**a**zo-me"
to **hurt:**		
▷ **that hurts**	με πονάει	"me po**na**-ee"
▷ **he is hurt**	έχει χτυπήσει	"**e**khee khtee-**pee**see"
▷ **my back hurts**	με πονάει η πλάτη μου	"me po**na**ee ee **pla**-tee moo"
husband	ο σύζυγος	"o **see**zee-ghos"
hydrofoil	το ιπτάμενο δελφίνι	"to eep**ta**-meno dhel-**fee**nee"
I	εγώ	"e**gho**"
ice	ο πάγος	"o **pa**ghos"

ice cream	το παγωτό	"to pagho-**to**"
iced (*drink*)	παγωμένος	"pagho-**me**nos"
if	αν	"an"
ignition	η ανάφλεξη	"ee **ana**-fleksee"
ill	άρρωστος	"**a**rostos"
immediately	αμέσως	"a-**me**sos"
important	σπουδαίος	"spoo**dhe**-os"
impossible	αδύνατο	"a**dhee**-nato"
in	σε	"se"
inch	ίντσα	"**een**tsa"
included	συμπεριλαμβανο- μένου	"seemberee-lamvano- **me**noo"
indicators (*on car*)	το φλας	"to flas"
indigestion	η δυσπεψία	"ee dheespe**psee**-a"
indoors	μέσα	"**me**sa"
infectious	μεταδοτικός	"meta-dhotee**khos**"
▷ **is it infectious?**	είναι μεταδοτικό;	"**ee**-ne meta-dhotee**kho**"
information	οι πληροφορίες	"ee pleero-fo**ree**-es"
▷ **I'd like some information about ...**	θα ήθελα πληροφορίες για ...	"the **ee**the-la pleero- fo**ree**-es ya"
information office	το γραφείο πληροφοριών	"to ghra**fee**-o pleero- toree-**on**"
injection	η ένεση	"ee **e**-nesee"
▷ **please give me an injection**	παρακαλώ, κάντε μου μία ένεση	"para-ka**lo ka**nde moo **mee**a e-nesee"
injured	τραυματισμένος	"travma-tees**me**nos"
▷ **he is seriously injured**	έχει χτυπήσει σοβαρά	"**e**khee khtee-**pee**see sova**ra**"
ink	το μελάνι	"to me-**la**nee"
insect	το έντομο	"to **en**-domo"

I don't understand	δεν καταλαβαίνω	"dhen kata-la**ve**no"
I don't speak Greek	δεν μιλάω ελληνικά	"dhen mee**la**-o elee-nee**ka**"
do you speak English?	μιλάτε αγγλικά;	"mee**la**-te anglee-**ka**"
more slowly please	πιο σιγά παρακαλώ	"**pee**o see**gha** para-ka**lo**"

insect bite	το τσίμπημα	"to **tseem**-beema"
insect repellent	η εντομοαπωθητική λοσιόν	"ee endomo-apothee-tee**kee** losee-**on**"
inside	το εσωτερικό	"to eso-teree**ko**"
▷ **inside the car**	μέσα στο αυτοκίνητο	"**me**sa sto afto-**kee**neeto"
▷ **it's inside**	είναι μέσα	"**ee**-ne **me**sa"
instant coffee	ο στιγμιαίος καφές	"o steeghmee-**eos** ka-**fes**"
instead	αντί	"an**dee**"
instructor	ο εκπαιδευτής	"o ekpe-dhef**tees**"
insulin	η ινσουλίνη	"ee eensoo-**lee**nee"
insurance	η ασφάλεια	"ee asfalee-a"
▷ **will the insurance pay for it?**	θα πληρώσει η ασφάλεια;	"tha plee**ro**see ee asfalee-a"
insurance certificate	το πιστοποιητικό ασφάλισης	"to peesto-pee-eetee**ko** asfa-**lee**sees"
▷ **can I see your insurance certificate, please?**	μπορώ να δω την ασφάλειά σας παρακαλώ;	"bo-**ro** na dho teen asfa-lee**a** sas para-ka**lo**"
to **insure**	ασφαλίζω	"asfa**lee**-zo"
▷ **can I insure my luggage?**	μπορώ να ασφαλίσω τις αποσκευές μου;	"bo-**ro** na asfa**lee**-so tees apo-ske**ves** moo"
interesting	ενδιαφέρων	"endhee-a**fe**ron"
international	διεθνής	"dhee-eth**nees**"
interpreter	ο/η διερμηνέας	"o/ee dhee-ermee**ne**-as"
into	σε	"se"
invitation	η πρόσκληση	"ee **pros**-kleesee"
to **invite**	προσκαλώ	"pros-ka**lo**"
invoice	το τιμολόγιο	"to teemo**lo**yo"
Ireland	η Ιρλανδία	"ee eerland**dhee**-a"

ABSOLUTE ESSENTIALS

I would like ...	θα ήθελα ...	"tha **ee**thela"
I need ...	χρειάζομαι ...	"khree-**a**zo-me"
where is ...?	πού είναι ...;	"poo **ee**-ne"
we're looking for ...	ψάχνουμε ...	"**psa**khnoo-me"

Irish *adj*	ιρλανδικός	"eerlan-dhee**kos**"
▷ **I'm Irish**	είμαι Ιρλανδός/	"**ee**-me eerlan-**dhos**/
	Ιρλανδέζα	eerlan-**dhe**za"
iron[1] *n (metal)*	το σίδερο	"to **see**dhero"
▷ **I need an iron**	χρειάζομαι ένα	"khree**a**zo-me **e**na
	σίδερο	**see**dhero"
to iron[2] *vb*	σιδερώνω	"seedhe**ro**no"
▷ **where can I get this skirt ironed?**	πού μπορούν να μου σιδερώσουν αυτή τη φούστα;	"poo bo**roon** na moo seedhee-**ro**soon af**tee** tee **foo**sta"
ironmonger's	το σιδηροπωλείο	"to seedheero-po**lee**-o"
is	είναι	"**ee**-ne"
island	το νησί	"to nee**see**"
it	αυτό	"af**to**"
Italian *adj*	ιταλικός	"eetalee**kos**"
(*language*)	ιταλικά	"eetalee**ka**"
Italy	η Ιταλία	"ee eeta**lee**-a"
itch	η φαγούρα	"ee fa-**ghoo**ra"
jack	ο γρύλος	"o **ghree**los"
jacket	το σακκάκι	"to sa-**ka**kee"
jam	η μαρμελάδα	"ee marme-**la**dha"
▷ **strawberry/apricot jam**	μαρμελάδα φράουλα/ βερύκοκο	"marme-**la**dha **fra**oola/ ve**ree**koko"
jammed	φρακαρισμένος	"frakarees-**me**nos"
▷ **the drawer is jammed**	το συρτάρι έχει φρακάρει	"to seer**ta**-ree **e**khee fraka-**ree**"
January	Ιανουάριος	"ee-anoo-**a**reeos"
jar	το βάζο	"to **va**zo"
jazz	η τζαζ	"ee dzaz"
jeans	το τζην	"to dzeen"

ABSOLUTE ESSENTIALS

do you have ...?	έχετε ...;	"**ekhe**-te"
is there ...?	υπάρχει ...;	"ee-**parkhee**"
are there ...?	υπάρχουν ...;	"ee-**parkhoon**"
how much is ...?	πόσο κάνει ...;	"**poso kanee**"

jelly	το ζελέ	"to zele"
jellyfish	η τσούχτρα	"ee tsookhtra"
▷ **I've been stung by a jellyfish**	με τσίμπησε μία τσούχτρα	"me tseem-bee-se meea tsookhtra"
jeweller's	το κοσμηματοπωλείο	"to kosmee-mato-polee-o"
jewellery	τα κοσμήματα	"ta kosmee-mata"
Jewish	Εβραίος	"evreos"
	Εβραία	"evrea"
job	η δουλειά	"ee dhoo-leea"
▷ **what is your job?**	τι δουλειά κάνετε;	"tee dhoo-leea kane-te"
jogging:		
▷ **to go jogging**	πηγαίνω για τζόκινγκ	"pee-yeno ya jogging"
to join (*a club*)	γίνομαι μέλος	"yeeno-me melos"
joke	το αστείο	"to astee-o"
journey	το ταξίδι	"to takseedhee"
▷ **how was your journey?**	είχατε καλό ταξίδι;	"eekha-te kalo takseedhee"
jug	η κανάτα	"ee kana-ta"
▷ **a jug of water**	μία κανάτα νερό	"meea kana-ta nero"
juice	ο χυμός	"o kheemos"
July	Ιούλιος	"ee-ooleeos"
jump leads	τα καλώδια μπαταρίας	"ta kalodhee-a bataree-as"
junction (*crossroads*)	η διασταύρωση	"ee dhee-astav-rosee"
June	Ιούνιος	"ee-ooneeos"
just:		
▷ **just two**	μόνο δύο	"mono dhee-o"
▷ **I've just arrived**	μόλις έφτασα	"molees eftasa"
to keep	κρατώ	"krato"

ABSOLUTE ESSENTIALS

yes (please)	ναι (παρακαλώ)	"ne (para-kalo)"
no (thank you)	όχι (ευχαριστώ)	"okhee (efkhareesto)"
hello	γεια σας	"ya sas"
goodbye	αντίο	"andee-o"

▷ may I keep it?	μπορώ να το κρατήσω;	"bo-**ro** na to kra**tee**-so"
▷ could you keep me a loaf of bread?	μπορείτε να μου κρατήσετε ένα καρβέλι ψωμί;	"bo**ree**-te na moo kra**tee**se-te **e**na kar**ve**lee pso**mee**"
kettle	ο βραστήρας	"o vras**tee**ras"
key	το κλειδί	"to klee**dhee**"
▷ which is the key for the front door?	ποιο είναι το κλειδί της μπροστινής πόρτας;	"pee**o ee**-ne to klee**dhee** tees brostee-**nees por**tas"
▷ I've lost my key	έχω χάσει το κλειδί μου	"ekho **kha**see to klee**dhee** moo"
▷ can I have my key?	μπορώ να έχω το κλειδί μου;	"bo-**ro** na ekho to klee**dhee** moo"
kidneys	τα νεφρά	"ta ne**fra**"
kilo	το κιλό	"to kee**lo**"
kilometre	το χιλιόμετρο	"to kheelee-**o**metro"
kind[1] *n (sort)*	το είδος	"to **ee**dhos"
▷ what kind of ...?	τι είδος ...;	"tee **ee**dhos"
kind[2] *adj*	καλός	"ka**los**"
▷ that's very kind of you	πολύ ευγενικό από μέρους σας	"po**lee** ev-ghenee**ko** apo **me**roos sas"
to **kiss**	φιλώ	"fee**lo**"
kitchen	η κουζίνα	"ee koo-**zee**na"
knife	το μαχαίρι	"to ma-**khe**ree"
to **know**	ξέρω	"**kse**ro"
▷ do you know where I can ...?	ξέρετε πού μπορώ να ...;	"**kse**re-te poo bo-**ro** na"
▷ I don't know	δεν ξέρω	"dhen **kse**ro"
lace	η δαντέλα	"ee dhan-**de**la"
laces *(for shoes)*	τα κορδόνια	"ta kor-**dho**neea"

ABSOLUTE ESSENTIALS

I don't understand	δεν καταλαβαίνω	"dhen kata-**la**veno"
I don't speak Greek	δεν μιλάω ελληνικά	"dhen meela-o elee-nee-ka"
do you speak English?	μιλάτε αγγλικά;	"meela-te anglee-**ka**"
more slowly please	πιο σιγά παρακαλώ	"pee**o** seegha para-ka**lo**"

ladder	η σκάλα	"ee **ska**la"
ladies'	γυναικών	"yee-ne**kon**"
▷ **where is the ladies'?**	πού είναι των γυναικών	"poo **ee**-ne ton yee-ne**kon**"
lady	η κυρία	"ee kee**ree**-a"
lager	η μπύρα	"ee **bee**ra"
lake	η λίμνη	"ee **leem**nee"
lamb	το αρνί	"to ar**nee**"
lamp	η λάμπα	"ee **lam**ba"
lane	το δρομάκι	"to dhro**ma**kee"
(*on road*)	η λωρίδα	"ee lo**ree**dha"
▷ **you are in the wrong lane**	είστε σε λάθος λωρίδα	"**ees**-te se **la**thos lo**ree**dha"
language	η γλώσσα	"ee **ghlo**sa"
large	μεγάλος	"me-**gha**los"
larger	μεγαλύτερος	"me-gha**lee**teros"
▷ **do you have a larger one?**	έχετε ένα μεγαλύτερο;	"**ekhe**-te ena me-gha**lee**tero"
last¹ *adj*	τελευταίος	"telef-**te**os"
▷ **last week**	η περασμένη βδομάδα	"ee peras**me**nee vdho**ma**dha"
to **last²** *vb*	διαρκώ	"dhee-ar**ko**"
▷ **how long will it last?**	πόσο θα διαρκέσει;	"**po**so tha dhee-ar**ke**see"
late (*in the day*)	αργά	"ar**gha**"
▷ **late last night**	αργά χθες το βράδυ	"ar**gha** khthes to **vra**dhee"
▷ **it's too late**	είναι πολύ αργά	"**ee**-ne po**lee** ar**gha**"
▷ **the train is 10 minutes late**	το τραίνο έχει καθυστέρηση 10 λεπτών	"to **tre**no ekhee kathee-**ste**reesee **dhe**ka lep**ton**"

ABSOLUTE ESSENTIALS

I would like ...	θα ήθελα ...	"tha **ee**thela"
I need ...	χρειάζομαι ...	"khree-**azo**-me"
where is ...?	πού είναι ...;	"poo **ee**-ne"
we're looking for ...	ψάχνουμε ...	"**psa**khnoo-me"

▷ **sorry we are late**	συγγνώμη που αργήσαμε	"seeghn**o**mee poo ar**yee**sa-me"
later	αργότερα	"ar**gho**-tera"
▷ **see you later**	θα σε δω αργότερα	"tha se dho **argho**-tera"
launderette	το δημόσιο πλυντήριο	"to dhee**mo**see-o pleen-**dee**ree-o"
laundry service	η υπηρεσία πλυντηρίου	"ee eepeere**see**a pleendee**ree**-oo"
▷ **is there a laundry service?**	έχετε υπηρεσία πλυντηρίου;	"**ekhe**-te eepeere**see**a pleendee**ree**-oo"
lavatory	το αποχωρητήριο	"to apokhoree-**tee**ree-o"
lawyer	ο/η δικηγόρος	"o/ee dheekee**gho**ros"
laxative	το καθαρτικό	"to kathar-tee**ko**"
lay-by	η βοηθητική λωρίδα	"ee vo-eetheetee**kee** lo**ree**dha"
lead (electric)	το καλώδιο	"to ka**lo**dhee-o"
leader (guide)	ο/η ξεναγός	"o/ee ksena**ghos**"
leak	η διαρροή	"ee dhee-aro-**ee**"
▷ **there is a leak in the petrol tank**	υπάρχει διαρροή στο ρεζερβουάρ	"ee**par**-khee dhee-aro-**ee** sto rezervoo-**ar**"
to **learn**	μαθαίνω	"ma-**the**no"
least:		
▷ **at least**	τουλάχιστο	"too**la**-kheesto"
leather	το δέρμα	"to **dher**ma"
to **leave**	φεύγω	"**fev**-gho"
▷ **when does the train leave?**	πότε φεύγει το τρένο;	"**po**-te **fev**yee to **tre**no"
▷ **I shall be leaving tomorrow morning**	θα φύγω αύριο το πρωί	"tha **fee**gho **av**ree-o to pro-**ee**"

do you have ...?	έχετε ...;	"**ekhe**-te"
is there ...?	υπάρχει ...;	"ee-**par**khee"
are there ...?	υπάρχουν ...;	"ee-**par**khoon"
how much is ...?	πόσο κάνει ...;	"**po**so **ka**nee"

▷ I left my bags in the taxi	ξέχασα τα πράγματά μου στο ταξί	"**kse**kha-sa ta **pra**-ghmata moo sto tak**see**"
▷ I left the keys in the car	ξέχασα τα κλειδιά μέσα στο αυτοκίνητο	"**kse**kha-sa ta klee-dhe**a me**sa sto afto-**kee**neeto"

left:

▷ on/to the left	αριστερά	"aree-ste**ra**"
left-luggage (*office*)	φύλαξη αποσκευών	"**fee**laxee apo-ske**von**"
leg	το πόδι	"to **po**dhee"
lemon	το λεμόνι	"to le**mo**nee"
lemonade	η λεμονάδα	"ee lemo-**na**dha"
lemon tea	το τσάι με λεμόνι	"to **tsa**-ee me le-**mo**nee"
to lend	δανείζω	"dha-**nee**zo"
▷ **could you lend me some money?**	μπορείτε να μου δανείσετε λίγα χρήματα;	"bo**ree**-te na moo dha**nee**se-te **lee**gha **khree**ma-ta"
lens	ο φακός	"o fa**kos**"
▷ **I wear contact lenses**	φοράω φακούς επαφής	"fora-o fa**koos** epa**fees**"

less:

▷ **less milk**	λιγότερο γάλα	"lee**gho**-tero **gha**la"
lesson	το μάθημα	"to **ma**thee-ma"
▷ **do you give lessons?**	παραδίδετε μαθήματα;	"para**dhee**-dhe-te ma**thee**-mata"
▷ **can we take lessons?**	μπορούμε να κάνουμε μαθήματα;	"bo**roo**-me na **ka**noo-me ma**thee**-mata"
to let (*allow*)	επιτρέπω	"epee-**tre**po"
(*hire out*)	ενοικιάζω	"eneekee-**a**zo"
letter	το γράμμα	"to **ghra**ma"

ABSOLUTE ESSENTIALS		
yes (please)	ναι (παρακαλώ)	"ne (para-ka**lo**)"
no (thank you)	όχι (ευχαριστώ)	"**okh**ee (efkharee**sto**)"
hello	γεια σας	"ya sas"
goodbye	αντίο	"an**dee**-o"

▷ **how much is a letter to England?**	πόσο κάνει ένα γράμμα για την Αγγλία;	"**po**so **ka**nee **e**na **ghra**ma ya teen ang**lee**-a"
lettuce	το μαρούλι	"to ma-**roo**lee"
library	η βιβλιοθήκη	"ee veevlee-o**thee**kee"
licence	η άδεια	"ee **a**dhee-a"
lid	το καπάκι	"to ka**pa**kee"
to **lie down**	ξαπλώνω	"ksa-**plo**no"
lifeboat	η ναυαγοσωστική λέμβος	"ee navagho-sostee**kee lem**vos"
lifeguard	ο ναυαγοσώστης	"o navagho**sos**tees"
life jacket	το σωσίβιο	"to so**see**vee-o"
lift	το ασανσέρ	"to asan-**ser**"
▷ **is there a lift in the building?**	υπάρχει ασανσέρ στο κτίριο;	"ee-**par**khee asan-**ser** sto **ktee**ree-o"
▷ **can you give me a lift to the garage?**	μπορείτε να με πάτε ως το συνεργείο;	"bo**ree**-te na me **pa**-te os to seener-**yee**-o"
light¹ *n*	το φως	"to fos"
▷ **may I take it over to the light?**	μπορώ να το δω στο φως;	"bo-**ro** na to dho sto fos"
▷ **have you got a light?**	έχετε φωτιά;	"**ekhe**-te fotee**a**"
light² *adj* (*colour*) (*weight*)	ανοιχτό ελαφρύς	"aneekh-**to**" "elaf-**rees**"
▷ **light blue/green**	ανοιχτό μπλε/ πράσινο	"aneekh-**to** ble/**pra**see-no"
light bulb	η λάμπα	"ee **lam**ba"
lighter (*for cigarettes*)	ο αναπτήρας	"o anap-**tee**ras"
lighter fuel	το υγρό αναπτήρα	"to eegh-**ro** anap-**tee**ra"
to **like**¹ *vb*:		
▷ **I like**	μου αρέσει	"moo a-**re**see"

ABSOLUTE ESSENTIALS

I don't understand	δεν καταλαβαίνω	"dhen kata-**la**veno"
I don't speak Greek	δεν μιλάω ελληνικά	"dhen meela-o elee-**nee**ka"
do you speak English?	μιλάτε αγγλικά;	"meela-te anglee-**ka**"
more slowly please	πιο σιγά παρακαλώ	"pee**o** seegha para-ka**lo**"

like² *prep*	σαν	"san"
▷ **like you**	σαν κι εσένα	"san ke**se**na"
▷ **like this**	σαν αυτό	"san af**to**"
line	η γραμμή	"ee ghra**mee**"
▷ **I'd like an outside line, please**	συνδέστε με με εξωτερική γραμμή, παρακαλώ	"seen-**dhes**-te me me ekso-teree**kee** ghra**mee** para-ka**lo**"
▷ **the line's engaged**	ο αριθμός μιλάει	"o areeth**mos** mee**la**-ee"
▷ **it's a bad line**	δεν ακούω καθαρά	"dhen a**koo**-o katha-**ra**"
lip salve	το βούτυρο-κακάο	"to **voo**teero-ka**ka**o"
lipstick	το κραγιόν	"to kra-**yon**"
liqueur	το λικέρ	"to lee**ker**"
▷ **what liqueurs do you have?**	τι λικέρ έχετε;	"tee lee**ker e**khe-te"
Lisbon	η Λισσαβώνα	"ee leesa**vo**-na"
to **listen to**	ακούω	"a**koo**-o"
litre	το λίτρο	"to **lee**tro"
little	μικρός	"mee-**kros**"
▷ **a little**	λίγο	"**lee**gho"
to **live**	μένω	"**me**no"
▷ **where do you live?**	πού μένετε;	"poo **me**ne-te"
▷ **he lives in London**	μένει στο Λονδίνο	"**me**nee sto lond-**dhee**no"
liver	το συκώτι	"to see-**ko**tee"
living room	το σαλόνι	"to sa**lo**nee"
loaf	το καρβέλι	"to kar-**ve**lee"
lobster	ο αστακός	"o asta-**kos**"
local	τοπικός	"topee-**kos**"
▷ **what's the local speciality?**	ποια είναι η τοπική σπεσιαλιτέ;	"**pee**a ee-ne ee topee**kee** spesee-alee-**te**"

ABSOLUTE ESSENTIALS		
I would like ...	θα ήθελα ...	"tha **ee**thela"
I need ...	χρειάζομαι ...	"khree-**a**zo-me"
where is ...?	πού είναι ...;	"poo **ee**-ne"
we're looking for ...	ψάχνουμε ...	"**psa**khnoo-me"

lock¹ *n* | η κλειδαριά | "ee klee-dharee-**a**"
▷ **the lock is broken** | έχει σπάσει η κλειδαριά | "**e**khee **spa**see ee klee-dharee-**a**"

to lock² *vb* | κλειδώνω | "klee**dho**no"
▷ **I have locked myself out of my room** | κλειδώθηκα έξω | "klee**dho**-thee-ka **e**kso"

lollipop | το γλειφιτζούρι | "to ghleefeed-**zoo**ree"

London | το Λονδίνο | "to lon-**dhee**no"

long | μακρύς | "mak**rees**"
▷ **for a long time** | για πολύ καιρό | "ya po**lee** ke**ro**"
▷ **how long will it take to get to ...?** | πόση ώρα θέλουμε για να φτάσουμε εκεί ...; | "**po**see **o**-ra **the**-loo-me ya na **fta**soo-me e**kee**"

long-sighted:
▷ **I'm long-sighted** | έχω πρεσβυωπία | "**e**kho presvee-**o**pee-a"

to look | κοιτάζω | "kee-**ta**zo"
▷ **I'm just looking** | απλώς βλέπω | "ap**los vle**po"

to look after | φροντίζω | "fron-**dee**zo"

to look at | κοιτάζω | "kee-**ta**zo"

to look for | ψάχνω | "**psa**khno"
▷ **we're looking for a hotel** | ψάχνουμε για ένα ξενοδοχείο | "**psa**khnoo-me ya **e**na ksenodho**khee**o"

lorry | το φορτηγό | "to fortee-**gho**"

to lose | χάνω | "**kha**no"

lost | χαμένος | "kha-**me**nos"
▷ **I have lost my wallet** | έχασα το πορτοφόλι μου | "**e**khasa to porto**fo**lee moo"
▷ **I am lost** | χάθηκα | "**kha**theeka"
▷ **my son is lost** | ο γιος μου έχει χαθεί | "o yos moo **e**khee kha**thee**"

ABSOLUTE ESSENTIALS

do you have ...?	έχετε ...;	"**e**khe-te"
is there ...?	υπάρχει ...;	"ee-**par**khee"
are there ...?	υπάρχουν ...;	"ee-**par**khoon"
how much is ...?	πόσο κάνει ...;	"**po**so **ka**nee"

lost property office	το γραφείο απολεσθέντων	"to ghra**fee**-o apoles-**then**don"
lot:		
▷ **a lot (of)**	πολύ	"po**lee**"
lotion	η λοσιόν	"ee losee-**on**"
loud	δυνατός	"dheena-**tos**"
▷ **it's too loud**	είναι πολύ δυνατά	"**ee**-ne polee dhee-na**ta**"
lounge (at airport)	η αίθουσα	"ee **eth**oo-sa"
(in hotel, house)	το σαλόνι	"to sa**lon**ee"
to **love**	αγαπώ	"agha-**po**"
▷ **I love swimming**	αγαπώ το κολύμπι	"agha-**po** to ko**leem**bee"
lovely	ωραίος	"ore-os"
▷ **it's a lovely day**	είναι υπέροχη μέρα	"**ee**-ne ee-**pe**rokhee **mera**"
low	χαμηλός	"khamee-**los**"
low-alcohol beer	μπύρα με λίγο αλκοόλ	"**beer**a me **lee**gho alko-**ol**"
low tide	η άμπωτη	"ee **am**-botee"
lucky	τυχερός	"teekhe**ros**"
luggage	οι αποσκευές	"ee apo-ske**ves**"
▷ **can you help me with my luggage, please?**	μπορείτε να με βοηθήσετε με τις αποσκευές μου, παρακαλώ	"bo**ree**-te na me vo-ee**thee**-se-te me tees apo-ske**ves** moo para-ka**lo**"
▷ **please take my luggage to a taxi**	παρακαλώ πηγαίνετε τις αποσκευές μου σε ένα ταξί	"para-ka**lo** pee**ye**ne-te tees apo-ske**ves** moo se ena ta**ksee**"
▷ **I sent my luggage on in advance**	έχω ήδη στείλει τις αποσκευές μου	"ekho **ee**dhee **stee**lee tees apo-ske**ves** moo"
▷ **our luggage has not arrived**	οι αποσκευές μας δεν έφτασαν	"ee apo-ske**ves** dhen **ef**tasan"

mains

▷ where do I check in my luggage?	πού είναι ο έλεγχος αποσκευών;	"poo ee-ne o elen-khos apo-skevon"
▷ could you have my luggage taken up?	μπορείτε να στείλετε τις αποσκευές μου πάνω;	"boree-te na steele-te tees apo-skevesmoo pano"
▷ please send someone to collect my luggage	παρακαλώ στείλτε κάποιον να παραλάβει τις αποσκευές μου	"para-kalo steel-te kapeeon na para-lavee tees apo-skevesmoo"
luggage rack	η σχάρο αποσκευών	"ee skhara apo-skevon"
luggage tag	η ετικέτα	"ee eteeketa"
luggage trolley	το καρότσι αποσκευών	"to ka-rotsee apo-skevon"
▷ are there any luggage trolleys?	υπάρχουν καρότσια για τις αποσκευές;	"eeparkhoon ka-rotseea ya tees apo-skeves"
lunch	το μεσημεριανό	"to mesee-meree-ano"
▷ what's for lunch?	τι έχει για μεσημεριανό;	"tee ekhee ya mesee-meree-ano"
luxury	η πολυτέλεια	"ee polee-telee-a"
macaroni	τα μακαρόνια	"ta makaronee-a"
machine	η μηχανή	"ee meekhanee"
madam	κυρία	"keeree-a"
Madrid	η Μαδρίτη	"ee madh-reetee"
magazine	το περιοδικό;	"to peree-odheeko"
▷ do you have any English magazines?	έχετε αγγλικά περιοδικά;	"ekhe-te angleeka peree-odheeka"
maid	η καμαριέρα	"ee kamaree-era"
main	κύριος	"keeree-os"
main course	το κύριο πιάτο	"to keereeo peeato"
mains (*electric*)	ο κεντρικός διακόπτης	"o kendree-kos dhee-akoptees"

ABSOLUTE ESSENTIALS

I don't understand	δεν καταλαβαίνω	"dhen kata-laveno"
I don't speak Greek	δεν μιλάω ελληνικά	"dhen meela-o elee-neeka"
do you speak English?	μιλάτε αγγλικά;	"meela-te anglee-ka"
more slowly please	πιο σιγά παρακαλώ	"peeo seegha para-kalo"

to **make**	κάνω	"**ka**no"

I make	κάνω	"**ka**no"
you make (*informal singular*)	κάνεις	"**ka**nees"
he/she/it makes	κάνει	"**ka**nee"
we make	κάνουμε	"**ka**noo-me"
you make (*plural or formal singular*)	κάνετε	"**ka**ne-te"
they make	κάνουν	"**ka**noon"

make-up	το μακιγιάζ	"makee-**yaz**"
make-up remover	η λοσιόν για ντεμακιγιάζ	"ee losee-**on** ya demakee-**yaz**"
man (*mankind*)	ο άνθρωπος	"o **an**thropos"
(*as opposed to woman*)	ο άνδρας	"o **an**dhras"
manager	ο διευθυντής	"o dhee-ef-theen**dees**"
▷ **I'd like to speak to the manager**	θέλω να μιλήσω στο διευθυντή	"**the**-lo na meelee-**so** sto dhee-ef-theen**dee** "
many	πολλοί	"po**lee**"
map	ο χάρτης	"o **khar**tees"
▷ **can you show me on the map?**	μπορείτε να μου δείξετε στο χάρτη	"bo**ree**-te na moo **dheek**-se-te sto **khar**tee"
▷ **I want a street map of the city**	θέλω έναν οδικό χάρτη της πόλης	"**the**-lo ena odhee-**ko khar**tee tees **po**lees"
▷ **I need a road map of ...**	χρειάζομαι έναν οδικό χάρτη της ...	"khree-**azo**-me enan odhee-**ko khar**tee tees"
▷ **where can I buy a map of the area?**	από πού μπορώ να αγοράσω έναν τοπικό χάρτη;	"**apo** poo bo-**ro** na agho-**raso** enan topee-**ko khar**tee"
March	Μάρτιος	"**mar**-teeos"

margarine	η μαργαρίνη	"ee margha-**reenee**"
mark	το σημάδι	"to seema-dhee"
market	η αγορά	"ee agho-**ra**"
▷ when is market day?	πότε έχει λαϊκή;	"**po**-te ekhee la-ee**kee**"
marmalade	η μαρμελάδα	"ee marme-**ladha**"
married	παντρεμένος	"pandre-**menos**"
	παντρεμένη	"pandre- **menee**"
Martini	το μαρτίνι	"to mar**teenee**"
mascara	η μάσκαρα	"ee **mas**kara"
mass (*religious service*)	η Θεία Λειτουργία	"ee **thee**-a leetoor-**yee**-a"
matches	τα σπίρτα	"ta **speer**ta"
material	το υλικό	"to eelee-**ko**"
▷ what is the material?	τι υλικό είναι;	"tee eelee-**ko ee**-ne"
to **matter**:		
▷ it doesn't matter	δεν πειράζει	"dhen pee-**razee**"
▷ what's the matter with you?	τι έχεις;	"tee **ekhees**"
May	Μάιος	"**ma**-eeos"
mayonnaise	η μαγιονέζα	"ee mayo-**neza**"
meal	το γεύμα	"to **yev**ma"
to **mean**	εννοώ	"eno-**o**"
▷ what does this mean?	τι σημαίνει αυτό;	"tee see**menee** af**to**"
measles	η ιλαρά	"ee eela**ra**"
to **measure**	μετρώ	"me**tro**"
▷ can you measure me, please?	μπορείτε να μου πάρετε τα μέτρα, παρακαλώ;	"bo**ree**-te na moo **pa**-re-te ta **me**tra para-ka**lo**"
meat	το κρέας	"to **kre**as"
▷ I don't eat meat	δεν τρώω κρέας	"dhen **tro**-o **kre**as"
mechanic	ο μηχανικός	"o meekha-nee**kos**"

ABSOLUTE ESSENTIALS

do you have ...?	έχετε ...;	"**ekhe**-te"
is there ...?	υπάρχει ...;	"ee-**parkhee**"
are there ...?	υπάρχουν ...;	"ee-**parkhoon**"
how much is ...?	πόσο κάνει ...;	"**poso kanee**"

▷ **can you send a mechanic?**	μπορείτε να στείλετε έναν μηχανικό;	"bo**ree**-te na **stee**-le-te enan meekhan-ee**ko**"
medicine	το φάρμακο	"to **far**mako"
medium (*wine*)	μέτριο γλυκύ	"**metree**-o ghlee**kee**"
(*steak*)	μέτριος	"**metree**-os"
(*size*)	μέτριος	"**metree**-os"
medium rare	μισοψημένος	"meesopsee-**me**nos"
to **meet**	συναντώ	"seenan-**do**"
▷ **where can we meet?**	πού μπορούμε να συναντηθούμε;	"poo bo**roo**-me na seenan-dee**thoo**-me"
▷ **pleased to meet you**	χαίρω πολύ	"**khe**ro po**lee**"
melon	το πεπόνι	"to pe-**po**nee"
(*watermelon*)	το καρπούζι	"to kar-**poo**zee"
member	το μέλος	"to **me**los"
▷ **do we need to be members?**	πρέπει να είμαστε μέλη;	"**pre**pee na **ee**ma-ste **me**lee"
men	οι άντρες	"ee **an**tres"
to **mention**	αναφέρω	"ana**fe**ro"
▷ **don't mention it**	παρακαλώ	"para-ka**lo**"
menu	το μενού	"to me**noo**"
▷ **may we see the menu?**	μπορούμε να δούμε τον κατάλογο;	"bo**roo**-me na **dhoo**-me ton ka**ta**-logho"
▷ **do you have a special menu for children?**	έχετε ειδικό μενού για παιδιά;	"**ekhe**-te eedhee-**ko** me**noo** ya pedhee-**a**"
▷ **we'll have the menu at ... drachmas**	θα πάρουμε το μενού με τις ... δραχμές	"tha **pa**roo-me to me**noo** me tees ... dhrakh**mes**"
message	το μήνυμα	"to **mee**neema"
▷ **can I leave a message?**	μπορώ να αφήσω ένα μήνυμα;	"bo-**ro** na a**fee**so ena **mee**neema"
meter	ο μετρητής	"to metree-**tees**"
metre	το μέτρο	"to **me**tro"

migraine	η ημικρανία	"ee eemee-kra**nee**-a"
▷ **I have a migraine**	έχω ημικρανία	"**ekho** eemee-kra**nee**-a"
milk	το γάλα	"to **ghala**"
milkshake	το μιλκσέικ	"to meelk-**se**-eek"
millimetre	το χιλιοστό	"to kheelee-o**sto**"
million	το εκατομμύριο	"to ekato-**mee**ree-o"
mince	ο κιμάς	"o kee**mas**"
to **mind:**		
▷ **do you mind if ...?**	σας ενοχλεί αν ...;	"sas enokh-**lee an**"
▷ **I don't mind**	δεν με πειράζει	"dhen me pee**ra**zee"
mine:		
▷ **this is not mine**	δεν είναι δικό μου	"dhen **ee**-ne dhee**ko** moo"
mineral water	το επιτραπέζιο νερό	"to epee-tra**pe**zee-o ne**ro**"
(*sparkling*)	το μεταλλικό νερό	"to meta-lee**ko** ne**ro**"
minimum	ελάχιστος	"e**la**-kheestos"
minister (*church*)	ο ιερέας	"o ee-e**re**-as"
minor road	ο δευτερεύων δρόμος	"o dhefte-**re**von **dhro**mos"
mint (*herb*)	ο δυόσμος	"o dhee-**o**smos"
minute	το λεπτό	"to lep**to**"
▷ **wait a minute**	περιμένετε ένα λεπτό	"peree**me**ne-te **e**na lep**to**"
mirror	ο καθρέφτης	"o kath-**ref**tees"
to **miss** (*train etc*)	χάνω	"**kha**no"
▷ **I've missed my train**	έχασα το τρένο μου	"**e**khasa to **tre**no moo"
Miss	Δεσποινίς	"dhespee-**nees**"
missing:		
▷ **my child/my handbag is missing**	έχασα το παιδί μου/ την τσάντα μου	"**e**khasa to pe**dhee** moo/ teen **tsan**-da moo"

ABSOLUTE ESSENTIALS

I don't understand	δεν καταλαβαίνω	"dhen kata-la**ve**no"
I don't speak Greek	δεν μιλάω ελληνικά	"dhen meela-o elee-**nee**ka"
do you speak English?	μιλάτε αγγλικά;	"**meela**-te anglee-**ka**"
more slowly please	πιο σιγά παρακαλώ	"**pee**o see**gha** para-ka**lo**"

mistake	το λάθος	"to **la**thos"
▷ **you've made a mistake in the change**	κάνατε λάθος τα ρέστα	"**ka**na-te **la**thos ta **re**sta"
misty:		
▷ **it's misty**	έχει ομίχλη	"**e**khee o**mee**khlee"
misunderstanding	η παρεξήγηση	"ee pare**ksee**yeesee"
modern	μοντέρνος	"mon**der**nos"
moisturizer	η υδατική κρέμα	"ee eedhatee-**kee kre**ma"
monastery	το μοναστήρι	"to mona-**stee**ree"
Monday	Δευτέρα	"dhef**te**ra"
money	τα χρήματα	"ta **khree**-mata"
▷ **I have run out of money**	δεν έχω άλλα λεφτά	"dhen **e**kho **a**la lef**ta**"
money order	η ταχυδρομική επιταγή	"ee takhee-dhromee**kee** epee-ta**yee**"
month	ο μήνας	"o **mee**nas"
monument	το μνημείο	"to mnee**mee**-o"
mop	η σφουγγαρίστρα	"ee sfooga-**ree**stra"
more	περισσότερος	"peree-**so**teros"
▷ **more wine, please**	κι άλλο κρασί, παρακαλώ	"kee**a**-lo kra-**see** para-ka**lo**"
morning	το πρωί	"to pro-**ee**"
▷ **in the morning**	το πρωί	"to pro-**ee**"
mosquito	το κουνούπι	"to koo-**noo**pee"
most	ο περισσότερος	"o peree-**so**teros"
▷ **the most popular discotheque**	η περισσότερο γνωστή ντισκοτέκ	"ee peree-**so**tero ghno-**stee** deesko-**tek**"
mother	η μητέρα	"ee mee-**te**ra"
motor	η μηχανή	"ee mee-kha**nee**"
motor boat	η βενζινάκατος	"ee venzee-**na**katos"

ABSOLUTE ESSENTIALS

I would like ...	θα ήθελα ...	"tha **ee**thela"
I need ...	χρειάζομαι ...	"khree-**a**zo-me"
where is ...?	πού είναι ...;	"poo **ee**-ne"
we're looking for ...	ψάχνουμε ...	"**psa**khnoo-me"

▷ can we rent a motor boat?	μπορούμε να νοικιάσουμε μία βάρκα με μηχανή;	"bo**roo**-me na neekee-**a**soo-me **mee**a varka me mee-kha**nee**"
motor cycle	η μοτοσικλέτα	"ee moto-see**kle**ta"
motorway	ο αυτοκινητόδρομος	"o afto-keenee-**to**dhromos"
▷ how do I get onto the motorway?	πώς μπορούμε να βγούμε στον αυτοκινητόδρομο;	"pos bo**roo**-me na **vghoo**-me ston afto-keenee-**to**dhromo"
▷ is there a toll on this motorway?	υπάρχουν διόδια σ'αυτόν τον αυτοκινητόδρομο;	"ee**par**-khoon dhee-**o**dhee-a saf**ton** ton afto-keenee-**to**dhromo"
mountain	το βουνό	"to voo**no**"
mousse	το μους	"to moos"
mouth	το στόμα	"to **sto**ma"
to **move**	κινούμαι	"kee**noo**-me"
▷ he can't move	δεν μπορεί να κινηθεί	"dhen bo**ree** na keenee-**thee**"
▷ I can't move my arm/leg	δεν μπορώ να κουνήσω το χέρι/ πόδι μου	"dhen bo-**ro** na koo-**nee**so to **khe**ree/ **po**dhee moo"
▷ don't move him	μην τον μετακινείτε	"meen ton meta-kee**nee**-te"
Mr	Κύριος	"**kee**ree-os"
Mrs	Κυρία	"kee**ree**-a"
much	πολύς	"po**lees**"
▷ that's too much	αυτό είναι πάρα πολύ	"af**to** ee-ne **pa**ra po**lee**"
▷ very much	πάρα πολύ	"**pa**ra po**lee**"
mumps	οι μαγουλάδες	"ee maghoo**la**dhes"
museum	το μουσείο	"to moo**see**-o"

ABSOLUTE ESSENTIALS

do you have ...?	έχετε ...;	"**ekhe**-te"
is there ...?	υπάρχει ...;	"ee-**parkhee**"
are there ...?	υπάρχουν ...;	"ee-**parkhoon**"
how much is ...?	πόσο κάνει ...;	"**poso kanee**"

▷ **the museum is open in the morning/ afternoon**	το μουσείο είναι ανοιχτό το πρωί/ απόγευμα	"to moosee-o ee-ne aneekh-to to pro-ee/ apoyevma"
mushroom	το μανιτάρι	"to manee-taree"
music	η μουσική	"ee mooseekee"
▷ **the music is too loud**	η μουσική είναι πολύ δυνατά	"ee mooseekee ee-ne polee dheenata"
mussel	το μύδι	"to meedhee"

must:

I must go	πρέπει να πάω	"prepee na pa-o"
you must go (*informal singular*)	πρέπει να πας	"prepee na pas"
he/she must go	πρέπει να πάει	"prepee na pa-ee"
we must go	πρέπει να πάμε	"prepee na pa-me"
you must go (*plural or formal singular*)	πρέπει να πάτε	"prepee na pa-te"
they must go	πρέπει να πάνε	"prepee na pa-ne"

mustard	η μουστάρδα	"ee moo-stardha"
mutton	το αρνί	"to arnee"
my	μου	"moo"
nail (*metal*)	το καρφί	"to karfee"
(*on finger, toe*)	το νύχι	"to neekhee"
nail polish	το βερνίκι νυχιών	"to verneekee neekheeon"
nail polish remover	το ασετόν	"to aseton"
naked	γυμνός	"yeemnos"
name	το όνομα	"to onoma"
▷ **what's your name?**	πώς σας λένε;	"pos sas le-ne"
▷ **my name is ...**	με λένε ...	"me le-ne"

napkin	η χαρτοπετσέτα	"ee kharto-pet-**seta**"
nappy	η πάνα	"ee **pa**na"
narrow	στενός	"**stenos**"
nationality	η εθνικότητα	"ee ethnee-**ko**teeta"
navy blue	μπλε	"ble"
near	κοντά	"kon**da**"
▷ **near the bank/the hotel**	κοντά στην τράπεζα/ στο ξενοδοχείο	"kon**da** steen **tra**-peza/sto kseno-dho**khee**-o"
necessary	απαραίτητος	"apa-**re**teetos"
neck	ο λαιμός	"o le**mos**"
necklace	το κολιέ	"to kolee-**e**"
to **need:**		
▷ **I need**	χρειάζομαι	"khree-**azo**-me"
needle	η βελόνα	"ee ve-**lo**na"
▷ **do you have a needle and thread?**	έχετε μία βελόνα και κλωστή;	"**ekhe**-te **mee**a ve**lo**na ke klos**tee**"
negative (*photography*)	το αρνητικό	"to arnee-tee**ko**"
neighbour	ο γείτονας η γειτόνισσα	"o **yee**-tonas" "ee yee**to**-neesa"
never	ποτέ	"po-**te**"
▷ **I never go there**	δεν πηγαίνω ποτέ εκεί	"dhen pee**ye**no po-**te** e**kee**"
new	καινούργιος	"ke**noor**-yos"
news (*TV, radio*)	οι ειδήσεις	"ee eedhee-sees"
newsagent's	το πρακτορείο εφημερίδων	"to prakto-**ree**o efee-me**ree**dhon"
newspaper	η εφημερίδα	"ee efee-me**ree**dha"
▷ **do you have any English newspapers?**	έχετε αγγλικές εφημερίδες;	"**ekhe**-te anglee**kes** efee-me**ree**dhes"

ABSOLUTE ESSENTIALS

I don't understand	δεν καταλαβαίνω	"dhen kata-la**ve**no"
I don't speak Greek	δεν μιλάω ελληνικά	"dhen meela-o elee-**nee**ka"
do you speak English?	μιλάτε αγγλικά;	"meela-te anglee-**ka**"
more slowly please	πιο σιγά παρακαλώ	"peeo see**gha** para-ka**lo**"

New Year	ο καινούργιος χρόνος	"o ke**noor**-yos **khro**nos"
▷ **Happy New Year!**	ευτιχισμένος ο καινούργιος χρόνος!	"eftee-khees-**me**nos o ke**noor**-yos **khro**nos"
New Zealand	η Νέα Ζηλανδία	"ee **ne**-a zeeland**hee**-a"
next	επόμενος	"e**po**menos"
▷ **the next stop**	η επόμενη στάση	"ee e**po**menee **sta**-see"
▷ **next week**	την άλλη βδομάδα	"teen alee vdho-**ma**dha"
▷ **take the next turning on the left**	κάντε στην επόμενη στροφή αριστερά	"**kan**-de steen e-**po**menee stro**fee** aree-stera"
▷ **when is the next bus to town?**	πότε είναι το επόμενο λεωφορείο για την πόλη;	"**po**-te **ee**-ne to e-**po**meno leo-fo**ree**-o ya teen **po**lee"
nice	ωραίος	"**ore**-os"
▷ **we are having a nice time**	περνάμε πολύ ωραία	"per-**na**-me po**lee ore**-a"
▷ **nice to have met you**	χαίρω πολύ	"**khe**ro po**lee**"
night	η νύχτα	"**neekh**-ta"
▷ **at night**	τη νύχτα	"tee **neekh**-ta"
▷ **last night**	χθες τη νύχτα	"khthes tee **neekh**-ta"
▷ **tomorrow night**	αύριο το βράδυ	"**avree**-o to **vra**dhee"
night club	το νυχτερινό κέντρο	"to neekh-teree**no ken**dro"
nightdress	το νυχτικό	"to neekh-tee**ko**"
nine	εννιά	"en**ya**"
nineteen	δεκαεννιά	"dheka-en**ya**"
ninety	ενενήντα	"e-ne**neen**da"
no	όχι	"**o**khee"
▷ **no thank you**	όχι ευχαριστώ	"**o**khee efkharee**sto**"
nobody	κανένας	"ka-**ne**nas"

noisy:

▷ it's too noisy — έχει πολύ θόρυβο — "**ekhee** po**lee tho**ree-vo"

non-alcoholic — μη οινοπνευματώδης — "mee eenop-nevma-**to**dhees"

none — κανένα — "ka-**ne**na"

▷ there's none left — δεν έχει μείνει κανένα — "then **ekhee mee**nee ka**ne**na"

non-smoking — μη καπνιστών — "mee kapnee-**ston**"

▷ I want to reserve a seat in a non-smoking compartment — θέλω να κλείσω θέση σε βαγόνι μη καπνιστών — "**the**-lo na **klee**so the**see** se va**gho**nee mee kapnee-**ston**"

north — ο βορράς — "o vo**ras**"

Northern Ireland — η Βόρεια Ιρλανδία — "ee **vo**ree-a eerland**hee**-a"

not — μη — "mee"

▷ I do not know — δεν ξέρω — "then **kse**ro"

note (*bank note*) — το χαρτονόμισμα — "to kharto**no**meesma"
  (*letter*) — το σημείωμα — "to see**mee**-oma"

note pad — το σημειωματάριο — "to semee-oma**ta**ree-o"

nothing — τίποτα — "**tee**-pota"

November — Νοέμβριος — "no-**em**vreeos"

now — τώρα — "**to**ra"

number — ο αριθμός — "o areeth-**mos**"

▷ car number — αριθμός αυτοκινήτου — "areeth-**mos** afto-kee**nee**too"

▷ what's the telephone number? — ποιος είναι ο αριθμός του τηλεφώνου; — "**pee**os **ee**-ne o areeth-**mos** too teele-**fo**noo"

▷ sorry, wrong number — συγγνώμη, λάθος νούμερο — "see-gh**no**mee **la**-thos **noo**mero"

nurse — η νοσοκόμα — "ee noso-**ko**ma"

nut (*peanut*) — το φυστίκι — "to fees**tee**kee"

ABSOLUTE ESSENTIALS

do you have ...?	έχετε ...;	"**ekhe**-te"
is there ...?	υπάρχει ...;	"ee-**parkhee**"
are there ...?	υπάρχουν ...;	"ee-**parkhoon**"
how much is ...?	πόσο κάνει ...;	"**poso kanee**"

(walnut)	το καρύδι	"to ka**ree**dhee"
(hazelnut)	το φουντούκι	"to foon**doo**kee"
(for bolt)	το παξιμάδι	"to paksee-**ma**dhee"
occasionally	κάπου-κάπου	"**ka**poo-**ka**poo"
o'clock:		
▷ **at 2 o'clock**	στις δύο η ώρα	"stees **dhee**o ee **o**-ra"
October	Οκτώβριος	"ok**to**-vreeos"
of course	βέβαια	"**ve**-ve-a"
off (light, machine etc)	σβηστός	"svee**stos**"
▷ **the lights are off**	το φως είναι σβηστό	"to fos ee-ne svee**sto**"
to **offer**	προσφέρω	"pros-**fero**"
office	το γραφείο	"to ghra**fee**-o"
▷ **I work in an office**	δουλεύω σε γραφείο	"dhoo-**levo** se ghra**fee**-o"
often	συχνά	"seekh-**na**"
oil	το λάδι	"to **la**dhee"
oil filter	το φίλτρο του λαδιού	"to **feel**tro too ladhee-**oo**"
ointment	η αλοιφή	"to alee**fee**"
OK	εντάξει	"en-**dak**see"
old (person)	ηλικιωμένος	"eeleekee-o**me**nos"
(thing)	παλιός	"palee-**os**"
▷ **how old are you?**	πόσων χρονών είστε;	"**po**son khro**non** ees-te"
olive oil	το ελαιόλαδο	"to ele-**o**ladho"
olives	οι ελιές	"ee elee-**es**"
omelette	η ομελέτα	"ee ome**le**ta"
on[1] adv (light, machine etc)	αναμένος	"ana**me**-nos"
on[2] prep	πάνω σε	"**pa**no se"
▷ **on the table**	πάνω στο τραπέζι	"**pa**no sto tra-**pe**zee"
once	μία φορά	"**mee**-a fo**ra**"

ABSOLUTE ESSENTIALS

yes (please)	ναι (παρακαλώ)	"ne (para-ka**lo**)"
no (thank you)	όχι (ευχαριστώ)	"**okhee** (efkharee**sto**)"
hello	γεια σας	"ya sas"
goodbye	αντίο	"an**dee**-o"

one	ένας	"**enas**"
	μία	"**mee**a"
	ένα	"**ena**"
(*numeral*)	ένα	"**ena**"
one-way (*street*)	ο μονόδρομος	"o **mono**-dhromos"
(*ticket*)	απλό	"ap**lo**"
onion	το κρεμμύδι	"to kre-**mee**dhee"
only	μόνο	"**mono**"
▷ **we only want 3**	θέλουμε μόνο τρία	"**the**-loo-me **mono tree**a"
open[1] *adj*	ανοικτός	"aneekh-**tos**"
▷ **is the castle open to the public?**	είναι το κάστρο ανοιχτό στο κοινό;	"**ee**-ne to **ka**stro aneekh-**to** sto kee**no**"
to **open**[2] *vb*	ανοίγω	"a**nee**-gho"
▷ **what time does the museum open?**	τι ώρα ανοίγει το μουσείο;	"tee **o**-ra a**nee**-yee to moo**see**-o"
▷ **I can't open the window**	δεν μπορώ να ανοίξω το παράθυρο	"dhen bo-**ro** na a**nee**kso to pa**ra**-theero"
opera	η όπερα	"ee **o**-pera"
operator (*telephone*)	η τηλεφωνήτρια	"ee teelefo-**nee**tree-a"
opposite	απέναντι	"a-**pe**nandee"
▷ **opposite the hotel**	απέναντι στο ξενοδοχείο	"a-**pe**nandee sto kseno-dho**khee**-o"
or	ή	"**ee**"
orange[1] *n* (*fruit*)	το πορτοκάλι	"to porto-**ka**lee"
orange[2] *adj*	πορτοκαλί	"porto-ka**lee**"
orange juice	ο χυμός πορτοκαλιού	"o khee**mos** porto-kalee-**oo**"
to **order**	παραγγέλνω	"pa-ran-**gel**no"
▷ **can I order now, please?**	μπορώ να παραγγείλω τώρα, παρακαλώ;	"bo-**ro** na paran-**gee**lo **to**ra para-ka**lo**"

ABSOLUTE ESSENTIALS

I don't understand	δεν καταλαβαίνω	"dhen kata-la-**ve**no"
I don't speak Greek	δεν μιλάω ελληνικά	"dhen **mee**la-o elee-nee**ka**"
do you speak English?	μιλάτε αγγλικά;	"**mee**la-te anglee-**ka**"
more slowly please	πιο σιγά παρακαλώ	"**pee**o see**gha** para-ka**lo**"

▷ **can you order me a taxi, please?**	μπορείτε να μου φωνάξετε ένα ταξί;	"bo**ree**-te na moo fo**nak**-se-te **e**na tak**see**"
oregano	η ρίγανη	"ee **ree**ghanee"
original	αρχικός	"arkhee-**kos**"
other	άλλος	"**a**los"
▷ **the other one**	ο άλλος	"o **a**los"
▷ **do you have any others?**	έχετε άλλα;	"**e**khe-te **a**la"
our	μας	"mas"
ours	δικός μας	"dhee-**kos** mas"
out (*light etc*)	σβησμένος	"svees-**me**nos"
▷ **he's out**	λείπει	"**lee**pee"
outdoors	στην ύπαιθρο	"steen **ee**-pethro"
outside	έξω	"**e**kso"
▷ **let's go outside**	ας βγούμε έξω	"as **vghoo**-me ekso"
▷ **an outside line, please**	μία εξωτερική γραμμή, παρακαλώ	"**mee**a ekso-teree**kee** ghra**mee** para-ka**lo**"
oven	ο φούρνος	"o **foor**nos"
over there	εκεί πέρα	"e**kee pe**ra"
to **overcharge**	παίρνω παραπάνω	"**per**no para-**pa**no"
to **overheat**	υπερθερμαίνω	"eeper-**ther-me**no"
▷ **the engine is overheating**	έχει υπερθερμανθεί η μηχανή	"**e**khee eeper-ther-man**thee** ee mee-kha**nee**"
overnight (*train*)	τη νύχτα νυχτερινός	"tee **nee**khta" "neekhteree**nos**"
to **owe**	χρωστάω	"khro**stao**"
▷ **you owe me ...**	μου χρωστάτε ...	"moo khrosta-te"
owner	ο ιδιοκτήτης η ιδιοκτήτρια	"o eedhee-ok**tee**tees" "ee eedhee-ok**tee**treea"

ABSOLUTE ESSENTIALS

I would like ...	θα ήθελα ...	"tha **ee**thela"
I need ...	χρειάζομαι ...	"khree-**a**zo-me"
where is ...?	πού είναι ...;	"poo **ee**-ne"
we're looking for ...	ψάχνουμε ...	"**psa**khnoo-me"

▷ could I speak to the owner?	μπορώ να μιλήσω στον ιδιοκτήτη/ στην ιδιοκτήτρια;	"bo-**ro** na mee**lee**-so ston eedhee-ok**tee**tee/steen eedhee-ok**tee**treea"
oyster	το στρείδι	"to **stree**dhee"
to **pack**	πακετάρω	"pake**ta**ro"
package	το δέμα	"to **dhe**ma"
package tour	η οργανωμένη εκδρομή	"ee orghano-**me**nee ek-dhro**mee**"
packed lunch	το πρόχειρο φαγητό	"to **pro**kheero fayee**to**"
packet	το πακέτο	"to pa-**ke**to"
▷ a packet of cigarettes	ένα πακέτο τσιγάρα	"ena pa-**ke**to tsee-**gha**-ra"
paddling pool	η πισινούλα για παιδιά	"ee peesee-**noo**la ya pedhee-**a**"
▷ is there a paddling pool for the children?	υπάρχει πισινούλα για τα παιδιά;	"eepar-**khee** peesee-**noo**la ya ta pedhee-**a**"
paid	πληρωμένος	"pleero-**me**nos"
pain:		
▷ I have a pain in my chest/here	πονάω στο στήθος/ εδώ	"pona-**o** sto **stee**thos/ e**dho**"
painkiller	το παυσίπονο	"to paf**see**-pono"
painting	ο πίνακας	"o **pee**nakas"
pair	το ζευγάρι	"to zev-**gha**ree"
▷ a pair of sandals	ένα ζευγάρι πέδιλα	"ena zev-**gha**ree **pe**dhee-la"
palace	το παλάτι	"to pa**la**tee"
pan	η κατσαρόλα	"ee katsa-**ro**la"
pancake	η τηγανίτα	"ee teegha-**nee**ta"
pants	τα εσώρουχα	"ta e-**so**rookha"

paper	το χαρτί	"to khartee"
parcel	το δέμα	"to **dhe**ma"
▷ **I want to send this parcel**	θέλω να στείλω αυτό το δέμα	"**the**-lo na **stee**-lo afto to **dhe**ma"
pardon:		
▷ **I beg your pardon?**	με συγχωρείτε	"me seenkho-**ree**-te"
parent	ο γονιός	"o ghonee-**os**"
Paris	το Παρίσι	"to pa**ree**-see"
park[1] _n_	το πάρκο	"to **par**ko"
to **park**[2] _vb (in car)_	παρκάρω	"par**ka**ro"
▷ **can we park our caravan here?**	μπορούμε να παρκάρουμε το τροχόσπιτό μας εδώ;	"bo**roo**-me na par**ka**-roo-me to trokho-spee**to** mas e**dho**"
▷ **where can I park?**	πού μπορώ να παρκάρω;	"poo bo-**ro** na par**ka**ro"
▷ **can I park here?**	μπορώ να παρκάρω εδώ;	"bo-**ro** na par**ka**ro e**dho**"
parking meter	το παρκόμετρο	"to par**ko**metro"
parsley	ο μαϊντανός	"o ma-eendan**os**"
part	το μέρος	"to **me**ros"
party _(group)_	η ομάδα	"ee om**a**dha"
(celebration)	το πάρτυ	"to party"
passenger	ο επιβάτης	"o epee-**va**tees"
passport	το διαβατήριο	"to dhee-ava-**tee**ree-o"
▷ **I have forgotten my passport**	ξέχασα το διαβατήριό μου	"**kse**-khasa to dhee-ava-**tee**ree-o moo"
▷ **please give me my passport back**	μου δίνετε το διαβατήριό μου, παρακαλώ	"moo **dhee**ne-te to dhee-ava-**tee**ree-o moo para-ka**lo**"

ABSOLUTE ESSENTIALS

yes (please)	ναι (παρακαλώ)	"ne (para-ka**lo**)"
no (thank you)	όχι (ευχαριστώ)	"**o**khee (efkharee**sto**)"
hello	γεια σας	"ya sas"
goodbye	αντίο	"an**dee**-o"

▷ **my wife/husband and I have a joint passport**	η/ο σύζυγός μου κι εγώ έχουμε οικογενειακό διαβατήριο	"ee/o seezee-**ghos** moo kee e**gho** ekhoo-me eeko-yenee-a**ko** dhee-ava-**tee**ree-o"
▷ **the children are on this passport**	τα παιδιά είναι σ'αυτό το διαβατήριο	"ta pedhee-**a** ee-ne sa**fto** to dhee-ava-**tee**ree-o"
▷ **my passport number is ...**	ο αριθμός διαβατηρίου μου είναι ...	"o areeth**mos** dhee-ava-tee**ree**-oo moo **ee**-ne"
passport control	ο έλεγχος διαβατηρίων	"o **elen**-khos dhee-ava-**tee**ree-on"
pasta	τα μακαρόνια	"ta maka**ro**nee-a"
pastry	η ζύμη	"ee **zee**-mee"
(*cake*)	το γλύκισμα	"to **ghlee**-keesma"
pâté	το πατέ	"to pa-**te**"
path	το μονοπάτι	"to mono-**pa**tee"
to **pay**	πληρώνω	"plee-**ro**no"
▷ **do I pay now or later?**	πληρώνω τώρα ή αργότερα;	"plee-**ro**no **to**ra ee ar-**gho**te-ra"
payment	η πληρωμή	"ee plee-ro**mee**"
peach	το ροδάκινο	"to ro**dha**-keeno"
peanut	το φυστίκι	"to fee-**stee**kee"
pear	το αχλάδι	"to akh-**la**dhee"
peas	τα μπιζέλια	"ta bee**ze**lee-a"
to **peel**	ξεφλουδίζω	"ksefloo-**dhee**zo"
peg (*for tent*)	ο πάσσαλος	"o **pa**-salos"
(*for clothes*)	το μανταλάκι	"to manda-**la**kee"
pen	το στυλό	"to stee**lo**"
pencil	το μολύβι	"to mo-**lee**vee"
penicillin	η πενικιλλίνη	"ee penee-kee-**lee**nee"

ABSOLUTE ESSENTIALS

I don't understand	δεν καταλαβαίνω	"dhen kata-la**ve**no"
I don't speak Greek	δεν μιλάω ελληνικά	"dhen meela-o elee-nee**ka**"
do you speak English?	μιλάτε αγγλικά;	"mee**la**-te anglee-**ka**"
more slowly please	πιο σιγά παρακαλώ	"**pee**o seegha para-ka**lo**"

▷ **I am allergic to penicillin**	είμαι αλλεργικός στην πενικιλλίνη	"**ee**-me aleryee**kos** steen penee-kee-**lee**nee"
penknife	ο σουγιάς	"o soo-**yas**"
pensioner	ο/η συνταξιούχος	"o/ee seendaksee-**oo**khos"
pepper (spice)	το πιπέρι	"to pee-**peree**"
per:		
▷ **per hour**	την ώρα	"teen **o**-ra"
▷ **per week**	τη βδομάδα	"tee vdho**ma**dha"
perfect	τέλειος	"**te**lee-os"
performance	η παράσταση	"ee para-**stasee**"
▷ **what time does the performance begin?**	τι ώρα αρχίζει η παράσταση;	"tee **o**-ra ar**khee**-zee ee para-**stasee**"
▷ **how long does the performance last?**	πόσο διαρκεί η παράσταση;	"**po**so dhee-ar**kee** ee para-**stasee**"
perfume	το άρωμα	"to **aroma**"
perhaps	ίσως	"**ee**sos"
period (menstruation)	η περίοδος	"ee pe**ree**-odhos"
perm	η περμανάντ	"ee perma**nand**"
▷ **my hair is permed**	τα μαλλιά μου έχουν περμανάντ	"ta malee-**a** moo **e**-khoon perma**nand**"
permit	άδεια	"**adhee**-a"
▷ **do I need a fishing permit?**	χρειάζομαι άδεια ψαρέματος;	"khree-**a**zo-me **adhee**-a psa**re**ma-tos"
person	το πρόσωπο	"to **pro**-sopo"
petrol	η βενζίνη	"ee ven-**zee**nee"
▷ **20 litres of unleaded petrol**	20 λίτρα αμόλυβδη	"**ee**kosee **lee**tra a**mo**leev-dhee"
▷ **I have run out of petrol**	έχω ξεμείνει απο βενζίνη	"**e**kho kse**mee**nee apo ven-**zee**nee"

ABSOLUTE ESSENTIALS

I would like ...	θα ήθελα ...	"tha **ee**thela"
I need ...	χρειάζομαι ...	"khree-**a**zo-me"
where is ...?	πού είναι ...;	"**poo ee**-ne"
we're looking for ...	ψάχνουμε ...	"**psa**khnoo-me"

petrol station	το πρατήριο βενζίνης	"to pra**tee**ree-o ven-**zee**nees"
phone	το τηλέφωνο	"to tee-**le**fo-no"
phone box	ο τηλεφωνικός θάλαμος	"o tee-lefo-nee**kos tha**lamos"
phonecard	η τηλεκάρτα	"ee tee-le**kar**-ta"
photocopy	η φωτοτυπία	"ee fototee**pee**-a"
▷ **where can I get some photocopying done?**	πού μπορώ να βγάλω μερικές φωτοτυπίες;	"poo bo-**ro** na **vgha**lo meree**kes** fototee**pee**-es"
photo(graph)	η φωτογραφία	"ee foto-ghra**fee**-a"
▷ **when will the photos be ready?**	πότε θα είναι έτοιμες οι φωτογραφίες;	"**po**-te tha **ee**-ne **e**teemes ee fotoghra**fee**-es"
▷ **can I take photos in here?**	μπορώ να βγάλω φωτογραφίες εδώ;	"bo-**ro** na **vgha**lo fotoghra**fee**-es e**dho**"
▷ **would you take a photo of us, please?**	μας βγάζετε μία φωτογραφία, παρακαλώ;	"mas **vgha**-ze-te **mee**a foto-ghra**fee**-a para-ka**lo**"
picnic	το πικ-νικ	"to picnic"
picture	η εικόνα	"ee ee**ko**na"
pie	η πίτα	"ee **pee**ta"
piece	το κομμάτι	"to ko-**ma**tee"
pill	το χάπι	"to **kha**pee"
pillow	το μαξιλάρι	"to maksee-**la**ree"
▷ **I would like an extra pillow**	θα ήθελα ένα μαξιλάρι επιπλέον	"tha **ee**the-la **e**na maksee-**la**ree epee**ple**-on"
pillowcase	η μαξιλαροθήκη	"ee maksee-laro-**thee**kee"
pin	η καρφίτσα	"ee kar**feet**-sa"
pine	το πεύκο	"to **pef**ko"
pineapple	ο ανανάς	"o ana**nas**"

ABSOLUTE ESSENTIALS

do you have ...?	έχετε ...;	"**ekh**e-te"
is there ...?	υπάρχει ...;	"ee-**par**khee"
are there ...?	υπάρχουν ...;	"ee-**par**khoon"
how much is ...?	πόσο κάνει ...;	"**poso ka**nee"

pink	ροζ	"roz"
pipe	η πίπα	"ee **pee**pa"
pipe tobacco	ο καπνός για πίπα	"o kap-**nos** ya **pee**pa"
pistachio nut	το φυστίκι Αιγίνης	"to fee-**stee**kee e-**yee**nees"
plane	το αεροπλάνο	"to aero-**pla**no"
▷ **my plane leaves at ...**	το αεροπλάνο μου φεύγει στις ...	"to aero-**pla**no moo **fev**-yee stees"
plaster (*for cut*)	ο λευκοπλάστης	"o lefko- **pla**stees"
(*for broken limb*)	ο γύψος	"o **yee**psos"
plastic	πλαστικός	"plastee-**kos**"
plate	το πιάτο	"to pee**a**to"
platform	η πλατφόρμα	"ee plat**for**ma"
▷ **which platform for the train to ...?**	σε ποια πλατφόρμα για το τρένο για ...;	"se pee**a** plat**for**ma ya to **tre**no ya"
to **play**	παίζω	"**pe**zo"
playroom	το δωμάτιο των παιδιών	"to dhomatee-o ton pedhee-**on**"
please	παρακαλώ	"para-ka**lo**"
▷ **yes, please**	παρακαλώ	"para-ka**lo**"
pleased	ευχαριστημένος	"efhareestee**me**nos"
▷ **pleased to meet you**	χαίρω πολύ	"**khe**ro polee"
pliers	η πένσα	"ee **pen**sa"
plug (*electric*)	η πρίζα	"ee **pree**za"
plum	το δαμάσκηνο	"to dhama-skeeno"
plumber	ο υδραυλικός	"o eedrav-lee**kos**"
points (*in car*)	οι πλατίνες	"ee pla-**tee**nes"
police	η αστυνομία	"ee astee-no**mee**-a"

ABSOLUTE ESSENTIALS

yes (please)	ναι (παρακαλώ)	"ne (para-ka**lo**)"
no (thank you)	όχι (ευχαριστώ)	"**o**khee (efkharee**sto**)"
hello	γεια σας	"ya sas"
goodbye	αντίο	"an**dee**-o"

▷ **we will have to report it to the police**	πρέπει να το αναφέρουμε στην αστυνομία	"**pre**pee na to a-na**fe**roo-me steen astee-no**mee**-a"
▷ **get the police**	φωνάξτε την αστυνομία	"fo**naks**-te teen astee-no**mee**-a"
policeman	ο αστυνομικός	"o astee-nomee**kos**"
police station	το αστυνομικό τμήμα	"to astee-nomee**ko tmee**ma"
▷ **where is the police station?**	πού είναι το αστυνομικό τμήμα;	"poo **ee**-ne to astee-nomee**ko tmee**ma"
polish (*for shoes*)	το βερνίκι	"to ver-**nee**kee"
polluted	μολυσμένος	"molees-**me**nos"
pool (*for swimming*)	η πισίνα	"ee pee-**see**na"
▷ **is there a children's pool?**	υπάρχει πισίνα για παιδιά;	"ee**par**-khee pee-**see**na ya pedhee-**a**"
▷ **is the pool heated?**	είναι θερμαινόμενη η πισίνα;	"**ee**-ne ther-me**no**menee ee pee-**see**na"
▷ **is it an outdoor pool?**	είναι ανοιχτή η πισίνα;	"**ee**-ne aneekh-**tee** ee pee-**see**na"
popular (*fashionable*)	κοσμικός	"kosmee-**kos**"
pork	το χοιρινό	"to kheeree-**no**"
port (*harbour*)	το λιμάνι	"to lee-**ma**nee"
porter	ο αχθοφόρος	"o akh-tho-**fo**ros"
Portugal	η Πορτογαλία	"ee porto-gha**lee**-a"
Portuguese *adj* (*language*)	πορτογαλικός πορτογαλικά	"portoghalee**kos**" "porto-ghalee**ka**"
possible	δυνατός	"dheena-**tos**"
▷ **as soon as possible**	το συντομότερο δυνατό	"to seen-do**mo**tero dhee-na**to**"
to **post** (*letter*)	ταχυδρομώ	"takhee-dhro**mo**"

ABSOLUTE ESSENTIALS

I don't understand	δεν καταλαβαίνω	"dhen kata-**la**veno"
I don't speak Greek	δεν μιλάω ελληνικά	"dhen meela-o elee-nee**ka**"
do you speak English?	μιλάτε αγγλικά;	"meela-te anglee-**ka**"
more slowly please	πιο σιγά παρακαλώ	"**pee**o see**gha** para-ka**lo**"

▷ where can I post these cards?	πού μπορώ να ταχυδρομήσω αυτές τις κάρτες;	"poo bo-**ro** na takhee-dhro**mee**-so a**ftes** tees **kar**tes"
postbox	το ταχυδρομικό κουτί	"to takhee-dhromee**ko** koo**tee**"
postcard	η καρτ-ποστάλ	"ee kart-po**stal**"
▷ do you have any postcards?	έχετε καρτ-ποστάλ;	"**ekhe**-te kart-po**stal**"
▷ where can I buy some postcards?	πού μπορώ να αγοράσω μερικές καρτ-ποστάλ;	"poo bo-**ro** na aghora-so meree**kes** kart-po**stal**"
postcode	ο ταχυδρομικός κώδικας	"o takhee-dhromee-**kos ko**dheekas"
post office	το ταχυδρομείο	"to takhee-dhro**mee**-o"
pot	η κατσαρόλα	"ee katsa-**ro**la"
potato	η πατάτα	"ee pa**ta**ta"
pottery	τα κεραμικά	"ta kera-mee**ka**"
pound (*money*) (*weight*)	η λίρα η λίμπρα	"ee **lee**ra" "ee **lee**bra"
powdered milk	το γάλα σε σκόνη	"to **gha**la se **sko**nee"
pram	το καροτσάκι	"to karot-**sa**kee"
prawn	η γαρίδα	"ee gha-**ree**dha"
to **prefer**	προτιμώ	"pro-tee**mo**"
▷ I'd prefer to go ...	θα προτιμούσα να πάω ...	"tha proteemoo-sa na **pa**-o"
pregnant	έγκυος	"**en**gee-os"
to **prepare**	ετοιμάζω	"etee-**ma**zo"
prescription	η συνταγή	"ee seenda-**yee**"
present (*gift*)	το δώρο	"to **dho**ro"

I would like ...	θα ήθελα ...	"tha **ee**thela"
I need ...	χρειάζομαι ...	"khree-**a**zo-me"
where is ...?	πού είναι ...;	"poo **ee**-ne"
we're looking for ...	ψάχνουμε ...	"**psa**khnoo-me"

▷ I want to buy a present for my husband/my wife	θέλω να αγοράσω ένα δώρο για τον άντρα μου/τη γυναίκα μου	"**the**-lo na agho-**ra**so **e**na **dho**ro ya ton **an**dra moo/tee yee-**ne**ka moo"
pretty	ωραίος	"**ore**-os"
price	η τιμή	"ee tee**mee**"
price list	ο τιμοκατάλογος	"o teemoka**ta**-loghos"
priest	ο ιερέας	"o ee-**ere**-as"
▷ I want to see a priest	θέλω να δω έναν ιερέα	"**the**-lo na dho **e**nan ee-**ere**-a"
private	ιδιωτικός	"eedhee-otee**kos**"
probably	πιθανώς	"peetha-**nos**"
problem	το πρόβλημα	"to **prov**-leema"
programme	το πρόγραμμα	"to **progh**rama"
to pronounce	προφέρω	"pro-**fe**ro"
▷ how do you pronounce this?	πώς το προφέρετε;	"pos to profe-re-te"
Protestant	διαμαρτυρόμενος διαμαρτυρόμενη	"dhee-amartee-**ro**menos" "dhee-amartee-**ro**menee"
prune	το δαμάσκηνο	"to dha**ma**-skeeno"
public	δημόσιος	"dhee**mosee**-os"
▷ is the castle open to the public?	είναι το κάστρο ανοιχτό στο κοινό;	"**ee**-ne to **ka**stro aneekh-**to** sto kee**no**"
public holiday	η αργία	"ee ar**yee**a"
pudding	η πουτίγκα	"ee poo-**teen**ga"
to pull	τραβώ	"tra**vo**"
pullover	το πουλόβερ	"to poo**lo**ver"
puncture	το τρύπημα	"to **tree**-peema"
purple	βιολετί	"vee-ole**tee**"
purse	το τσαντάκι	"tsan-**da**kee"
▷ I've lost my purse	έχασα το τσαντάκι μου	"**e**khasa to tsan-**da**kee moo"

ABSOLUTE ESSENTIALS

do you have ...?	έχετε ...;	"**ekhe**-te"
is there ...?	υπάρχει ...;	"ee-**par**khee"
are there ...?	υπάρχουν ...;	"ee-**par**khoon"
how much is ...?	πόσο κάνει ...;	"**po**so **ka**nee"

to **push**	σπρώχνω	"**sprokh**-no"
to **put**	βάζω	"**va**zo"
to **put down**	βάζω κάτω	"**va**zo **ka**to"
▷ put it down over there, please	βάλτε το εκεί κάτω, παρακαλώ	"**val**-te to e**kee ka**to para-ka**lo**"
pyjamas	οι πυζάμες	"ee pee-**za**-mes"
quarter:		
▷ quarter to 10	10 παρά τέταρτο	"**dhe**ka para **te**tar-to"
▷ quarter past 3	3 και τέταρτο	"trees ke **te**tar-to"
queue	η ουρά	"ee oo**ra**"
▷ is this the end of the queue?	εδώ είναι η αρχή της ουράς;	"**edho** ee-ne ee ar-**khee** tees oo**ras**"
quick	γρήγορος	"**ghree**ghoros"
quickly	γρήγορα	"**ghree**-ghora"
quiet	ήσυχος	"**ee**see-khos"
quilt	το πάπλωμα	"to **pa**plo-ma"
quite (*rather*)	μάλλον	"**ma**lon"
(*completely*)	απολύτως	"apo-**lee**tos"
rabbit	το κουνέλι	"to koo-**ne**lee"
racket	η ρακέτα	"ee ra**ke**ta"
radiator (*heater*)	το καλοριφέρ	"to kalo-ree**fer**"
(*car part*)	το ψυγείο	"to psee**yee**-o"
radio	το ραδιόφωνο	"to radhee-**o**fono"
▷ is there a radio in the car?	υπάρχει ραδιόφωνο στο αυτοκίνητο;	"ee**par**-khee radhee-**o**fono sto afto-**kee**neeto"
radish	το ραπανάκι	"to rapa-**na**kee"
railway station	ο σιδηροδρομικός σταθμός	"o seedheero-dhromee**kos** stath-**mos**"

rain	η βροχή	"ee vrokhee"
▷ is it going to rain?	θα βρέξει;	"tha **vre**ksee"
raincoat	το αδιάβροχο	"to adhee-**a**vrokho"
raining:		
▷ it's raining	βρέχει	"**vre**khee"
raisin	η σταφίδα	"ee sta-**fee**dha"
rare	σπάνιος	"**spa**nee-os"
(*steak*)	μισοψημένος	"meesop-see**me**nos"
raspberries	τα βατόμουρα	"ta vato-**moo**ra"
rate	ο ρυθμός	"o reeth-**mos**"
▷ what is the daily/ weekly rate?	πόσο την ημέρα/ εβδομάδα;	"**po**so teen ee**me**ra/ev-dho-**ma**dha"
▷ do you have a special rate for children?	έχετε μειωμένες τιμές για παιδιά;	"**ekhe**-te mee-o**me**nes tee**mes** ya pedhee-**a**"
▷ what is the rate for sterling/dollars?	ποια είναι η ισοτιμία για τη λίρα/το δολάριο;	"peea **ee**-ne ee eeso-tee**mee**-a ya tee **lee**ra/to dho**la**ree-o"
▷ rate of exchange	τιμή του συναλλάγματος	"tee**mee** too seenal**agh**-matos"
raw	ωμός	"o**mos**"
razor	το ξυράφι	"to ksee-**ra**fee"
razor blades	τα ξυραφάκια	"ta kseera**fa**-keea"
ready	έτοιμος	"**etee**-mos"
	έτοιμη	"**etee**-mee"
▷ I'm ready	είμαι έτοιμος	"**ee**-me **etee**-mos"
real	πραγματικός	"praghma-tee**kos**"
receipt	η απόδειξη	"ee apo-**dhee**ksee"
▷ I'd like a receipt, please	θα ήθελα απόδειξη, παρακαλώ	"tha **ee**thela apo-**dhee**ksee para-ka**lo**"
recently	τελευταία	"telef**te**-a"
reception (desk)	η ρεσεψιόν	"ee resepsee-**on**"

recipe	η συνταγή	"ee seenda-**yee**"
to **recommend**	συνιστώ	"seenee-**sto**"
▷ what do you recommend?	τι έχετε να μας συστήσετε;	"tee **ekhe**-te na mas see**stee**-se-te"
record (music etc)	ο δίσκος	"o **dhee**skos"
red	κόκκινος	"**ko**kee-nos"
reduction	η έκπτωση	"ee **ek**-ptosee"
▷ is there a reduction for children/for senior citizens?	υπάρχει έκπτωση για παιδιά/ συνταξιούχους;	"ee**par**khee **ek**-ptosee ya pedhee-**a**/seen-daksee-**oo**khoos"
refill	το ανταλλακτικό	"to anda-laktee**ko**"
▷ do you have a refill for my gas lighter?	έχετε ανταλλακτικό για τον αναπτήρα μου;	"**ekhe**-te anda-laktee**ko** ya ton anap**tee**ra moo"
refund	η επιστροφή χρημάτων	"ee epee-stro**fee** khree-**ma**ton"
registered	συστημένο	"seestee**me**no"
regulations	οι κανονισμοί	"ee kano-nees**mee**"
▷ I didn't know the regulations	δεν ήξερα τους κανονισμούς	"dhen **eek**-sera toos kano-nees**moos**"
to **reimburse**	επιστρέφω τα χρήματα	"e-pee**stre**-fo ta **khree**ma-ta"
relations (family)	οι συγγενείς	"ee seenge**nees**"
to **relax**	χαλαρώνω	"kha-la**ro**-no"
reliable (person) (car, method)	αξιόπιστος δοκιμασμένος	"aksee-**o**peestos" "dhokee-mas**me**nos"
to **remain**	απομένω	"apo-**me**no"
to **remember**	θυμάμαι	"theema-me"
to **rent**	νοικιάζω	"neekee-**azo**"

ABSOLUTE ESSENTIALS		
I would like ...	θα ήθελα ...	"tha **ee**thela"
I need ...	χρειάζομαι ...	"khree-**azo**-me"
where is ...?	πού είναι ...;	"poo **ee**-ne"
we're looking for ...	ψάχνουμε ...	"**psa**khnoo-me"

▷ **I'd like to rent a room/villa**	θα ήθελα να νοικιάσω ένα δωμάτιο/μία βίλλα	"the **ee**thela na neekee-**a**so **e**na dhomatee-o/**mee**a **vee**-la"
rental	το νοίκι	"to **nee**kee"
to repair	επιδιορθώνω	"epeedhee-**or**thono"
▷ **can you repair this?**	μπορείτε να το διορθώσετε αυτό;	"bo**ree**-te na to dhee-**or**tho-se-te af**to**"
to repeat	επαναλαμβάνω	"epana-**lam**vano"
▷ **please repeat that**	επαναλαμβάνετε παρακαλώ	"epana-lam**va**-ne-te para-ka**lo**"
Republic of Ireland	η Ιρλανδία	"ee eerland**dhee**-a"
reservation	η κράτηση	"ee **kra**tee-see"
to reserve	κλείνω	"**klee**-no"
▷ **we'd like to reserve two seats for tonight**	θέλουμε να κλείσουμε δύο θέσεις για απόψε	"**the**-loo-me na **klee**soo-me **dhee**-o **the**sees ya a**pop**-se"
▷ **I have reserved a room in the name of ...**	έχω κλείσει δωμάτιο στο όνομα ...	"**ekho klee**see dhomatee-o sto **o**noma"
▷ **I want to reserve a single room/a double room**	θέλω να κλείσω ένα μονόκλινο/δίκλινο δωμάτιο	"**the**-lo na **klee**so ena mo**no**kleeno/ **dhee**kleeno dhomatee-o"
reserved	κρατημένος	"kratee-**me**nos"
rest¹ *n*	ξεκούραση	"kse**koo**-rasee"
▷ **the rest**	οι υπόλοιποι	"ee ee**po**-leepee"
to rest² *vb*	ξεκουράζομαι	"ksekoo-**ra**zo-me"
restaurant	το εστιατόριο	"to estee-a**to**ree-o"
restaurant car	το βαγόνι-εστιατόριο	"to va**gho**nee estee-a**to**reeo"
to return (*go back, give back*)	επιστρέφω	"epee-**stre**fo"

ABSOLUTE ESSENTIALS

do you have ...?	έχετε ...;	"**ekhe**-te"
is there ...?	υπάρχει ...;	"ee-**par**khee"
are there ...?	υπάρχουν ...;	"ee-**par**khoon"
how much is ...?	πόσο κάνει ...;	"**poso ka**nee"

return ticket	το εισιτήριο με επιστροφή	"to eesee-**tee**ree-o me epee-stro**fee**"
▷ **a return ticket to ..., first class**	με επιστροφή για ..., πρώτη θέση	"me epee-stro**fee** ya ... **pro**tee **the**see"
reverse charge call	κλήση πληρωτέα από τον παραλήπτη	"**klee**see pleerotea apo ton para-**lee**ptee"
rheumatism	οι ρευματισμοί	"ee rhevma-tees**mee**"
rice	το ρύζι	"to **ree**zee"
riding (equestrian)	η ιππασία	"ee eepa**see**-a"
▷ **can we go riding?**	μπορούμε να πάμε για ιππασία;	"bo**roo**-me na **pa**me ya eepa**see**-a"
right[1] n	δεξιά	"dhe-ksee-**a**"
▷ **to/on the right**	δεξιά	"dheksee-**a**"
right[2] adj	σωστός	"sos**tos**"
ring	το δαχτυλίδι	"to dhakhtee-**lee**dhee"
ripe	ώριμος	"**o**ree-mos"
river	το ποτάμι	"to po-**ta**mee"
▷ **can one swim in the river?**	μπορεί κανείς να κολυμπήσει στο ποτάμι;	"bo**ree** ka**nees** na koleem-**bee**see sto pota-mee"
road	ο δρόμος	"o **dhro**mos"
▷ **which road do I take for ...?**	ποιο δρόμο πρέπει να πάρω για ...;	"pee**o dhro**mo **pre**pee na **pa**ro ya"
▷ **when will the road be clear?**	πότε θα ανοίξει ο δρόμος;	"**po**-te tha a**neek**-see o **dhro**mos"
road map	ο οδικός χάρτης	"o odhee-**kos khar**tees"
roast	το ψητό	"to psee**to**"
to **rob**	ληστεύω	"lees**te**vo"
▷ **I've been robbed**	με λήστεψαν	"me **lee**step-san"
roll (of bread)	το ψωμάκι	"to pso-**ma**kee"

ABSOLUTE ESSENTIALS

yes (please)	ναι (παρακαλώ)	"ne (para-ka**lo**)"
no (thank you)	όχι (ευχαριστώ)	"**o**khee (efkharee**sto**)"
hello	γεια σας	"**ya sas**"
goodbye	αντίο	"an**dee**-o"

Rome	η Ρώμη	"ee **ro**-mee"
roof	η στέγη	"ee **ste**-yee"
▷ the roof leaks	η στέγη στάζει	"ee **ste**-yee **sta**-zee"
roof rack	η σχάρα	"ee **skha**ra"
room (in house etc)	το δωμάτιο	"to dho**ma**tee-o"
(space)	ο χώρος	"o **kho**ros"
room service	η υπηρεσία δωματίου	"ee eepee-re**see**-a dhoma**tee**-oo"
rope	το σχοινί	"to skhee**nee**"
rosé (wine)	ροζέ	"ro-**se**"
rough (sea)	τρικυμισμένη	"treekee-mees**me**nee"
round (shape)	στρογγυλός	"stron-gee**los**"
▷ round the corner	στη γωνία	"stee gho**nee**-a"
▷ round the house/ Greece	γύρω στο σπίτι/στην Ελλάδα	"**yee**ro sto **spee**tee/steen e**la**dha"
route	ο δρόμος	"o **dhro**mos"
▷ is there a route that avoids the traffic?	υπάρχει παράκαμψη για την κίνηση;	"ee**par**-khee para**kamp**-see ya teen **kee**nee-see"
rowing boat	η βάρκα με κουπιά	"**ee var**ka me koo**pee**-a"
rubber band	το λαστιχάκι	"to lastee-**kha**kee"
rubbish	τα σκουπίδια	"ta skoo**pee**dhee-a"
rucksack	ο σάκκος	"o **sa**kos"
ruins	τα ερείπια	"ta e**ree**pee-a"
rum	το ρούμι	"to **roo**mee"
to **run**	τρέχω	"**tre**kho"
rush hour	η ώρα αιχμής	"ee **o**-ra ekh**mees**"
saccharine	η ζαχαρίνη	"ee zakha**ree**-nee"

ABSOLUTE ESSENTIALS

I don't understand	δεν καταλαβαίνω	"dhen kata-la**ve**no"
I don't speak Greek	δεν μιλάω ελληνικά	"dhen meela-o elee-**nee**ka"
do you speak English?	μιλάτε αγγλικά;	"meela-te anglee-**ka**"
more slowly please	πιο σιγά παρακαλώ	"pee**o** see**gha** para-ka**lo**"

safe¹ *n*	το χρηματοκιβώτιο	"to khreemato-kee**vo**tee-o"
safe² *adj* (*medicine*)	αβλαβής	"avla-**vees**"
▷ **is it safe to swim here?**	μπορεί κανείς να κολυμπήσει εδώ άφοβα;	"bo**ree** ka**nees** na koleem-**bee**see e**dho a**fova"
▷ **is it safe for children?** (*medicine*)	βλάπτει τα παιδιά;	"**vla**ptee ta pedhee-**a**"
safety pin	η παραμάνα	"ee para-**ma**na"
▷ **I need a safety pin**	θέλω μία παραμάνα	"**the**-lo **mee**a para-**ma**na"
to sail	αποπλέω	"apo-**ple**-o"
▷ **when do we sail?**	πότε φεύγουμε;	"**po**-te **fev**ghoo-me"
sailboard	η ιστιοσανίδα	"ee eestee-osa**nee**dha"
sailing	η ιστιοπλοΐα	"ee eestee-oplo-**ee**-a"
▷ **I'd like to go sailing**	θα ήθελα να κάνω ιστιοπλοΐα	"tha **ee**-the-la na **ka**no eestee-oplo-**ee**-a"
▷ **what time is the next sailing?**	τι ώρα φεύγει το επόμενο πλοίο;	"tee **o**-ra **fev**-yee to e**po**-meno **plee**-o"
salad	η σαλάτα	"ee sa**la**ta"
salad dressing	το λαδολέμονο	"to ladho-**le**mono"
saline solution for contact lenses	το αλκαλικό διάλυμα	"alka-lee**ko** dhee-a**lee**-ma"
salmon	ο σολομός	"o solo-**mos**"
salt	το αλάτι	"to a**la**tee"
same	ίδιος	"**ee**dhee-os"
▷ **I'll have the same**	θα πάρω το ίδιο	"tha **pa**-ro to **ee**dhee-o"
sand	η άμμος	"ee **a**mos"
sandals	τα πέδιλα	"ta **pe**dhee-la"
sandwich	το σάντουιτς	"to **san**doo-eets"

I would like ...	θα ήθελα ...	"tha **ee**thela"
I need ...	χρειάζομαι ...	"khree-**azo**-me"
where is ...?	πού είναι ...;	"poo **ee**-ne"
we're looking for ...	ψάχνουμε ...	"**psakh**noo-me"

▷ **what kind of sandwiches do you have?**	τι σάντουιτς έχετε;	"tee **san**doo-eets **e**khe-te"
sandy:		
▷ **a sandy beach**	μία παραλία με άμμο	"**mee**a para-**lee**-a me **a**-mo"
sanitary towel	η σερβιέτα	"ee servee-**e**ta"
sardine	η σαρδέλα	"ee sar**dhe**la"
Saturday	Σάββατο	"**sa**va-to"
sauce	η σάλτσα	"ee **sal**tsa"
saucepan	η κατσαρόλα	"ee katsa-**ro**la"
saucer	το πιατάκι	"to peeata**ke**e"
sauna	η σάουνα	"ee **sa**-oona"
sausage	το λουκάνικο	"to loo**ka**-neeko"
savoury	πικάντικος	"pee**kan**-deekos"
to **say**	λέω	"**le**-o"
scallop	το χτένι	"to **kht**enee"
scarf (long)	το κασκόλ	"to kas**kol**"
(square)	το σάλι	"to **sa**lee"
school	το σχολείο	"to skho**lee**-o"
(for 12-15 year olds)	το Γυμνάσιο	"to yeem**na**see-o"
(for 15-18 year-olds)	το Λύκειο	"to **lee**kee-o"
scissors	το ψαλίδι	"to psa-**lee**dhee"
Scotland	η Σκωτία	"ee sko**tee**-a"
Scottish adj	σκωτσέζικος	"skot-**se**zeekos"
▷ **I'm Scottish**	είμαι Σκωτσέζος/ Σκωτσέζα	"**ee**-me skot-**se**zos/skot-**se**za"
screw	η βίδα	"ee **vee**dha"
▷ **the screw has come loose**	η βίδα έχει ξεβιδωθεί	"ee **vee**dha **e**khee ksevee-dho**thee**"

do you have ...?	έχετε ...;	"**e**khe-te"
is there ...?	υπάρχει ...;	"ee-**par**khee"
are there ...?	υπάρχουν ...;	"ee-**par**khoon"
how much is ...?	πόσο κάνει ...;	"**po**so **ka**nee"

screwdriver	το κατσαβίδι	"to katsa-**vee**dhee"
sculpture	το γλυπτό	"to ghleep-**to**"
sea	η θάλασσα	"ee **tha**-lasa"
seafood	τα θαλασσινά	"ta thala-see**na**"
▷ **do you like seafood?**	σας αρέσουν τα θαλασσινά;	"sas a-**re**soon ta thala-see**na**"
seasickness	η ναυτία	"ee naf**tee**-a"
season ticket	το εισιτήριο διαρκείας	"to eesee-**tee**ree-o dhee-ar-**kee**as"
seat (*in theatre*)	η θέση	"ee **the**see"
(*in car etc*)	το κάθισμα	"to **ka**thees-ma"
▷ **is this seat free?**	είναι ελεύθερη αυτή η θέση;	"**ee**-ne el**ef**-theree af**tee** ee **the**see"
▷ **is this seat taken?**	είναι πιασμένη αυτή η θέση;	"**ee**-ne peea-**sme**nee af**tee** ee **the**see"
▷ **we'd like to reserve two seats for tonight**	θέλουμε να κλείσουμε δύο θέσεις για απόψε	"**the**-loo-me na **klee**see-me **dhee**-o **the**sees ya a**pop**-se"
▷ **I have a seat reservation**	έχω κλείσει θέση	"ekho **klee**see **the**see"
second	δεύτερος	"**dhef**-teros"
second class (*ticket etc*)	δεύτερη θέση	"**dhef**-teree **the**see"
to see	βλέπω	"**vle**po"
▷ **see you soon**	θα τα πούμε σύντομα	"tha ta **poo**-me **seen**-doma"
▷ **what is there to see here?**	τι μπορούμε να δούμε εδώ;	"tee bo**roo**-me na **dhoo**-me e**dho**"
self-service	σελφ-σέρβις	"self-**ser**vees"
to sell	πουλώ	"poo**lo**"
▷ **do you sell stamps?**	πουλάτε γραμματόσημα;	"poo**la**-te ghra-ma**to**see-ma"

Sellotape®	το σελοτέιπ	"to selote-eep"
to **send**	στέλνω	"**stel**no"
▷ please send my mail/ luggage on to this address	στείλτε τα γράμματά μου/τις αποσκευές μου σ'αυτή τη διεύθυνση παρακαλώ	"▷ **steel**-te ta **ghra**ma-**ta** moo/tees apo-ske**ves** moo sa**ftee** tee dhee-**ef**theen-see para-ka**lo**"
senior citizen	ο/η συνταξιούχος	"o/ee seentaksee-**oo**khos"
▷ is there a reduction for senior citizens?	κάνετε έκπτωση σε συνταξιούχους;	"**ka**-ne-te **ek**-ptosee se seen-daksee-**oo**khoos"
separate	χωριστός	"khoree-**stos**"
September	Σεπτέμβριος	"sep**tem**-vreeos"
serious	σοβαρός	"sova-**ros**"
seriously:		
▷ he is seriously injured	έχει χτυπήσει σοβαρά	"ekhee khtee-**pee**see so-va**ra**"
to **serve**	σερβίρω	"ser-**vee**ro"
▷ we are still waiting to be served	περιμένουμε ακόμα να παραγγείλουμε	"peree-**me**noo-me a**ko**ma na paran-**gee**loo-me"
service (*in restaurant etc*)	η εξυπηρέτηση	"ee ekseepee-**re**teesee"
▷ is service included?	συμπεριλαμβάνεται το φιλοδώρημα;	"seem-beree-lam**va**-ne-te to feelo**dho**-reema"
▷ what time is the service? (*church*)	τι ώρα είναι η λειτουργία;	"tee **o**-ra **ee**-ne ee leetoor-**yee**-a"
service charge	το φιλοδώρημα	"to feelo**dho**-reema"
seven	εφτά	"ef-**ta**"
seventeen	δεκαεφτά	"dheka-ef-**ta**"
seventy	εβδομήντα	"ev-dho**meen**da"
shade	η σκιά	"ee skee-**a**"

ABSOLUTE ESSENTIALS

I don't understand	δεν καταλαβαίνω	"dhen kata-la**ve**no"
I don't speak Greek	δεν μιλάω ελληνικά	"dhen meela-o elee-nee**ka**"
do you speak English?	μιλάτε αγγλικά;	"meela-te anglee-**ka**"
more slowly please	πιο σιγά παρακαλώ	"pee**o** see**gha** para-ka**lo**"

▷ in the shade	στη σκιά	"stee skee-**a**"
shallow	ρηχός	"ree**khos**"
shampoo	το σαμπουάν	"to samboo-**an**"
shampoo and set	λούσιμο και χτένισμα	"**loo**seemo ke **khte**neesma"
to **share**	μοιράζω	"mee-**ra**zo"
▷ we could share a taxi	μπορούμε να μοιραστούμε ένα ταξί	"bo**roo**-me na mee-ra**stoo**-me **e**na tak**see**"
to **shave**	ξυρίζομαι	"kseeree-zo-me"
shaving brush	το πινέλο ξυρίσματος	"to pee**ne**-lo kseerees-matos"
shaving cream	η κρέμα ξυρίσματος	"ee **kre**ma kseerees-matos"
she	αυτή	"af**tee**"
sheet	το σεντόνι	"to sen-**do**nee"
shellfish	τα θαλασσινά	"ta thala-see**na**"
sherry	το σέρρυ	"to sherry"
ship	το πλοίο	"to **plee**-o"
shirt	το πουκάμισο	"to poo**ka**-meeso"
shock absorber	το αμορτισέρ	"to amor-tee**ser**"
shoe	το παπούτσι	"to pa-**poot**see"
▷ there is a hole in my shoe	το παπούτσι μου έχει τρυπήσει	"to pa-**poot**see moo **e**khee tree-**pee**see"
▷ can you reheel these shoes?	μπορείτε να βάλετε τακούνια σ'αυτά τα παπούτσια;	"bo**ree**-te na **va**le-te ta**koo**nee-a **saf**ta ta pa-**poot**see-a"
shoe laces	τα κορδόνια για παπούτσια	"ta kor-**dho**nee-a ya pa-**poot**see-a"

ABSOLUTE ESSENTIALS

I would like ...	θα ήθελα ...	"tha **ee**thela"
I need ...	χρειάζομαι ...	"khree-**a**zo-me"
where is ...?	πού είναι ...;	"poo **ee**-ne"
we're looking for ...	ψάχνουμε ...	"**psa**khnoo-me"

shoe polish	το βερνίκι για παπούτσια	"to ver**nee**-kee ya pa-**poo**tsee-a"
shop	το μαγαζί	"to magha-**zee**"
▷ what time do the shops close?	τι ώρα κλείνουν τα μαγαζιά;	"tee **o**-ra **klee**noon ta maghazee-**a**"
shopping	τα ψώνια	"ta **pso**nee-a"
▷ to go shopping	ψωνίζω	"pso-**nee**zo"
▷ where is the main shopping area?	πού είναι η αγορά;	"poo **ee**-ne ee agho-**ra**"
shopping centre	το εμπορικό κέντρο	"to em-boree**ko ken**-dro"
short	κοντός	"kon**dos**"
short cut	ο συντομότερος δρόμος	"o seendo-**mo**teros **dhro**mos"
short-sighted:		
▷ I'm short-sighted	έχω μυωπία	"ekho mee-o**pee**-a"
shorts	το σορτς	"to shorts"
shoulder	ο ώμος	"o **o**-mos"
show[1] n (in theatre etc)	η παράσταση	"ee para-stasee"
to **show**[2] vb	δείχνω	"**dheekh**-no"
▷ could you show me please?	μπορείτε να μου δείξετε, παρακαλώ,	"bo**ree**-te na moo **dheek**se-te para-ka**lo**"
shower (in bath)	το ντους	"to doos"
(rain)	η μπόρα	"ee **bo**ra"
▷ how does the shower work?	πώς λειτουργεί το ντους;	"pos leetoor-**yee** to doos"
▷ I'd like a room with a shower	θα ήθελα ένα δωμάτιο με ντους	"tha **ee**the-la **e**na dho**ma**tee-o me doos"
shrimp	η γαρίδα	"ee gha-**ree**dha"
sick (ill)	άρρωστος	"**a**ro-stos"
▷ I feel sick	είμαι άρρωστος	"**ee**-me aro-stos"

ABSOLUTE ESSENTIALS

do you have ...?	έχετε ...;	"**ekhe**-te"
is there ...?	υπάρχει ...;	"ee-**park**hee"
are there ...?	υπάρχουν ...;	"ee-**park**hoon"
how much is ...?	πόσο κάνει ...;	"**poso kanee**"

▷ **she has been sick**	έκανε εμετό	"**eka**-ne e-me**to**"

sightseeing:

▷ **to go sightseeing**	επισκέπτομαι τα αξιοθέατα	"epee-**skep**to-me ta aksee-o**the**-ata"
▷ **are there any sightseeing tours?**	γίνονται εκδρομές στα αξιοθέατα;	"**yee**-non-te ekdhro-**mes** sta aksee-o**the**-ata"
sign[1] n (*roadsign, notice etc*)	η πινακίδα	"ee peena**kee**dha"
to **sign**[2] *vb*	υπογράφω	"eepo**ghra**-fo"
▷ **where do I sign?**	πού υπογράφω;	"poo eepo**ghra**-fo"
signature	η υπογραφή	"ee eepo-ghra**fee**"
silk	το μετάξι	"to me-**taksee**"
silver	ασημένιος	"asee-**me**nee-os"
similar	παρόμοιος	"pa**ro**mee-os"
simple	απλός	"ap**los**"
single (*not married*) (*not double*)	ελεύθερος μονός	"e**lef**-theros" "mo**nos**"
▷ **a single to ..., second class**	ένα απλό για ..., δεύτερη θέση	"ena ap**lo** ya ... **dhef**-teree **the**see"
single bed	το μονό κρεβάτι	"to mo**no** kre**va**tee"
single room	το μονόκλινο δωμάτιο	"to mo**no**-kleeno dho**ma**tee-o"
▷ **I want to reserve a single room**	θέλω να κλείσω ένα μονόκλινο δωμάτιο	"**the**-lo na **klee**so ena mo**no**-kleeno dho**ma**tee-o"
sir	κύριε	"**kee**ree-e"
sister	η αδελφή	"ee adhel-**fee**"
to **sit** (*down*)	κάθομαι	"**katho**-me"
▷ **please sit down**	καθήστε παρακαλώ	"ka**thee**-ste para-ka**lo**"
six	έξι	"**e**-ksee"

ABSOLUTE ESSENTIALS

yes (please)	ναι (παρακαλώ)	"ne (para-ka**lo**)"
no (thank you)	όχι (ευχαριστώ)	"**okhee** (efkharee**sto**)"
hello	γεια σας	"ya sas"
goodbye	αντίο	"an**dee**-o"

sixteen	δεκαέξι	"dheka-**e**-ksee"
sixty	εξήντα	"e-**kseen**da"
size (*of clothes, shoes*)	το μέγεθος	"to **me**-yethos"
▷ **I take a size ...**	φοράω νούμερο ...	"fora-o **noo**-mero"
▷ **do you have this in a bigger/smaller size?**	το έχετε σε μεγαλύτερο/ μικρότερο μέγεθος;	"to **ekhe**-te se megha-**lee**te-ro/meek**ro**-te-ro **me**-yethos"
skate (*sportswear*)	το πατίνι	"to pa-**tee**nee"
skating	το πατινάζ	"to pa-tee**naz**"
ski[1] *n*	το σκι	"to skee"
▷ **can we hire skis here?**	μπορούμε να νοικιάσουμε σκι εδώ;	"bo**roo**-me na neekee-**a**soo-me skee **edho**"
to **ski**[2] *vb*	κάνω σκι	"**ka**no skee"
ski boot	οι μπότες του σκι	"ee **bo**-tes too skee"
skimmed milk	το αποβουτυρωμένο γάλα	"to apo-vootee-ro**me**no **gha**la"
skin	το δέρμα	"to **dher**ma"
skin diving	το υποβρύχιο κολύμπι	"to eepov**ree**khee-o ko**leem**pee"
skirt	η φούστα	"ee **foo**sta"
ski suit	τα ρούχα του σκι	"ta **roo**kha too skee"
sledge	το έλκηθρο	"to **el**kee-thro"
to **sleep**	κοιμάμαι	"kee**ma**-me"
▷ **I can't sleep for the noise/heat**	δεν μπορώ να κοιμηθώ απο τη φασαρία/τη ζέστη	"dhen bo-**ro** na keemee-**tho** apo tee fasa**ree**-a/ tee **zes**-tee"
sleeper	το βαγκόν-λι	"to va**gon**-lee"
sleeping bag	το σλίπινγκ-μπαγκ	"to **sleep**ing-bag"
sleeping car	η κλινάμαξα	"ee klee**na**-ma-ksa"

I don't understand	δεν καταλαβαίνω	"dhen kata-la**ve**no"
I don't speak Greek	δεν μιλάω ελληνικά	"dhen meela-o elee-**nee**ka"
do you speak English?	μιλάτε αγγλικά;	"mee**la**-te anglee-**ka**"
more slowly please	πιο σιγά παρακαλώ	"pee**o** see**gha** para-ka**lo**"

sleeping pill	το υπνωτικό χάπι	"to eepno-tee**ko kha**pee"
slice	η φέτα	"ee **fe**ta"
slide (*photography*)	το σλάιντ	"to slide"
slow	αργός	"ar-**ghos**"
slowly	σιγά	"see**gha**"
small	μικρός	"mee**kros**"
smaller	μικρότερος	"mee**kro**-teros"
smell	η μυρωδιά	"ee meerodhee-**a**"
smoke[1] *n*	ο καπνός	"o kap**nos**"
to **smoke**[2] *vb*	καπνίζω	"kap-**nee**zo"
▷ **do you mind if I smoke?**	σας πειράζει να καπνίσω;	"sas peera-zee na kap-**nee**so"
▷ **do you smoke?**	καπνίζετε;	"kap-**nee**ze-te"
▷ **I'd like a no smoking room/seat**	θα ήθελα ένα δωμάτιο/μία θέση μη καπνιστών	"tha **ee**the-la ena dho**ma**tee-o/**mee**a **the**see mee kap-nee**ston**"
smoked	καπνιστός	"kap-nee**stos**"
snack bar	το σνακ-μπαρ	"to snack-bar"
snorkel	ο αναπνευστήρας	"o anap-nef**stee**-ras"
snow	το χιόνι	"to khee-**o**nee"
▷ **the snow is very icy/heavy**	το χιόνι είναι παγωμένο/πυκνό	"to khee-**o**nee **ee**-ne pagho**me**-no/pee-**kno**"
▷ **is it going to snow?**	θα χιονίσει;	"tha khee-o**nee**see"
snowed up	αποκλεισμένος από το χιόνι	"apo-klees**me**nos a**po** to khee-**o**nee"
snowing:		
▷ **it's snowing**	χιονίζει	"khee-o**nee**zee"
so	γι' αυτό	"ya**fto**"
▷ **so much**	τόσο πολύ	"**to**so po**lee**"
▷ **so pretty**	τόσο ωραίος	"**to**so o-**re**-os"

I would like ...	θα ήθελα ...	"tha **ee**thela"
I need ...	χρειάζομαι ...	"khree-**a**zo-me"
where is ...?	πού είναι ...;	"poo **ee**-ne"
we're looking for ...	ψάχνουμε ...	"**psa**khnoo-me"

soap	το σαπούνι	"to sa-**poo**nee"
▷ **there is no soap**	δεν έχει σαπούνι	"dhen **e**khee sa**poo**-nee"
soap powder	το απορρυπαντικό	"to a-poree-pandee**ko**"
sober	ξεμέθυστος	"kse**me**thee-stos"
sock	η κάλτσα	"ee **kalt**sa"
socket (*electrical*)	η πρίζα	"ee **pree**za"
▷ **where is the socket for my electric razor?**	πού είναι η πρίζα για την ξυριστική μου μηχανή;	"poo **ee**-ne ee **pree**za ya teen kseeree-stee**kee** moo mee-kha**nee**"
soda (water)	η σόδα	"ee **so**dha"
soft	μαλακός	"mala-**kos**"
soft drink	το αναψυκτικό	"to anapseek-tee**ko**"
sole (*for shoe*)	η σόλα	"ee **so**-la"
solution	το διάλυμα	"to dhee-**a**lee-ma"
▷ **cleansing solution for contact lenses**	διάλυμα καθαρισμού φακών επαφής	"dhee-**a**lee-ma katha-rees**moo** fa**kon** epa**fees**"
some	μερικοί	"meree-**kee**"
someone	κάποιος	"**ka**pee-os"
something	κάτι	"**ka**tee"
sometimes	κάποτε	"**ka**po-te"
son	ο γιος	"o yos"
song	το τραγούδι	"to tra-**ghoo**dhee"
soon	σύντομα	"**seen**-doma"
▷ **as soon as possible**	το συντομότερο	"to seendo-**mo**-tero"
▷ **sooner**	νωρίτερα	"no**ree**-tera"
sore:		
▷ **it's sore**	πονάει	"pona-ee"
▷ **I have a sore throat**	έχω πονόλαιμο	"**e**kho po**no**-lemo"

ABSOLUTE ESSENTIALS

do you have ...?	έχετε ...;	"**e**khe-te"
is there ...?	υπάρχει ...;	"ee-**par**khee"
are there ...?	υπάρχουν ...;	"ee-**par**khoon"
how much is ...?	πόσο κάνει ...;	"**po**so **ka**nee"

sorry:

▷ **I'm sorry!** (*apology*)   συγγνώμη   "seegh-**no**mee"
   (*regret*)   λυπάμαι   "lee**pa**-me"

sort   το είδος   "to **ee**dhos"
▷ **what sort of cheese?**   τι είδος τυρί;   "tee **ee**dhos tee-**ree**"

soup   η σούπα   "ee **soo**pa"
▷ **what is the soup of the day?**   τι είναι η σούπα της ημέρας;   "tee **ee**-ne ee **soo**pa tees ee**me**ras"

south   ο νότος   "o **no**tos"

souvenir   το σουβενίρ   "to soove**neer**"

space (*room*)   ο χώρος   "o **kho**ros"

spade   το φτυάρι   "to ftee-**a**ree"

Spain   η Ισπανία   "ee eespa**nee**-a"

Spanish *adj*   ισπανικός   "eespanee**kos**"
  (*language*)   ισπανικά   "eespanee**ka**"

spare wheel   η ρεζέρβα   "ee re**zer**va"

sparkling (*wine*)   αφρώδης   "a**fro**dhees"

spark plug   το μπουζί   "to boo**zee**"

to speak   μιλάω   "meela-o"
▷ **can I speak to ...?**   μπορώ να μιλήσω στον/στην ...;   "bo-**ro** na mee-**lee**so ston/steen"

special   ειδικός   "eedhee-**kos**"
▷ **do you have a special menu for children?**   έχετε ειδικό μενού για παιδιά;   "**ekhe**-te eedhee-**ko** me**noo** ya pedhee-**a**"

speciality (*in restaurant*)   σπεσιαλιτέ   "spesee-alee-**te**"

▷ **is there a local speciality?**   έχετε τοπική σπεσιαλιτέ;   "ekhe-te topee-**kee** spesee-alee-**te**"
▷ **what is the chef's speciality?**   ποια είναι η σπεσιαλιτέ;   "peea **ee**-ne ee spesee-alee-**te**"

speed	η ταχύτητα	"ee ta**khee**-teeta"
speed limit	το όριο ταχύτητας	"to **o**ree-o ta**khee**-teetas"
▷ **what is the speed limit on this road?**	ποιο είναι το όριο ταχύτητας σ'αυτόν το δρόμο;	"peeo **ee**-ne to oree-o ta**khee**-teetas saf**ton** to **dhro**mo"
to **spell:**		
▷ **how do you spell it?**	πώς γράφεται;	"pos **ghra**-fe-te"
spicy	αρωματισμένος	"aroma-teesm**e**nos"
spinach	το σπανάκι	"to spa-**na**kee"
spirits	τα οινοπνευματώδη	"ta eenop-nevma-**to**dhee"
sponge	το σφουγγάρι	"to sfoon-**ga**ree"
spoon	το κουτάλι	"to koo-**ta**lee"
sport	το σπορ	"to spor"
▷ **which sports activities are available here?**	τι σπορ έχει εδώ;	"tee spor **e**khee e**dho**"
spring (*season*)	η άνοιξη	"ee **a**neek-see"
square (*in town*)	η πλατεία	"ee pla**tee**-a"
squash (*sport*)	το σκουός	"to skoo-**os**"
▷ **orange squash**	πορτοκαλάδα	"porto-ka**la**dha"
stain	ο λεκές	"o le**kes**"
▷ **this stain is coffee/ blood**	ο λεκές είναι από καφέ/αίμα	"o le-**kes ee**-ne a**po** ka-**fe**/e-ma"
▷ **can you remove this stain?**	μπορείτε να βγάλετε αυτό το λεκέ;	"bo**ree**-te na **vgha**-le-te af**to** to le-**ke**"
stairs	η σκάλα	"ee **ska**la"
stalls (*in theatre*)	η πλατεία	"ee pla**tee**-a"
stamp	το γραμματόσημο	"to ghrama-**to**seemo"
▷ **do you sell stamps?**	πουλάτε γραμματόσημα;	"poo**la**-te ghrama-**to**seema"

ABSOLUTE ESSENTIALS

I don't understand	δεν καταλαβαίνω	"dhen kata-la**ve**no"
I don't speak Greek	δεν μιλάω ελληνικά	"dhen meela-o elee-nee**ka**"
do you speak English?	μιλάτε αγγλικά;	"meela-te anglee-**ka**"
more slowly please	πιο σιγά παρακαλώ	"peeo see**gha** para-ka**lo**"

▷ I'd like six stamps for postcards to Great Britain, please	θα ήθελα έξι γραμματόσημα για κάρτες στη Βρετανία, παρακαλώ	"tha **ee**-thela eksee ghrama-**to**seema ya **kar**-tes stee vretanee-a para-ka**lo**"
▷ twelve 35-drachma stamps, please	δώδεκα γραμματόσημα των 35, παρακαλώ	"**dho**-dheka ghrama-**to**seema ton tree-**an**da **pen**-de para-ka**lo**"
to **start**	αρχίζω	"ar-**khee**zo"
▷ when does the film/ show start?	τι ώρα αρχίζει η ταινία/το σόου;	"tee **o**-ra ar**khee**-zee ee te**nee**-a/to show"
starter (*in meal*)	το ορεκτικό	"to orek-tee**ko**"
station	ο σταθμός	"o stath-**mos**"
▷ to the main station, please	στο σταθμό, παρακαλώ	"to stath-**mo** para-ka**lo**"
stationer's	το χαρτοπωλείο	"to kharto-po**lee**-o"
to **stay**	μένω	"**me**no"
▷ I'm staying at a hotel	μένω σε ξενοδοχείο	"**me**-no se kseno-dho**khee**o"
▷ I want to stay an extra night	θέλω να μείνω μία νύχτα ακόμη	"**the**-lo na **mee**no **mee**a **nee**-khta a-**ko**mee"
steak	η μπριζόλα	"ee bree**zo**la"
steep	ανηφορικός	"anee-foree**kos**"
sterling	η λίρα στερλίνα	"ee **lee**ra ster**lee**na"
▷ what is the rate for sterling?	ποια είναι η ισοτιμία για τη λίρα;	"pee**a ee**-ne ee eeso-tee**mee**-a ya tee **lee**-ra"
stew	το κρέας με χορταρικά στην κατσαρόλα	"to **kre**-as me khorta-ree**ka** steen katsa-**ro**la"
steward (*on a ship*)	ο καμαρότος	"o kama-**ro**tos"
(*on a plane*)	ο αεροσυνοδός	"o aero-seeno**dhos**"
stewardess (*on plane*)	η αεροσυνοδός	"ee aero-seeno**dhos**"

ABSOLUTE ESSENTIALS		
I would like ...	θα ήθελα ...	"tha **ee**thela"
I need ...	χρειάζομαι ...	"khree-**a**zo-me"
where is ...?	πού είναι ...;	"poo **ee**-ne"
we're looking for ...	ψάχνουμε ...	"**psa**khnoo-me"

sticking plaster	ο λευκοπλάστης	"o lefko-**plas**tees"
still (*yet*)	ακόμα	"a**ko**ma"
(*immobile*)	ακίνητος	"a**kee**-neetos"
sting	το κεντρί	"to ken-**dhree**"
stockings	οι κάλτσες	"ee **kalt**-ses"

stolen:
▷ **my passport/my watch has been stolen**	μου έκλεψαν το διαβατήριο/το ρολόι μου	"moo **e**klepsan to dheea-va**tee**reeo/to ro**lo**-ee moo"

stomach	το στομάχι	"to sto-**ma**khee"

stomach ache:
▷ **I have a stomach ache**	με πονάει το στομάχι μου	"me po**na**-ee to sto-**ma**khee moo"

stomach upset:
▷ **I have a stomach upset**	έχω στομαχική διαταραχή	"**e**kho stoma-khee**kee** dhee-atara-**khee**"

to **stop**	σταματώ	"stama-**to**"
▷ **please stop here/at the corner**	σταματήστε εδώ/στη γωνία, σας παρακαλώ	"stama**tees**-te e**dho**/stee gho**nee**-a sas para-ka**lo**"
▷ **do we stop at ...?**	σταματάμε στο ...;	"stama**ta**-me sto"
▷ **where do we stop for lunch?**	πού σταματάμε για μεσημεριανό;	"poo stama**ta**-me ya mesee-meree-a**no**"
▷ **please stop the bus**	παρακαλώ σταματήστε το λεωφορείο	"para-ka**lo** stama**tee**-ste to leo-fo**ree**-o"

stopover (*in air travel*)	ο ενδιάμεσος σταθμός	"o endhee-**a**mesos stath-**mos**"
storm	η καταιγίδα	"ee ka-te-**yee**dha"
straight on	κατευθείαν	"katef-**thee**-an"
straw (*for drinking*)	το καλαμάκι	"to kala-**ma**kee"

ABSOLUTE ESSENTIALS

do you have ...?	έχετε ...;	"**ekhe**-te"
is there ...?	υπάρχει ...;	"ee-**parkhee**"
are there ...?	υπάρχουν ...;	"ee-**parkhoon**"
how much is ...?	πόσο κάνει ...;	"**poso kanee**"

strawberry	η φράουλα	"ee **fra**-oola"
street	ο δρόμος	"o **dhro**mos"
street map	ο οδικός χάρτης	"o odhee-**kos khar**tees"
string	ο σπάγγος	"o **span**gos"
strong	δυνατός	"dheena-**tos**"
stuck:		
▷ **it's stuck**	έχει κολλήσει	"**ekhee** ko**lee**see"
student	ο φοιτητής	"o feetee-**tees**"
	η φοιτήτρια	"ee fee-**tee**tree-a"
stung:		
▷ **he has been stung by ...**	τον τσίμπησε ...	"ton **tseem**bee-se"
stupid	βλάκας	"**vla**kas"
suddenly	ξαφνικά	"ksaf-nee**ka**"
suede	το καστόρι	"to kas**to**ree"
sugar	η ζάχαρη	"ee **za**kharee"
suit (*man's*)	το κοστούμι	"to ko-**stoo**mee"
(*woman's*)	το ταγιέρ	"to ta-**yer**"
suitcase	η βαλίτσα	"ee va**leet**-sa"
▷ **my suitcase was damaged in transit**	η βαλίτσα μου έπαθε ζημιά στη μεταφορά	"ee va**leet**-sa moo **epa**-the zee**mee**-a stee meta-fo**ra**"
summer	το καλοκαίρι	"to kalo-**ke**ree"
sun	ο ήλιος	"o **eelee**-os"
to **sunbathe**	κάνω ηλιοθεραπεία	"**ka**no eelee-o-thera**pee**-a"
sunburn (*painful*)	το κάψιμο από τον ήλιο	"to **kap**-seemo a**po** ton **eelee**-o"
▷ **can you give me something for sunburn?**	έχετε κάτι για το κάψιμο απο τον ήλιο;	"**ekhe**-te **ka**tee ya to **kap**-seemo apo ton **eelee**-o"

Sunday	Κυριακή	"keeree-a**kee**"
sunglasses	τα γυαλιά του ηλίου	"ta yalee-**a** too eelee-oo"
sunny	ηλιόλουστος	"eelee-**o**loostos"
▷ **it's sunny**	έχει ήλιο	"**ekhee eelee**-o"
sunshade	η ομπρέλα	"ee om**bre**la"
sunstroke	η ηλίαση	"ee eelee-asee"
suntan lotion	το αντηλιακό	"to andee-leea**ko**"
supermarket	το σούπερ-μάρκετ	"to supermarket"
supper	το δείπνο	"to **dhee**pno"
supplement	το συμπλήρωμα	"to seem**blee**-roma"
▷ **is there a supplement to pay?**	πρέπει να πληρώσω επιπλέον;	"**pre**pee na plee**ro**so epee-**ple**on"
sure	βέβαιος	"**ve**-ve-os"
surface mail	απλό ταχυδρομείο	"**aplo** takheedhro**mee**-o"
surfboard	το σερφ	"to serf"
▷ **can I rent a surfboard?**	μπορώ να νοικιάσω ένα σερφ;	"bo-**ro** na nee-kee**a**so ena serf"
surfing	το σέρφινγκ	"to surfing"
▷ **I'd like to go surfing**	θέλω να κάνω σέρφινγκ	"**the**-lo na **ka**no surfing"
surname	το επώνυμο	"to e**po**-neemo"
suspension	η ανάρτηση	"ee a**nar**-teesee"
sweater	το πουλόβερ	"to poo**lo**ver"
sweet[1] n	το γλυκό	"to ghlee**ko**"
sweet[2] adj (taste)	γλυκός	"ghlee**kos**"
sweetener	το γλυκαντικό	"to ghleekandee**ko**"
sweets	οι καραμέλες	"ee kara**me**-les"
to **swim**	κολυμπώ	"koleem-**bo**"
▷ **let's go swimming**	πάμε για κολύμπι	"**pa**-me ya ko**leem**-bee"

ABSOLUTE ESSENTIALS

I don't understand	δεν καταλαβαίνω	"dhen kata-**la**veno"
I don't speak Greek	δεν μιλάω ελληνικά	"dhen meela-o elee-nee**ka**"
do you speak English?	μιλάτε αγγλικά;	"meela-te anglee-**ka**"
more slowly please	πιο σιγά παρακαλώ	"**peeo** seegha para-ka**lo**"

English	Greek	Pronunciation
▷ can one swim in the river?	μπορεί κανείς να κολυμπήσει στο ποτάμι;	"boree kanees na koleem-beesee sto pota-mee"
swimming pool	η πισίνα	"ee pee-seena"
▷ is there a swimming pool?	υπάρχει πισίνα;	"eepar-khee peesee-na"
swimsuit	το μαγιό	"to ma-yo"
switch	ο διακόπτης	"o dhee-akoptees"
to **switch off**	σβήνω	"sveeno"
▷ can I switch the light off?	μπορώ να σβήσω το φως;	"bo-ro na sveeso to fos"
to **switch on**	ανάβω	"anavo"
▷ can I switch the light on?	μπορώ να ανάψω το φως;	"bo-ro na anapso to fos"
Switzerland	η Ελβετία	"ee elvetee-a"
Swiss *adj*	ελβετικός	"el-veteekos"
synagogue	η συναγωγή	"ee seenagho-yee"
table	το τραπέζι	"to tra-pezee"
▷ a table for four, please	ένα τραπέζι για τέσσερις, παρακαλώ	"ena tra-pezee ya te-serees para-kalo"
▷ the table is booked for ... o'clock this evening	το τραπέζι είναι κλεισμένο για τις ... το βράδυ	"to tra-pezee ee-ne klees-meno ya tees ... to vradhee"
tablecloth	το τραπεζομάντηλο	"to tra-pezo-mandeelo"
tablespoon	το κουτάλι	"to koo-talee"
tablet	το χάπι	"to khapee"
table tennis	το πινγκ-πονγκ	"to peeng pong"
to **take**	παίρνω	"perno"
▷ how long does the journey take?	πόση ώρα παίρνει το ταξίδι;	"posee o-ra pernee to taksee-dhee"

▷ **I take a size ...**	φοράω νούμερο ...	"fora-o **noo**-mero"
▷ **I'd like to take a shower**	θα ήθελα να κάνω ένα ντους	"tha **ee**-thela na **ka**no **e**na doos"
▷ **could you take a photograph of us?**	μπορείτε να μας βγάλετε μία φωτογραφία;	"bo**ree**-te na mas **vgha**-le-te **mee**a foto-gra**fee**-a"
talc	το ταλκ	"to talk"
to **talk**	μιλάω	"meela-o"
tall	ψηλός	"psee**los**"
▷ **how tall are you/is it?**	πόσο ύψος έχετε/ έχει;	"**po**so **ee**psos **e**khe-te/ **e**khee"
tampons	τα ταμπόν	"ta tam**bon**"
tap	η βρύση	"ee **vree**see"
tape (*cassette*)	η κασέτα	"ee ka**se**-ta"
(*video*)	η βιντεοκασέτα	"ee vide-o-ka**se**-ta"
(*ribbon*)	η ταινία	"ee te**nee**-a"
tape recorder	το μαγνητόφωνο	"to maghnee-**to**fono"
tart (*sweet*)	η τάρτα	"ee **tar**-ta"
tartar sauce	η σως ταρτάρ	"ee sos tar**tar**"
taste[1] *n*	η γεύση	"ee **yef**see"
to **taste**[2] *vb*	δοκιμάζω	"dhokee-**ma**zo"
▷ **can I taste it?**	μπορώ να το δοκιμάσω;	"bo-**ro** na to dho-kee**ma**-so"
tax	ο φόρος	"o **fo**ros"
taxi	το ταξί	"to tak**see**"
▷ **can you order me a taxi?**	μπορείτε να μου φωνάξετε ένα ταξί;	"bo**ree**-te na moo fonak-se-te **e**na tak**see**"
taxi rank	η πιάτσα των ταξί	"ee pee-**a**tsa ton tak**see**"
tea	το τσάι	"to **tsa**-ee"
tea bag	το φακελάκι τσάι	"to fa-ke**la**-kee **tsa**-ee"
to **teach**	διδάσκω	"dhee-**dhas**ko"

ABSOLUTE ESSENTIALS

do you have ...?	έχετε ...;	"**ekhe**-te"
is there ...?	υπάρχει ...;	"ee-**parkhee**"
are there ...?	υπάρχουν ...;	"ee-**parkhoon**"
how much is ...?	πόσο κάνει ...;	"**po**so **kanee**"

teacher	ο δάσκαλος	"o **dhas**ka-los"
	η δασκάλα	"ee dhas**kala**"
teapot	η τσαγιέρα	"ee tsa-**yera**"
teaspoon	το κουταλάκι	"to koo-ta**lakee**"
tee shirt	το φανελάκι	"to fa-ne**la**-kee"
teeth	τα δόντια	"ta **dhon**dee-a"
telegram	το τηλεγράφημα	"to teele-**ghra**feema"
▷ **I want to send a telegram**	θέλω να στείλω ένα τηλεγράφημα	"**the**-lo na **stee**-lo ena teele-**ghra**feema"
telephone[1] *n*	το τηλέφωνο	"to tee**le**-fono"
telephone[2] *vb*	τηλεφωνώ	"teele-fo**no**"
▷ **how much is it to telephone Britain/the USA?**	πόσο κάνει ένα τηλεφώνημα στη Βρετανία/στις Ηνωμένες Πολιτείες;	"**poso kanee** ena tee-le**fo**-neema stee vreta**nee**-a/stees eeno-**me**-nes polee**tee**-es"
telephone book	ο τηλεφωνικός κατάλογος	"o teele-fonee**kos** katalo-ghos"
telephone box	ο τηλεφωνικός θάλαμος	"o teele-fonee**kos** thala-mos"
telephone call	το τηλεφώνημα	"to teele-**fo**neema"
▷ **I'd like to make a telephone call**	θέλω να κάνω ένα τηλεφώνημα	"**the**-lo na **kano** ena teele-**fo**neema"
telephone directory	ο τηλεφωνικός κατάλογος	"o teele-fonee**kos** kata-lo-ghos"
television	η τηλεόραση	"ee teele-**o**rasee"
television set	η τηλεόραση	"ee teele-**o**rasee"
telex	το τέλεξ	"to telex"
to **tell**	λέω	"**leo**"
temperature	η θερμοκρασία	"ee thermo-kra**see**-a"

ABSOLUTE ESSENTIALS

yes (please)	ναι (παρακαλώ)	"ne (para-ka**lo**)"
no (thank you)	όχι (ευχαριστώ)	"**okhee** (efkharee**sto**)"
hello	γεια σας	"ya sas"
goodbye	αντίο	"an**dee**-o"

▷ **to have a temperature**	έχω πυρετό	"**e**kho pee-re**to**"
▷ **what is the temperature?**	τι θερμοκρασία έχει;	"tee thermo-kra**see**-a **e**khee"
temporary	προσωρινός	"proso-ree**nos**"
ten	δέκα	"**dhe**ka"
tennis	το τέννις	"to tennis"
▷ **where can we play tennis?**	πού μπορούμε να παίξουμε τέννις;	"poo boo**roo**-me na **pe**ksoo-me tennis"
tennis ball	το μπαλάκι του τέννις	"to ba**la**-kee too tennis"
tennis court	το γήπεδο του τέννις	"to **yee**-pedho too tennis"
tennis racket	η ρακέτα του τέννις	"ee ra-**ke**ta too tennis"
tent	η σκηνή	"ee skee**nee**"
▷ **can we pitch our tent here?**	μπορούμε να στήσουμε τη σκηνή μας εδώ;	"bo**roo**-me na **stee**-soo-me tee skee**nee** mas e**dho**"
tent peg	ο πάσσαλος της σκηνής	"o **pa**sa-los tees skee**nees**"
terminus	το τέρμα	"to **ter**ma"
terrace	η ταράτσα	"ee tara**tsa**"
than	από	"a**po**"
▷ **better than this**	καλύτερο από αυτό	"ka**lee**-tero a**po** af**to**"
thank you	ευχαριστώ	"ef-kharee-**sto**"
▷ **thank you very much**	ευχαριστώ πολύ	"ef-kharee-**sto** po**lee**"
▷ **no thank you**	όχι, ευχαριστώ	"**o**khee ef-kharee-**sto**"
that	εκείνος	"e**kee**-nos"
	εκείνη	"e**kee**-nee"
	εκείνο	"e**kee**-no"
▷ **that one**	εκείνο	"e**kee**-no"

ABSOLUTE ESSENTIALS

I don't understand	δεν καταλαβαίνω	"dhen kata-la**ve**no"
I don't speak Greek	δεν μιλάω ελληνικά	"dhen mee**la**-o elee-nee**ka**"
do you speak English?	μιλάτε αγγλικά;	"mee**la**-te anglee-**ka**"
more slowly please	πιο σιγά παρακαλώ	"**pee**o see**gha** para-ka**lo**"

theatre	το θέατρο	"to **the**-atro"
their	τους	"toos"
theirs	δικός τους	"dhee-**kos** toos"
then	τότε	"**to**-te"
there	εκεί	"ekee"
▷ **there is a bed**	υπάρχει ένα κρεβάτι	"ee-**park**hee ena kre-**vatee**"
▷ **there are two chairs**	υπάρχουν δύο καρέκλες	"ee-**park**hoon **dhee**-o karekles"
thermometer	το θερμόμετρο	"to thermo-metro"
these	αυτοί	"**aftee**"
	αυτές	"**aftes**"
	αυτά	"**afta**"
they	αυτοί	"**aftee**"
	αυτές	"**aftes**"
	αυτά	"**afta**"
thief	ο κλέφτης	"o **klef**tees"
thing	το πράγμα	"to **pragh**ma"
▷ **my things**	τα πράγματά μου	"ta **pragh**-mata moo"
to **think**	σκέφτομαι	"**skef**to-me"
third	τρίτος	"**tree**tos"
thirsty:		
▷ **I'm thirsty**	διψάω	"dheep**sao**"
thirteen	δεκατρία	"dheka-**tree**-a"
thirty	τριάντα	"tree-**anda**"
this	αυτός	"**aftos**"
	αυτή	"**aftee**"
	αυτό	"**afto**"
▷ **this one**	αυτό	"**afto**"
▷ **this book**	αυτό το βιβλίο	"**afto** to vee**vlee**-o"

ABSOLUTE ESSENTIALS

I would like ...	θα ήθελα ...	"tha **ee**thela"
I need ...	χρειάζομαι ...	"khree-**azo**-me"
where is ...?	πού είναι ...;	"poo **ee**-ne"
we're looking for ...	ψάχνουμε ...	"**psakh**noo-me"

ticket

those	εκείνοι	"e**kee**-nee"
	εκείνες	"e**kee**nes"
	εκείνα	"e**kee**na"
▷ those books	εκείνα τα βιβλία	"e**kee**na ta vee**vlee**-a"
thousand	χίλια	"**kheel**eea"
thread	η κλωστή	"ee klo**stee**"
three	τρία	"**tree**-a"
throat	ο λαιμός	"o le**mos**"
▷ I want something for a sore throat	θέλω κάτι για πονόλαιμο	"**the**-lo **ka**tee ya po**no**-lemo"
throat lozenges	οι παστίλιες για το λαιμό	"ee pa**steel**ee-es ya to le**mo**"
through	διαμέσου	"dhee-a**me**soo"
▷ I can't get through	δεν μπορώ να πιάσω γραμμή	"dhen bo-**ro** na pee-**a**so ghra**mee**"
thunder	ο κεραυνός	"o kerav-**nos**"
thunderstorm	η καταιγίδα	"ee ka-te-**yee**dha"
▷ will there be a thunderstorm?	θα έχει καταιγίδα;	"tha **e**khee ka-te-**yee**dha"
Thursday	Πέμπτη	"**pem**-ptee"
ticket	το εισιτήριο	"to eeee**too**roo o"
▷ a single ticket	ένα απλό εισιτήριο	"**e**na ap-**lo** eesee**tee**ree-o"
▷ a return ticket	ένα εισιτήριο με επιστροφή	"**e**na eesee**tee**ree-o me epee-stro**fee**"
▷ can you book the tickets for us?	μπορείτε να μας κρατήσετε εισιτήρια;	"bo**ree**-te **na mas** kra**tee**-se-te eesee-**tee**ree-a"
▷ where do I buy a ticket?	από πού αγοράζω εισιτήριο;	"**apo** poo agho-**ra**zo eesee-**tee**ree-o"
▷ can I buy the tickets here?	μπορώ να αγοράσω τα εισιτήρια εδώ;	"bo-**ro** na aghora-so ta eesee-**tee**ree-a e**dho**"

ticket collector	ο ελεγκτής	"o eleng-**tees**"
ticket office	η θυρίδα	"ee thee-**ree**dha"
tide	η παλίρροια	"ee pal**ee**ree-a"
tie	η γραβάτα	"ee ghra-**va**ta"
tights	το καλσόν	"to kal**son**"
till[1] *n*	το ταμείο	"to tam**ee**-o"
till[2] *prep* (*until*)	μέχρι	"**mekh**ree"
▷ **I want to stay three nights from ... till ...**	θέλω να μείνω για τρεις νύχτες από ... μέχρι ...	"**the**-lo na **mee**no ya trees **neekh**-tes a**po** ... **mekh**ree"
time (*by the clock*)	η ώρα	"ee **o**-ra"
(*duration*)	ο καιρός	"o ker**os**"
▷ **this time**	αυτή την ώρα	"af**tee** teen **o**-ra"
▷ **what time is it?**	τι ώρα είναι;	"tee **o**-ra **ee**-ne"
▷ **do we have time to visit the town?**	έχουμε ώρα να επισκεφτούμε την πόλη;	"**ekh**oo-me **o**-ra na epee-skef**too**-me teen pol**ee**"
▷ **what time do we get to ...?**	τι ώρα φτάνουμε ...;	"tee **o**-ra **fta**noo-me"
timetable board	ο πίνακας δρομολογίων	"o **pee**nakas dhromo-lo**yee**-on"
tin	η κονσέρβα	"ee kon-**ser**va"
tinfoil	το αλουμινόχαρτο	"to aloomee**no**-kharto"
tin-opener	το ανοιχτήρι για κονσέρβες	"to aneekh-**tee**ree ya kon-**ser**-ves"
tip[1] *n*	το φιλοδώρημα	"to feelo-**dho**reema"
▷ **is the tip included?**	συμπεριλαμβάνεται το φιλοδώρημα;	"seem-bereelam-**va**-ne-te to feelo-**dho**reema"
to **tip**[2] *vb* (*waiter etc*)	δίνω φιλοδώρημα	"**dhee**no feelo-**dho**reema"

▷ **is it usual to tip?**	συνηθίζεται να δίνει κανείς φιλοδώρημα;	"seenee-**thee**-ze-te na **dhee**nee ka**nees** feelo-**dho**reema"
▷ **how much should I tip?**	πόσο πρέπει να δώσω για φιλοδώρημα;	"**po**so **pre**pee na **dho**so ya feelo-**dho**reema"
tipped (*cigarettes*)	με φίλτρο	"me **feel**tro"
tired	κουρασμένος	"kooras-**me**nos"
tiring	κουραστικός	"koora-stee**kos**"
tissue	το χαρτομάντηλο	"to kharto-**man**deelo"
to	σε	"se"
▷ **to Greece**	στην Ελλάδα	"steen e**la**dha"
toast	η φρυγανιά	"ee freeghanee-**a**"
tobacco	ο καπνός	"o kap**nos**"
tobacconist's	το καπνοπωλείο	"to kapno-po**lee**-o"
today	σήμερα	"**see**-mera"
▷ **is it open today?**	είναι ανοιχτό σήμερα;	"**ee**-ne aneekh-**to see**-mera"
together	μαζί	"ma**zee**"
toilet	η τουαλέτα	"ee too-a-**le**ta"
▷ **is there a toilet for the disabled?**	υπάρχει τουαλέτα για ανάπηρους;	"ee**par**-khee too-a-**le**ta ya a**na**-peeroos"
▷ **where are the toilets, please?**	πού είναι οι τουαλέτες, παρακαλώ;	"poo **ee**-ne ee too-a-**le**tes para-ka**lo**"
▷ **is there a toilet on board?**	υπάρχει τουαλέτα;	"ee**par**-khee too-a-**le**ta"
▷ **the toilet won't flush**	το καζανάκι δεν δουλεύει	"to kaza-**na**kee dhen dhoo-**le**vee"
toilet paper	το χαρτί υγείας	"to khar**tee** ee**yee**- as"
▷ **there is no toilet paper**	δεν υπάρχει χαρτί υγείας	"dhen ee**par**-khee khar**tee** ee**yee**-as"
toll	τα διόδια	"ta dhee-**o**dhee-a"

ABSOLUTE ESSENTIALS

I don't understand	δεν καταλαβαίνω	"dhen kata-la**ve**no"
I don't speak Greek	δεν μιλάω ελληνικά	"dhen meela-o elee-**nee**ka"
do you speak English?	μιλάτε αγγλικά;	"meela-te anglee-**ka**"
more slowly please	πιο σιγά παρακαλώ	"**peeo** see**gha** para-ka**lo**"

▷ is there a toll on this motorway?	υπάρχουν διόδια σ'αυτόν τον αυτοκινητόδρομο;	"ee**par**-khoon dhee-**o**dhee-a saf**ton** ton afto-keenee**to**-dhromo"
tomato	η ντομάτα	"ee do**ma**-ta"
tomato juice	ο τοματοχυμός	"o tomato-khee**mos**"
tomorrow	αύριο	"**a**-vree-o"
▷ **tomorrow morning**	αύριο το πρωί	"**a**-vree-o to pro-**ee**"
▷ **is it open tomorrow?**	είναι ανοιχτό αύριο;	"**ee**-ne aneekh-**to a**-vree-o"
tongue	η γλώσσα	"ee **ghlo**sa"
tonic water	το τόνικ	"to **to**neek"
tonight	απόψε	"a**pop**-se"
too (*also*)	επίσης	"e**pee**-sees"
(*too much*)	πολύ	"po**lee**"
▷ **it's too big**	είναι πολύ μεγάλο	"**ee**-ne po**lee** me**gha**lo"
tooth	το δόντι	"to **dhon**dee"
▷ **I've broken a tooth**	μου έσπασε ένα δόντι	"moo **e**-spa-se **e**na **dhon**dee"
toothache	ο πονόδοντος	"o pono-**dhon**dos"
▷ **I have toothache**	έχω πονόδοντο	"**e**kho pono-**dhon**do"
▷ **I want something for toothache**	θέλω κάτι για τον πονόδοντο	"**the**-lo **ka**tee ya ton pono-**dhon**do"
toothbrush	η οδοντόβουρτσα	"ee odhon-**do**voortsa"
toothpaste	η οδοντόκρεμα	"ee odhon-**do**krema"
toothpick	η οδοντογλυφίδα	"ee odhon-doghlee-**fee**dha"
top[1] *n*	το πάνω μέρος	"to **pa**-no **me**ros"
(*of mountain*)	η κορυφή	"ee koree-**fee**"
top[2] *adj*	πάνω	"**pa**-no"
▷ **the top floor**	ο τελευταίος όροφος	"o telef-**te**os **o**rofos"

torch	ο φακός	"o fak**os**"
torn	σκισμένος	"skees-**me**nos"
total	το σύνολο	"to **see**-nolo"
tough (of meat)	σκληρός	"sklee**ros**"
tour	η ξενάγηση	"ee ksena-**yee**see"
▷ how long does the tour take?	πόση ώρα κρατάει η ξενάγηση;	"**po**see **o**-ra krata-ee ee kse**na**-yeesee"
▷ the tour starts at ...	η ξενάγηση αρχίζει στις ...	"ee kse**na**-yeesee ar**khee**zee stees"
tourist	ο τουρίστας η τουρίστρια	"o too-**ree**stas" "ee too-**ree**stree-a"
tourist office	το τουριστικό γραφείο	"to tooree-**stee**ko ghra**fee**-o"
▷ I'm looking for the tourist information office	ψάχνω τις τουριστικές πληροφορίες	"**psakh**-no tees tooree-stee**kes** pleero-fo**ree**-es"
tourist ticket	το τουριστικό εισιτήριο	"to tooree-**stee**ko eesee-**tee**ree-o"
to tow	ρυμουλκώ	"reemool-**ko**"
▷ can you tow me to a garage?	μπορείτε να με τραβήξετε σ'ένα συνεργείο;	"bo**ree**-te na me tra**vee**-kse-te **se**na seener-**yee**-o"
towel	η πετσέτα	"ee pet-**se**ta"
▷ the towels have run out	τέλειωσαν οι πετσέτες	"**te**lee-osan ee pet**se**-tes"
town	η πόλη	"ee **po**lee"
town centre	το κέντρο της πόλης	"to **ken**dro tees **po**lees"
town plan	ο χάρτης της πόλης	"o **khar**tees tees **po**lees"
tow rope	το σχοινί ρυμούλκησης	"to skhee**nee** reemool-**kee**sees"

do you have ...?	έχετε ...;	"**ekhe**-te"
is there ...?	υπάρχει ...;	"ee-**parkhee**"
are there ...?	υπάρχουν ...;	"ee-**parkhoon**"
how much is ...?	πόσο κάνει ...;	"**poso kanee**"

toy	το παιγνίδι	"to pegh-**nee**dhee"
traditional	παραδοσιακός	"para-dhosee-a**kos**"
traffic	η κυκλοφορία	"ee keeklo-fo**ree**-a"
▷ is the traffic heavy on the motorway?	έχει κίνηση ο αυτοκινητόδρομος;	"**e**khee **kee**nee-see o afto-keenee**to**-dhromos"
▷ is there a route that avoids the traffic?	υπάρχει δρόμος για να αποφύγεις την κίνηση;	"ee**par**-khee **dhro**mos ya na apo**fee**-yees teen **kee**nee-see"
traffic jam	το μποτιλιάρισμα	"to boteelee-**a**reesma"
trailer	το ρυμουλκούμενο	"to reemool-**koo**meno"
train	το τρένο	"to **tre**no"
▷ is this the train for ...?	αυτό είναι το τρένο για ...;	"af**to ee**-ne to **tre**no ya"
▷ what time is the train?	τι ώρα έχει τρένο;	"tee **o**-ra **e**khee **tre**no"
▷ does this train go to ...?	αυτό το τρένο πηγαίνει ...;	"af**to** to **tre**no pee-**ye**nee"
▷ how frequent are the trains to town?	πόσο συχνά έχει τρένο για την πόλη;	"**po**so seekh**na e**khee **tre**no ya teen **po**lee"
training shoes	τα αθλητικά παπούτσια	"ta athleetee**ka** pa**poo**tseea"
tram	το τραμ	"to tram"
to transfer	μεταφέρω	"meta-**fe**ro"
▷ I should like to transfer some money from my account	θα ήθελα να μεταφέρω μερικά χρήματα από τον λογαριασμό μου	"tha **ee**the-la na meta-**fe**ro meree**ka khree**mata apo ton loghareea-**smo** moo"
to translate	μεταφράζω	"meta-**fra**zo"
▷ could you translate this for me?	μπορείτε να μου το μεταφράσετε;	"bo**ree**-te na moo to meta-**fra**-se-te"
translation	η μετάφραση	"ee meta-frasee"
to travel	ταξιδεύω	"taksee-**dhe**vo"

▷ **I'm travelling alone**	ταξιδεύω μόνος	"taksee-**dhe**vo **mo**nos"
travel agent	ο ταξιδιωτικός πράκτορας	"o takseedhee-otee**kos prak**-toras"
traveller's cheques	το ταξιδιωτικό τσεκ;	"to tak-seedhee- otee**ko** tsek"
▷ **do you accept traveller's cheques?**	δέχεστε ταξιδιωτικά τσεκ	"**dhe**-khes-te tak-seedhee-otee**ka** tsek"
tray	ο δίσκος	"o **dhee**skos"
tree	το δέντρο	"to **dhen**-dro"
trim (hair)	το κόψιμο	"to **kop**-seemo"
trip	η εκδρομή	"ee ek-dhro**mee**"
▷ **this is my first trip to ...**	αυτό είναι το πρώτο μου ταξίδι ...	"af**to ee**-ne to **pro**to moo tak-**see**-dhee"
trolley bus	το τρόλλεϋ	"to **tro**-le-ee"
trouble:		
▷ **I am in trouble**	έχω πρόβλημα	"ekho **prov**-leema"
▷ **I'm having trouble with the phone/key**	έχω πρόβλημα με το τηλέφωνο/το κλειδί	"ekho **prov**-leema me to tee**le**-fono/to klee-**dhee**"
trousers	το παντελόνι	"to pande-**lo**nee"
true	αληθινός	"alee-thee**nos**"
trunk	το μπαούλο	"to ba-**oo**lo"
trunks	το μαγιό	"to ma-**yo**"
to **try**	προσπαθώ	"pros-pa**tho**"
to **try on**	δοκιμάζω	"dhokee-**ma**zo"
▷ **may I try on this dress?**	μπορώ να δοκιμάσω αυτό το φόρεμα;	"bo-**ro** na dhokee-**ma**so af**to** to **fo**-rema"
T-shirt	το φανελάκι	"to fa-nela-kee"
Tuesday	Τρίτη	"**tree**tee"

tuna	ο τόννος	"o **to**nos"
tunnel	η σήραγγα	"o **see**-ranga"
turkey	η γαλοπούλα	"ee ghalo-**poo**la"
turn[1] *n*	η σειρά	"ee see**ra**"
▷ it's my/her turn	είναι η σειρά μου/της	"**ee**-ne ee see**ra** moo/tees"
to **turn**[2] *vb*	γυρίζω	"yee-**ree**zo"
to **turn down** (*sound, heating etc*)	χαμηλώνω	"kha-mee**lo**no"
turning	η στροφή	"ee stro**fee**"
▷ is this the turning for ...?	από δω πρέπει να στρίψω για ...;	"**a**po dho **pre**pee na st**reep**-so ya"
turnip	το γογγύλι	"to gho-**gee**lee"
to **turn off** (*on a journey*)	στρίβω	"**stree**vo"
(*engine, light*)	σβήνω	"**svee**no"
▷ I can't turn the heating off	δεν μπορώ να σβήσω το καλοριφέρ	"dhen bo-**ro** na **svee**so to kalo-ree**fer**"
to **turn on** (*radio etc*)	ανοίγω	"a**nee**-gho"
(*engine, light*)	ανάβω	"a**na**vo"
▷ I can't turn the heating on	δεν μπορώ να ανάψω το καλοριφέρ	"dhen bo-**ro** na a**na**pso to kalo-ree**fer**"
to **turn up** (*sound, heating etc*)	δυναμώνω	"dhee-na**mo**no"
tweezers	το τσιμπίδι	"to tseem-**bee**dhee"
twelve	δώδεκα	"**dho**-dheka"
twenty	είκοσι	"**ee**-kosee"
twenty one	εικοσιένα	"ee-kosee-**e**na"
twenty two	εικοσιδύο	"ee-kosee**dhee**-o"
twice	δύο φορές	"**dhee**-o fo-**res**"

twin	δίδυμος	"**dhee**-dheemos"
twin-bedded	δίκλινο	"**dhee**-kleeno"
two	δύο	"**dhee**-o"
typical	χαρακτηριστικός	"kharak-teeree-stee**kos**"
▷ **have you anything typical of this town/ region?**	έχετε κάτι χαρακτηριστικό της πόλης/περιοχής;	"**ekhe**-te **kate** kharak-teeree-stee**ko** tees **po**lees/pereeo-**khees**"
tyre	το λάστιχο	"to **la**stee-kho"
tyre pressure	η πίεση στα λάστιχα	"ee **pee**-esee sta **la**stee-kha"
umbrella	η ομπρέλα	"ee om**bre**la"
uncomfortable	άβολος	"**a**-volos"
▷ **the bed is uncomfortable**	το κρεβάτι είναι άβολο	"to kre-**va**tee **ee**-ne **a**-volo"
unconscious	αναίσθητος	"a-**nes**-theetos"
under	κάτω από	"**ka**to a**po**"
underground (railway)	ο υπόγειος	"o ee**po**yee-os"
underpass	η υπόγεια διάβαση	"ee ee**po**yee-a dhee-a**va**see"
to **understand**	καταλαβαίνω	"kata-la**ve**no"
▷ **I don't understand**	δεν καταλαβαίνω	"dhen kata-la**ve**no"
underwear	τα εσώρουχα	"ta e-**so**rookha"
United States	οι Ηνωμένες Πολιτείες	"ee eeno-**me**-nes poleetee**-es**"
university	το Πανεπιστήμιο	"to panepee-**stee**mee-o"
unleaded petrol	η αμόλυβδη βενζίνη	"ee amoleev-dhee ven**zee**-nee"
to **unpack**	ξεπακετάρω	"kse-pake**ta**-ro"
up (out of bed)	σηκωμένος	"seeko-**me**nos"
▷ **go up**	ανεβαίνω	"a-ne-**ve**no"

ABSOLUTE ESSENTIALS

do you have ...?	έχετε ...;	"**ekhe**-te"
is there ...?	υπάρχει ...;	"ee-**park**hee"
are there ...?	υπάρχουν ...;	"ee-**park**hoon"
how much is ...?	πόσο κάνει ...;	"**poso** kanee"

▷ up there	εκεί πάνω	"e**kee** pano"
upstairs	πάνω	"**pa**no"
urgently	επειγόντως	"epee-**ghon**dos"
USA	ΗΠΑ	"**ee**pa"
to **use**	χρησιμοποιώ	"khreesee-mopee-**o**"
▷ **may I use your phone?**	μπορώ να χρησιμοποιήσω το τηλέφωνό σας;	"bo-**ro** na khree-seemopee-**ee**so to teele-fono sas"
useful	χρήσιμος	"**khree**see-mos"
usual	συνηθισμένος	"seenee-thees**me**nos"
usually	συνήθως	"see-**nee**thos"
vacancy	το άδειο δωμάτιο	"to a-dhee-o dhomatee-o"
▷ **do you have any vacancies?** (*campsite*)	έχετε θέσεις;	"ekhe-te **the**sees"
to **vacate**	αδειάζω	"a-dhee-**azo**"
▷ **when do I have to vacate the room?**	πότε πρέπει να αδειάσω το δωμάτιο;	"**po**-te **pre**pee na a-dhee-**aso** to dhomatee-o"
vacuum cleaner	η ηλεκτρική σκούπα	"ee eelek-tree**kee skoo**pa"
valid	έγκυρος	"**engee**-ros"
valley	η κοιλάδα	"ee kee-**la**dha"
valuable	πολύτιμος	"po**lee**teemos"
valuables	τα πολύτιμα αντικείμενα	"ta po**lee**teema andee**kee**me-na"
van	το φορτηγάκι	"to fortee-**gha**kee"
vase	το βάζο	"to **va**zo"
VAT	ο ΦΠΑ	"o fee-pee-a"
veal	το μοσχάρι	"to mos-**kha**ree"

vegetables	τα λαχανικά	"ta lakha-nee**ka**"
vegetarian	ο χορτοφάγος	"o khorto-**fa**ghos"
▷ **do you have any vegetarian dishes?**	έχετε φαγητά για χορτοφάγους;	"**ekhe**-te fa-yee**ta** ya khorto-**fa**ghoos"
ventilator	ο εξαεριστήρας	"o eksa-eree-**stee**ras"
vermouth	το βερμούτ	"to ver**moot**"
vertigo	ο ίλιγγος	"o **ee**lee-gos"
very	πολύ	"po**lee**"
vest	η φανέλα	"ee fa-**ne**la"
via	μέσω	"**me**so"
video	το βίντεο	"to **vee**de-o"
videocassette	η βιντεοκασέτα	"ee veede-oka**se**ta"
Vienna	η Βιέννη	"ee vee-**e**nee"
view	η θέα	"ee **the**-a"
▷ **I'd like a room with a view of the sea/the mountains**	θα ήθελα δωμάτιο με θέα στη θάλασσα/ στα βουνά	"tha **ee**the-la dhomatee-o me **the**-a stee **tha**la-sa/sta voo**na**"
villa	η βίλλα	"ee villa"
village	το χωριό	"to khoree**o**"
vinegar	το ξύδι	"to **ksee**dhee"
vineyard	ο αμπελώνας	"o ambe**lo**nas"
visa	η βίζα	"ee visa"
▷ **I have an entry visa**	έχω βίζα	"**ekho vee**za"
to visit	επισκέπτομαι	"epees**ke**pto-me"
▷ **can we visit the vineyard/church?**	μπορούμε να επισκεφτούμε τον αμπελώνα/την εκκλησία	"bo**roo**-me na epeeskef**too**-me ton ambe**lo**na/teen eklee**see**-a"
vitamin	η βιταμίνη	"ee veeta-**mee**nee"
vodka	η βότκα	"ee **vot**ka"

ABSOLUTE ESSENTIALS

I don't understand	δεν καταλαβαίνω	"dhen kata-la**ve**no"
I don't speak Greek	δεν μιλάω ελληνικά	"dhen meela-o elee-nee**ka**"
do you speak English?	μιλάτε αγγλικά;	"meela-te anglee-**ka**"
more slowly please	πιο σιγά παρακαλώ	"pee**o** see**gha** para-ka**lo**"

volleyball	το βόλεϊ	"to **vole**-ee-ee"
voltage	η τάση	"ee **ta**see"
▷ **what's the voltage?**	πόσα βολτ είναι το ρεύμα;	"**po**sa volt **ee**-ne to **rev**ma"
waist	η μέση	"ee **me**see"
waistcoat	το γιλέκο	"to yee**le**ko"
to **wait (for)**	περιμένω	"peree-**me**no"
▷ **can you wait here for a few minutes?**	μπορείτε να περιμένετε εδώ για λίγα λεπτά;	"bo**ree**-te na peree-**me**-ne-te e**dho** ya **lee**gha lep**ta**"
waiter	το γκαρσόνι	"to gar-**so**nee"
waiting room	η αίθουσα αναμονής	"ee **etho**o-sa ana-mo**nees**"
waitress	η σερβιτόρα	"ee servee-**to**ra"
to **wake**	ξυπνάω	"kseep**na**-o"
▷ **please wake me up at ...**	παρακαλώ ξυπνήστε με στις ...	"para-ka**lo** kseep**nees**-te me stees"
▷ **wake up**	ξυπνάω	"kseep**na**-o"
Wales	η Ουαλία	"ee oo-a**lee**-a"
walk[1] *n*	ο περίπατος	"o pe**ree**-patos"
▷ **to go for a walk**	πάω για περίπατο	"**pa**-o ya pe**ree**-pato"
▷ **are there any interesting walks nearby?**	υπάρχει καλό μέρος για περίπατο εδώ κοντά;	"ee**par**-khee ka-**lo me**ros ya pe**ree**-pato e**dho** kon**da**"
to **walk**[2] *vb*	περπατώ	"per-pa**to**"
wallet	το πορτοφόλι	"to porto-**fo**lee"
walnut	το καρύδι	"to ka-**ree**dhee"
to **want**	θέλω	"**the**-lo"
warm	ζεστός	"ze**stos**"
warning triangle	το τρίγωνο αυτοκινήτου	"to **tree**-ghono afto-kee**nee**too"

ABSOLUTE ESSENTIALS		
I would like ...	θα ήθελα ...	"tha **ee**thela"
I need ...	χρειάζομαι ...	"khree-**a**zo-me"
where is ...?	πού είναι ...;	"poo **ee**-ne"
we're looking for ...	ψάχνουμε ...	"**psa**khnoo-me"

water

to **wash** (clothes)	πλένω	"**ple**no"
(oneself)	πλένομαι	"**ple**no-me"
▷ **where can I wash my clothes/my hands?**	πού μπορώ να πλύνω τα ρούχα μου/τα χέρια μου;	"poo bo-**ro** na **plee**no ta **roo**-kha moo/ta **khe**ree-a moo"

washable:

▷ **is it washable?**	πλένεται;	"**ple**-ne-te"

washbasin	ο νιπτήρας	"o neep-**tee**ras"
▷ **the washbasin is dirty**	ο νιπτήρας είναι λερωμένος	"o neep-**tee**ras **ee**-ne lero-**me**nos"

washing	το πλύσιμο	"to **plee**seemo"
▷ **where can I do some washing?**	πού μπορώ να πλύνω μερικά ρούχα;	"poo bo-**ro** na **plee**no meree-**ka roo**kha"

washing machine	το πλυντήριο	"to pleen**dee**ree-o"
washing powder	το απορρυπαντικό	"to a-poree-pandee**ko**"
washing-up liquid	το υγρό για τα πιάτα	"to ee**ghro** ya ta pee**a**ta"

wasp	η σφήκα	"ee **sfee**ka"

waste bin	ο σκουπιδοτενεκές	"o skoopee-dho-te-ne**kes**"

watch[1] *n*	το ρολόι	"to rolo-ee"
▷ **I think my watch is slow/fast**	νομίζω ότι το ρολόι μου πάει πίσω/μπροστά	"no**mee**-zo **o**tee to rolo-ee moo **pa**-ee **pee**so/bro-**sta**"
▷ **my watch has stopped**	το ρολόι μου σταμάτησε	"to rol**o**-ee moo sta**ma**tee-se"

to **watch**[2] *vb* (TV)	βλέπω	"**vle**-po"
(someone's luggage)	προσέχω	"pro-**se**kho"
▷ **could you watch my bag for a minute please?**	μπορείτε να προσέχετε την τσάντα μου για ένα λεπτό παρακαλώ;	"bo**ree**-te na prose-**khe**-te teen **tsan**da moo ya **e**na lep**to** para-ka**lo**"

water	το νερό	"to ne**ro**"

ABSOLUTE ESSENTIALS

do you have ...?	έχετε ...;	"**ekhe**-te"
is there ...?	υπάρχει ...;	"ee-**park**hee"
are there ...?	υπάρχουν ...;	"ee-**park**hoon"
how much is ...?	πόσο κάνει ...;	"**po**so **ka**nee"

▷ there is no hot water	δεν υπάρχει ζεστό νερό	"dhen ee**par**-khee ze**sto** nero"
▷ a glass of water	ένα ποτήρι νερό	"ena po**tee**-ree nero"
▷ a bottle of water	μία μπουκάλα νερό	"**mee**a booka-la nero"
waterfall	ο καταρράκτης	"o kata-**rak**tees"
water heater	ο θερμοσίφωνας	"o thermo-**see**fonas"
water melon	το καρπούζι	"to kar-**poo**zee"
waterproof	αδιάβροχος	"adhee-**a**vrokhos"
water-skiing	το σκι	"to skee"
▷ is it possible to go water-skiing?	μπορεί να πάει κανείς για σκι;	"bo**ree** na **pa**-ee ka**nees** ya skee"
wave (on sea)	το κύμα	"to **kee**ma"
wax	το κερί	"to ke**ree**"
way	ο δρόμος	"o **dhro**-mos"
(method)	ο τρόπος	"o **tro**pos"
▷ this way	από δω	"apo **dho**"
▷ that way	από κει	"apo **kee**"
▷ which is the way to ...?	πώς πάνε για ...;	"pos **pa**-ne ya"
▷ what's the best way to get to ...?	ποιος είναι ο καλύτερος τρόπος για να πάω ...;	"pee**os** ee-ne o kalee-teros **tro**pos ya na **pa**-o"
we	εμείς	"e**mees**"
weak	αδύνατος	"adhee-natos"
to wear	φοράω	"fora-o"
▷ what should I wear?	τι να φορέσω;	"tee na fo**re**so"
weather	ο καιρός	"o ke**ros**"
▷ what dreadful weather!	τι απαίσιος καιρός!	"tee a-**pe**see-os ke**ros**"
▷ is the weather going to change?	θα αλλάξει ο καιρός;	"tha a**lak**see o ke**ros**"
wedding	ο γάμος	"o **gha**mos"

ABSOLUTE ESSENTIALS

yes (please)	ναι (παρακαλώ)	"ne (para-kalo)"
no (thank you)	όχι (ευχαριστώ)	"okhee (efkharee**sto**)"
hello	γεια σας	"ya sas"
goodbye	αντίο	"andee-o"

Wednesday	Τετάρτη	"te-**tar**tee"
week	η βδομάδα	"ee vdho-**ma**dha"
▷ **this week**	αυτή τη βδομάδα	"a**ftee** tee vdho-**ma**dha"
▷ **for one/two weeks**	για μία/δύο βδομάδες	"ya **mee**a/**dhee**o vdho-**ma**dhes"
weekday	η καθημερινή	"ee kathee-meree**nee**"
weekend	το σαββατοκύριακο	"to savato-**kee**ree-ako"
weekly rate	η εβδομαδιαία τιμή	"ee ev-dhomadhee-**e**-a tee**mee**"
weight	το βάρος	"to **va**ros"
welcome	καλώς ήρθατε	"ka**los eer**tha-te"
well (*healthy*)	υγιής	"eeyee-**ees**"
▷ **he's not well**	δεν είναι καλά	"then **ee**-ne ka-**la**"
well done (*steak*)	καλοψημένος	"ka-lopsee-**me**nos"
Welsh *adj*	ουαλικός	"oo-alee**kos**"
▷ **I'm Welsh**	είμαι Ουαλός/Ουαλή	"**ee**-me oo-a**los**/oo-a**lee**"
west	η δύση	"ee **dhee**see"
wet (*damp*)	βρεγμένος	"vregh**me**nos"
(*weather*)	βροχερός	"vro-khe**ros**"
wetsuit	η στολή για καταδύσεις	"ee sto**lee** ya ka-ta**dhee**-sees"
what	τι	"tee"
▷ **what is it?**	τι είναι;	"tee **ee**-ne"
▷ **what book?**	ποιο βιβλίο;	"pee**o** vee**vlee**-o"
wheel	η ρόδα	"ee **ro**dha"
wheelchair	η αναπηρική καρέκλα	"ee ana-peeree**kee** ka-**re**kla"
when	πότε	"**po**-te"
where	πού	"**poo**"

ABSOLUTE ESSENTIALS

I don't understand	δεν καταλαβαίνω	"dhen kata-la**ve**no"
I don't speak Greek	δεν μιλάω ελληνικά	"dhen mee**la**-o elee-nee**ka**"
do you speak English?	μιλάτε αγγλικά;	"mee**la**-te anglee-**ka**"
more slowly please	πιο σιγά παρακαλώ	"pee**o** see**gha** para-ka**lo**"

▷ where are you from?	από πού είστε;	"apo poo ees-te"
which	ποιος	"peeos"
▷ which is it?	ποιο είναι;	"peeo ee-ne"
while¹ *n:*		
▷ in a while	σε λίγο	"se leegho"
while² *conj*	όσο	"oso"
▷ can you do it while I wait?	μπορείτε να το κάνετε όσο περιμένω;	"boree-te na to ka-ne-te oso pereeme-no"
whipped cream	η σαντιγύ	"ee santee-yee"
whisky	το ουίσκι	"to oo-eeskee"
▷ I'll have a whisky	θα πάρω ένα ουίσκι	"tha paro ena oo-eeskee"
white	άσπρος	"aspros"
who	ποιος	"peeos"
▷ who is it?	ποιος είναι;	"peeos ee-ne"
whole	όλος	"olos"
wholemeal bread	το μαύρο ψωμί	"to mavro psomee"
whose:		
▷ whose is it?	ποιου είναι;	"peeoo ee-ne"
why	γιατί	"yatee"
wide	πλατύς	"platees"
wife	η σύζυγος	"ee seezee-ghos"
window	το παράθυρο	"to para-theero"
▷ I'd like a window seat	θα ήθελα θέση σε παράθυρο	"tha eethela thesee se para-theero"
▷ I can't open the window	δεν μπορώ να ανοίξω το παράθυρο	"dhen bo-ro na aneekso to para-theero"
▷ I have broken the window	έσπασα το παράθυρο	"espasa to para-theero"

ABSOLUTE ESSENTIALS

i would like ...	θα ήθελα ...	"tha eethela"
i need ...	χρειάζομαι ...	"khree-azo-me"
where is ...?	πού είναι ...;	"poo ee-ne"
we're looking for ...	ψάχνουμε ...	"psakhnoo-me"

wine list

English	Greek	Pronunciation
▷ may I open the window?	μπορώ να ανοίξω το παράθυρο;	"bo-**ro** na a**nee**k-so to pa**ra**-theero"
windscreen	το παρμπρίζ	"to par-**breez**"
▷ could you clean the windscreen?	μπορείτε να καθαρίσετε το παρμπρίζ;	"bo**ree**-te na katha-**ree**se-te to par-**breez**"
▷ the windscreen has shattered	το παρμπρίζ έσπασε	"to par-**breez e**spa-se"
windscreen washers	οι υαλοκαθαριστήρες	"ee eealo-katharee-**stee**-res"
▷ top up the windscreen washers	γεμίστε το νερό των καθαριστήρων	"ye**mee**-ste to ne**ro** ton katha-ree**stee**ron"
windsurfing	το γουιντσέρφινγκ	"to windsurfing"
▷ can I go windsurfing?	μπορώ να πάω για γουιντσέρφινγκ;	"bo-**ro** na **pa**-o ya windsurfing"
windy:		
▷ it's (too) windy	φυσάει (πολύ)	"fee**sa**-ee (po**lee**)"
wine	το κρασί	"to kra**see**"
▷ this wine is not chilled	αυτό το κρασί δεν είναι κρύο	"af**to** to kra**see** dhen **ee**-ne **kree**-o"
▷ can you recommend a good red/white/rosé wine?	έχετε να μας συστήσετε ένα καλό κόκκινο/άσπρο/ροζέ κρασί;	"**ekhe**-te na mas see**stee**-se-te **e**na ka-**lo ko**kee-no/**a**spro/ro-**ze** kra**see**"
▷ a bottle/carafe of house wine	ένα μπουκάλι/μια καράφα κρασί χύμα	"**e**na boo**ka**lee/**mee**a kara-fa kra**see** khee**ma**"
▷ red/white/rosé wine	κόκκινο/άσπρο/ροζέ κρασί	"**ko**kee-no/**a**-spro/ro-**ze** kra**see**"
wine list	ο κατάλογος κρασιών	"o **ka**ta-loghos krasee-**on**"

ABSOLUTE ESSENTIALS

do you have ...?	έχετε ...;	"**ekhe**-te"
is there ...?	υπάρχει ...;	"ee-**par**khee"
are there ...?	υπάρχουν ...;	"ee-**par**khoon"
how much is ...?	πόσο κάνει ...;	"**po**so **ka**nee"

▷ **may we see the wine list, please?**	μπορούμε να δούμε τον κατάλογο με τα κρασιά, παρακαλώ;	"boroo-me na dhoo-me ton kata-logho me ta krasee-a para-kalo"
winter	ο χειμώνας	"o khee-monas"
with	με	"me"
without	χωρίς	"khorees"
woman	η γυναίκα	"ee yee-neka"
wood	το ξύλο	"to kseelo"
wool	το μαλλί	"to malee"
word	η λέξη	"ee leksee"
▷ **what is the word for ...?**	ποια είναι η λέξη για ...;	"peea ee-ne ee leksee ya"
to **work** (person) (machine)	δουλεύω λειτουργώ	"dhoo-levo" "leetoor-gho"
▷ **where do you work?**	πού δουλεύετε;	"poo dhoo-leve-te"
▷ **this does not work**	αυτό εδώ δεν λειτουργεί	"afto edho dhen leetoor-yee"
worried	ανήσυχος	"anee-seekhos"
worse	χειρότερος	"kheero-teros"
worth:		
▷ **2000 drachmas worth of petrol**	2000 δραχμές βενζίνη	"thee-o kheelee-adhes dhrakhmes venzeenee"
▷ **it's worth 2000 drachmas**	αξίζει 2000 δραχμές	"akseezee thee-o kheelee-adhes dhrakhmes"
to **wrap (up)**	τυλίγω	"tee-leegho"
▷ **could you wrap it up for me, please?**	μπορείτε να μου το τυλίξετε, παρακαλώ;	"boree-te na moo to tee-leekse-te para-kalo"
wrapping paper	το χαρτί περιτυλίγματος	"to khartee peree-teeleegh-matos"

to **write**	γράφω	"**ghra**fo"
▷ **could you write that down?**	μπορείτε να μου το γράψετε;	"**boree**-te na moo to **ghra**-pse-te"
writing paper	το χαρτί αλληλογραφίας	"to khartee aleelo-ghrafee-as"
wrong	λάθος	"**la**thos"
▷ **there is something wrong with the brakes**	κάτι δεν πάει καλά με τα φρένα	"**ka**tee dhen **pa**-ee ka**la** me ta **fre**na"
▷ **I think you've given me the wrong change**	νομίζω πως μου έχετε δώσει λάθος ρέστα	"no**mee**zo pos moo **e**khe-te **dho**see **la**thos **re**sta"
yacht	το γιωτ	"to yot"
year	ο χρόνος	"o **khro**nos"
▷ **this year**	φέτος	"**fe**tos"
▷ **last year**	πέρσι	"**per**-see"
▷ **next year**	του χρόνου	"too **khro**noo"
yellow	κίτρινος	"**kee**tree-nos"
yes	ναι	"ne"
▷ **yes, please**	ναι, παρακαλώ	"ne para-ka**lo**"
yesterday	χθες	"khthes"
yet	ακόμα	"a**ko**ma"
▷ **not yet**	όχι ακόμα	"**o**khee a**ko**ma"
yoghurt	το γιαούρτι	"to ya-**oor**tee"
you (*informal singular*)	εσύ	"e-**see**"
(*plural or formal singular*)	εσείς	"e-**sees**"
young	νέος	"**ne**-os"
your (*informal singular*)	σου	"soo"
(*plural or formal singular*)	σας	"sas"
yours (*informal singular*)	δικός σου	"dhee-**kos** soo"
(*plural or formal singular*)	δικός σας	"dhee-**kos** sas"

ABSOLUTE ESSENTIALS

I don't understand	δεν καταλαβαίνω	"dhen kata-**la**veno"
I don't speak Greek	δεν μιλάω ελληνικά	"dhen meela-o elee-nee**ka**"
do you speak English?	μιλάτε αγγλικά;	"meela-te anglee-**ka**"
more slowly please	πιο σιγά παρακαλώ	"peeo see**gha** para-ka**lo**"

youth hostel	ο ξενώνας νεότητας	"o ksenonas neotee-tas"
zebra crossing	η διάβαση πεζών	"ee dhee-a-vasee pezon"
zero	μηδέν	"mee-dhen"
zip	το φερμουάρ	"to fermoo-ar"
zoo	ο ζωολογικός κήπος	"o zo-olo-yeekos keepos"

In the pronunciation system used in this book, Greek sounds are represented by spellings of the nearest possible sounds in English. Hence, when you read out the pronunciation – shown in the third column, after the translation – sound the letters as if you were reading an English word. Whenever we think it is not sufficiently clear where to stress a word or phrase, we have used **bold** to highlight the syllable to be stressed. The following notes should help you:

	REMARKS	EXAMPLE	PRONUNCIATION
gh	Like a rough g	γάλα	**gh**ala
dh	Like th in this	δάκτυλο	**dhak**-teelo
th	Like th in thin	θέατρο	**the**-atro
ks	Like x in fox	ξένος	**ks**enos
r	Slightly trilled r	ρόδα	**r**odha
kh	Like ch in loch	χάνω	**kh**ano
	or like a rough h	χέρι	**kh**eree
ps	Like ps in lapse	ψάρι	**ps**aree

Greek spelling is very regular and if you can master the alphabet you may find yourself reading straight from the translations. The alphabet is as follows:

GREEK LETTER	CLOSEST ENGLISH SOUND	SHOWN BY	EXAMPLE	
Α, α	hand	a	άνθρωπος	**an**-thropos
Β, β	vine	v	βούτυρο	**voo**-teero
Γ, γ	see above	gh	γάλα	**gh**ala
	or yes	y	για	ya
Δ, δ	this	dh	δάκτυλο	**dhak**-teelo
Ε, ε	met	e	έτοιμος	**e**-teemos
Ζ, ζ	zone	z	ζώνη	**zo**nee
Η, η	meet	ee	ήλιος	**ee**-leeos
Θ, θ	thin	th	θέατρο	**the**-atro
Ι, ι	meet	ee	ίππος	**ee**pos
Κ, κ	key	k	και	ke

GREEK LETTER	CLOSEST ENGLISH SOUND	SHOWN BY	EXAMPLE	
Λ, λ	*log*	l	λάδι	*ladhee*
Μ, μ	*mat*	m	μάτι	*matee*
Ν, ν	*not*	n	νύχτα	*neekh-ta*
Ξ, ξ	*rocks*	ks	ξένος	*ksenos*
Ο, ο	*cot*	o	όχι	*okhee*
Π, π	*pat*	p	πόλη	*polee*
Ρ, ρ	*carrot*	r	ρόδα	*rodha*
Σ, σ (, ς)	*sat*	s	σήμα	*seema*
Τ, τ	*top*	t	τράπεζα	*tra-peza*
Υ, υ	*meet*	ee	ύπνος	*eepnos*
Φ, φ	*fat*	f	φούστα	*foosta*
Χ, χ	*see above*	kh	χάνω	*khano*
		kh	χέρι	*kheree*
Ψ, ψ	*lapse*	ps	ψάρι	*psaree*
Ω, ω	*cot*	o	ώρα	*ora*

There are a few combinations of letters which you might find tricky:

αι	*met*	e	γυναίκα	*yee-neka*
αυ	*café*	af	αυτό	*afto*
	or have	av	αύριο	*av-reeo*
γγ	*angle*	ng	Αγγλία	*anglee-a*
γκ	*get*	g	γκάζι	*gazee*
μπ	*bag*	b	μπλούζα	*blooza*
οι	*meet*	ee	πλοίο	*plee-o*
ου	*moon*	oo	ούζο	*oozo*

You will notice from the phrases that a Greek question mark is the same as an English semi-colon.

In the weight and length charts the middle figure can be either metric or imperial. Thus 3.3 feet = 1 metre, 1 foot = 0.3 metres, and so on.

feet		metres	inches		cm	lbs		kg
3.3	1	0.3	0.39	1	2.54	2.2	1	0.45
6.6	2	0.61	0.79	2	5.08	4.4	2	0.91
9.9	3	0.91	1.18	3	7.62	6.6	3	1.4
13.1	4	1.22	1.57	4	10.6	8.8	4	1.8
16.4	5	1.52	1.97	5	12.7	11.0	5	2.2
19.7	6	1.83	2.36	6	15.2	13.2	6	2.7
23.0	7	2.13	2.76	7	17.8	15.4	7	3.2
26.2	8	2.44	3.15	8	20.3	17.6	8	3.6
29.5	9	2.74	3.54	9	22.9	19.8	9	4.1
32.9	10	3.05	3.9	10	25.4	22.0	10	4.5
			4.3	11	27.9			
			4.7	12	30.1			

°C	0	5	10	15	17	20	22	24	26	28	30	35	37	38	40	50	100
°F	32	41	50	59	63	68	72	75	79	82	86	95	98.4	100	104	122	212

Km	10	20	30	40	50	60	70	80	90	100	110	120
Miles	6.2	12.4	18.6	24.9	31.0	37.3	43.5	49.7	56.0	62.0	68.3	74.6

Tyre pressures

lb/sq in	15	18	20	22	24	26	28	30	33	35
kg/sq cm	1.1	1.3	1.4	1.5	1.7	1.8	2.0	2.1	2.3	2.5

Liquids

gallons	1.1	2.2	3.3	4.4	5.5	pints	0.44	0.88	1.76
litres	5	10	15	20	25	litres	0.25	0.5	1

CAR PARTS

air conditioning	ο κλιματισμός	"o kleema-tees**mos**"
antifreeze	το αντιπηκτικό υγρό	"to andee-peektee**ko** ee**ghro**"
automatic	αυτόματος	"**afto**-matos"
battery	η μπαταρία	"bata**ree**-a"
boot	το πορτ–μπαγκάζ	"to port-ba**gaz**"
brake fluid	το υγρό των φρένων	"to ee**ghro** ton **fre**non"
brakes	τα φρένα	"ta **fre**na"
car	το αυτοκίνητο	"to afto-**kee**neeto"
carburettor	το καρμπυρατέρ	"to karbeera-**ter**"
car number	ο αριθμός αυτοκινήτου	"o a-reeth**mos** afto-kee**nee**too"
car wash	το πλυντήριο αυτοκινήτων	"to pleen**tee**reeo afto-kee**nee**ton"
chain	η αλυσίδα	"ee alee-**see**dha"
engine	η μηχανή	"ee mee-kha**nee**"
exhaust pipe	η εξάτμιση	"ee **eksat**-meesee"
fan belt	το λουρί του ανεμιστήρα	"to loo**ree** too anemees-**tee**ra"
fuel pump	η αντλία καυσίμων	"ee and**lee**-a kaf-**see**mon"
garage	το συνεργείο	"to seener-**yeeo**"
gears	οι ταχύτητες	"ee ta**khee**-teetes"
headlights	οι προβολείς	"ee provo**lees**"
indicator	το φλας	"to flas"
jack	ο γρύλος	"o **ghree**los"
jump leads	τα καλώδια μπαταρίας	"ta ka**lo**dhee-a bata**ree**-as"
leak	η διαρροή	"ee dhee-aro-**ee**"
oil filter	το φίλτρο του λαδιού	"to **feel**tro too ladhee-**oo**"
petrol	η βενζίνη	"ee ven-**zee**nee"
points	οι πλατίνες	"ee pla-**tee**nes"
radiator	το ψυγείο	"to psee**yee**-o"
roof rack	η σχάρα	"ee **skha**ra"
shock absorber	το αμορτισέρ	"to amor-tee**ser**"
spare wheel	η ρεζέρβα	"ee re**zer**va"
spark plug	το μπουζί	"to boo**zee**"
suspension	η ανάρτηση	"ee a**nar**-teesee"
tyre	το λάστιχο	"to **la**stee-kho"
tyre pressure	η πίεση στα λάστιχα	"ee **pee**-esee sta **la**stee-kha"
warning triangle	το τρίγωνο αυτοκινήτου	"to **tree**-ghono afto-kee**nee**too"
windscreen	το παρμπρίζ	"to par-**breez**"
windscreen washers	οι υαλοκαθαριστήρες	"ee eealo-katharee-**stee**-res"

COLOURS

black	μαύρος	**"mavros"**
blue	μπλε	**"ble"**
brown	καφέ	**"kafe"**
colour	το χρώμα	**"to khroma"**
dark	σκούρο	**"skooro"**
green	πράσινος	**"prasee-nos"**
grey	γκρίζος	**"greezos"**
light	ανοιχτό	**"aneekh-to"**
navy blue	μπλε	**"ble"**
orange	πορτοκαλί	**"porto-kalee"**
pink	ροζ	**"roz"**
purple	βιολετί	**"vee-oletee"**
red	κόκκινος	**"kokee-nos"**
white	άσπρος	**"aspros"**
yellow	κίτρινος	**"keetree-nos"**

COUNTRIES

America	η Αμερική	"ee ameree-**kee**"
Australia	η Αυστραλία	"ee af-stra**lee**-a"
Austria	η Αυστρία	"ee af**stree**a"
Belgium	το Βέλγιο	"to **vel**gheeo"
Britain	η Βρετανία	"ee vreta**nee**-a"
Canada	ο Καναδάς	"o kana-**dhas**"
England	η Αγγλία	"ee ang**lee**-a"
Europe	η Ευρώπη	"ee ev**ro**pee"
France	η Γαλλία	"ee gha**lee**-a"
Germany	η Γερμανία	"ee yerma**nee**-a"
Greece	η Ελλάδα	"ee e**ladha**"
Ireland	η Ιρλανδία	"ee eerland**hee**-a"
Italy	η Ιταλία	"ee eeta**lee**-a"
New Zealand	η Νέα Ζηλανδία	"ee **ne**-a zeeland**hee**-a"
Northern Ireland	η Βόρεια Ιρλανδία	"ee **voree**-a eerland**hee**-a"
Portugal	η Πορτογαλία	"ee porto-gha**lee**-a"
Scotland	η Σκωτία	"ee sko**tee**-a"
Spain	η Ισπανία	"ee eespa**nee**-a"
Switzerland	η Ελβετία	"ee elve**tee**-a"
United States	οι Ηνωμένες Πολιτείες	"ee eeno-**me**-nes polee**tee**-es"
USA	οι ΗΠΑ	"ee **ee**pa"
Wales	η Ουαλία	"ee oo-a**lee**-a"

DRINKS

alcohol	το οινόπνευμα	"to **eeno**-pnevma"
alcoholic	οινοπνευματώδης	"eenop-nevma-**to**dhees"
apéritif	το απεριτίφ	"aperee-**teef**"
beer	η μπύρα	"ee **bee**ra"
brandy	το κονιάκ	"to konee-**ak**"
champagne	η σαμπάνια	"ee sambanee-a"
cider	ο μηλίτης	"o mee**lee**tees"
cocktail	το κοκτέιλ	"to kokte-**eel**"
cocoa	το κακάο	"to **kaka**-o"
coffee	ο καφές	"o ka-**fes**"
coke®	η Κόκα Κόλα	"ee **koka kola**"
draught beer	βαρελίσια μπύρα	"vare-**lee**seea **bee**ra"
drinking chocolate	η σοκολάτα ρόφημα	"ee soko-**la**ta rofeema"
drinking water	το πόσιμο νερό	"to **poseemo** nero"
fruit juice	ο φρουτοχυμός	"o frooto-kheemos"
gin	το τζιν	"to jin"
gin and tonic	τζιν με τόνικ	"jin me tonic"
juice	ο χυμός	"o khee**mos**"
lager	η μπύρα	"ee **bee**ra"
lemonade	η λεμονάδα	"ee lemo-**na**dha"
lemon tea	το τσάι με λεμόνι	"to **tsa**-ee me le-**mo**nee"
liqueur	το λικέρ	"to lee**ker**"
milk	το γάλα	"to **gha**la"
milkshake	το μιλκσέικ	"to meelk-**se**-eek"
mineral water	το επιτραπέζιο νερό	"to epee-trapezee-o nero"
non-alcoholic	μη οινοπνευματώδης	"mee eenop-nevma-**to**dhees"
orange juice	ο χυμός πορτοκαλιού	"o khee**mos** porto-kalee-**oo**"
rosé (wine)	ροζέ	"ro-**se**"
sherry	το σέρρυ	"to sherry"
skimmed milk	το αποβουτυρωμένο γάλα	"to apo-vootee-rom**e**no **gha**la"
soda	η σόδα	"ee **so**dha"
soft drink	το αναψυκτικό	"to anapseek-tee**ko**"
spirits	τα οινοπνευματώδη	"ta eenop-nevma-**to**dhee"
squash	η πορτοκαλάδα	"ee porto-ka**la**dha"
tea	το τσάι	"to **tsa**-ee"
tomato juice	ο τοματοχυμός	"o tomato-khee**mos**"
tonic water	το τόνικ	"to **to**neek"
vermouth	το βερμούτ	"to ver**moot**"
vodka	η βότκα	"ee **vot**ka"
whisky	το ουίσκι	"to oo-**ee**skee"
wine	το κρασί	"to kra**see**"

FISH AND SEAFOOD

caviar	το χαβιάρι	"to khavee-**aree**"
crab	το καβούρι	"to ka-**voo**ree"
fish	το ψάρι	"to **psa**ree"
herring	η ρέγγα	"ee **ren**-ga"
lobster	ο αστακός	"o asta-**kos**"
mussel	το μύδι	"to **mee**dhee"
oyster	το στρείδι	"to **stree**dhee"
prawn	η γαρίδα	"ee gha-**ree**dha"
salmon	ο σολομός	"o solo-**mos**"
sardine	η σαρδέλα	"ee sar**dhe**la"
scallop	το χτένι	"to **khte**nee"
seafood	τα θαλασσινά	"ta thala-**see**na"
shellfish	τα θαλασσινά	"ta thala-**see**na"
shrimp	η γαρίδα	"ee gha-**ree**dha"
tuna	ο τόννος	"o **to**nos"

FRUIT AND NUTS

almond	το αμύγδαλο	"to **ameegh**-dhalo"
apple	το μήλο	"to **meelo**"
apricot	το βερύκοκκο	"to **veree**-koko"
banana	η μπανάνα	"ee ba**nana**"
blackcurrant	το μαύρο φραγκοστάφυλο	"to **ma**-vro frango-**stafeelo**"
cherry	το κεράσι	"to ke**rasee**"
chestnut	το κάστανο	"to **kastano**"
coconut	η καρύδα	"ee ka**reedha**"
currant	η σταφίδα	"ee sta-**feedha**"
date	ο χουρμάς	"o khoor-**mas**"
fruit	τα φρούτα	"ta **froota**"
grape	το σταφύλι	"to sta**feelee**"
grapefruit	το γκρέιπ–φρουτ	"to grapefruit"
hazelnut	το φουντούκι	"to foon-**dookee**"
lemon	το λεμόνι	"to le**monee**"
melon	το πεπόνι	"to pe-**ponee**"
olive	η ελιά	"ee elee-**a**"
orange	το πορτοκάλι	"to porto-**kalee**"
peach	το ροδάκινο	"to ro**dha**-keeno"
peanut	το φυστίκι	"to fee-**steekee**"
pear	το αχλάδι	"to akh-**ladhee**"
pineapple	ο ανανάς	"o ana**nas**"
pistachio	το φυστίκι Αιγίνης	"to fee-**steekee** e-**yee**nees"
plum	το δαμάσκηνο	"to dhama-skeeno"
prune	το δαμάσκηνο	"to dhama-skeeno"
raisin	η σταφίδα	"ee sta-**feedha**"
raspberry	το βατόμουρο	"to **vato**-mooro"
strawberry	η φράουλα	"ee **fra**-oola"
walnut	το καρύδι	"to ka-**reedhee**"
watermelon	το καρπούζι	"to kar-**poozee**"

MEATS

bacon	το μπαίηκον	"to **be**-eekon"
beef	το βοδινό	"to vodhee-**no**"
breast	το στήθος	"to **stee**thos"
chicken	το κοτόπουλο	"to koto-**poolo**"
chop	η μπριζόλα	"ee bree**zo**la"
duck	η πάπια	"ee **papee**-a"
goose	η χήνα	"ee **khee**-na"
ham	το ζαμπόν	"to zam**bon**"
kidneys	τα νεφρά	"ta ne**fra**"
liver	το συκώτι	"to see-**ko**tee"
meat	το κρέας	"to **kre**as"
mince	ο κιμάς	"o kee**mas**"
mutton	το αρνί	"to ar**nee**"
pâté	το πατέ	"to pa-**te**"
pork	το χοιρινό	"to kheeree-**no**"
rabbit	το κουνέλι	"to koo-**ne**lee"
sausage	το λουκάνικο	"to **loo**ka-neeko"
steak	η μπριζόλα	"ee bree**zo**la"
stew	το κρέας με χορταρικά στην κατσαρόλα	"to **kre**-as me khorta-ree**ka** steen katsa-**ro**la"
turkey	η γαλοπούλα	"ee ghalo-**poo**la"
veal	το μοσχάρι	"to mos-**kha**ree"

SHOPS

baker's	ο φούρνος	"o **foor**nos"
barber	ο κουρέας	"o koo**re**-as"
bookshop	το βιβλιοπωλείο	"to veevlee-opo**lee**-o"
butcher's	το κρεοπωλείο	"to kreo-po**lee**-o"
café	το καφενείο	"to ka-fe**nee**-o"
chemist's	το φαρμακείο	"to farma**kee**-o"
dry-cleaner's	το καθαριστήριο	"to katharee-**steer**ee-o"
duty-free shop	το κατάστημα αφορολόγητων	"to ka**ta**-steema afo-**rolo**-yeeton"
grocer's	το μπακάλικο	"to **baka**-leeko"
hairdresser	ο κομμωτής	"o komo-**tees**"
	η κομμώτρια	"ee ko**mo**tree-a"
ironmonger's	το σιδηροπωλείο	"to seedheero-po**lee**-o"
jeweller's	το κοσμηματοπωλείο	"to kosmee-mato-po**lee**-o"
launderette	το δημόσιο πλυντήριο	"to dhee**mo**see-o pleen-**deer**ee-o"
market	η αγορά	"ee agho-**ra**"
newsagent	το πρακτορείο εφημερίδων	"to prakto-**ree**o efee-me**reed**hon"
post office	το ταχυδρομείο	"to takhee-dhro**mee**-o"
shop	το μαγαζί	"to magha-**zee**"
stationer's	το χαρτοπωλείο	"to kharto-po**lee**-o"
supermarket	το σούπερ–μάρκετ	"to supermarket"
tobacconist's	το καπνοπωλείο	"to kapno-po**lee**-o"

VEGETABLES

artichoke	η αγκινάρα	"ee angee**nar**a"
asparagus	το σπαρράγγι	"to spa-**ran**gee"
aubergine	η μελιτζάνα	"ee meleed-**zan**a"
avocado	το αβοκάντο	"to avo-**kan**do"
bean	το φασόλι	"to fa**so**lee"
beetroot	το παντζάρι	"to pand-**zar**ee"
broccoli	το μπρόκολο	"to **bro**kolo"
cabbage	το λάχανο	"to **lak**hano"
carrot	το καρότο	"to ka**ro**to"
cauliflower	το κουνουπίδι	"to koonoo-**peed**hee"
celery	το σέλινο	"to **se**leeno"
courgette	το κολοκυθάκι	"to kolokee-**thak**ee"
cucumber	το αγγούρι	"to a**goo**ree"
French beans	τα φασολάκια	"ta faso-**lak**ee-a"
garlic	το σκόρδο	"to **skor**dho"
onion	το κρεμμύδι	"to kre-**meed**hee"
parsley	ο μαϊντανός	"o ma-eendan**os**"
peas	τα μπιζέλια	"ta beez**el**ee-a"
potato	η πατάτα	"ee pa**ta**ta"
radish	το ραπανάκι	"to rapa-**nak**ee"
spinach	το σπανάκι	"to spa-**nak**ee"
tomato	η ντομάτα	"ee do**ma**-ta"
turnip	το γογγύλι	"to gho-**geel**ee"
vegetables	τα λαχανικά	"ta lakha-**nee**ka"
vegetarian	ο χορτοφάγος	"o khorto-**fa**ghos"

GREEK–ENGLISH

Α, α

αβάσιμος/η/ο groundless
άβαφος/η/ο unpainted
αβέβαιος/η/ο uncertain
αβεβαίωτος/η/ο unconfirmed
αβλαβής/ής/ές harmless
αβοήθητος/η/ο unassisted
αγαθά (τα) riches
άγαλμα (το) statue
αγάπη (η) love
αγαπώ to love
αγγείο (το) vessel, urn
αγγειοπλαστική (η) pottery
αγγελία (η) announcement
άγγελος (ο) angel
αγγίζω to touch
Αγγλία (η) England
αγγλικός/ή/ό English (*thing*)
Άγγλος/ίδα (ο/η) Englishman/-woman
αγγούρι (το) cucumber
αγγουροντομάτα (η) cucumber and
  tomato salad
αγελάδα (η) cow
αγένεια (η) discourtesy
αγέννητος/η/ο unborn
αγέραστος/η/ο youthful
αγιάτρευτος/η/ο incurable
άγιος/α/ο holy; saint
Άγιον Όρος (το) the Holy Mountain
αγκάλιασμα (το) hug
αγκινάρα (η) artichoke

αγκίστρι (το) fishing hook
άγκυρα (η) anchor
αγκώνας (ο) elbow
αγνότητα (η) purity
άγνοια (η) ignorance
αγνώριστος/η/ο unrecognisable
άγνωστος/η/ο unknown
αγορά (η) agora, market
αγοράζω to buy
αγορανομικός έλεγχος price control
αγοραστής (ο) buyer
αγόρι young boy
αγράμματος/η/ο illiterate
άγριος/α/ο wild
αγρόκτημα (το) farm
αγρός (ο) field
αγρότης (ο) peasant
αγώνας (ο) struggle
αγωνία (η) anguish
άδεια (η) permit, licence || **άδεια
οδηγήσεως** driving licence || **άδεια
φωτογραφήσεως** permit to take
photographs
αδειάζω to empty
άδειος/α/ο empty
αδελφή (η) sister
αδελφός (ο) brother
αδέξιος/α/ο clumsy
αδέσμευτος/η/ο uncommitted, non-
aligned
΄Αδης (ο) Hades
αδιάβατος/η/ο impassable
αδιάβροχο (το) raincoat
αδιαθεσία (η) indisposition
αδιάκοπος/η/ο constant
αδιακρισία (η) indiscretion
αδιαντροπιά (η) impudence
αδιαφανής/ής/ές opaque
αδιαφορία (η) indifference
αδιέξοδος (ο) cul-de-sac; no through
road

A	α	"a"
B	β	"v"
Γ	γ	"gh" *or* "y"
Δ	δ	"dh"
E	ε	"e"
Z	ζ	"z"
H	η	"ee"
Θ	θ	"th"
I	ι	"ee"
K	κ	"k"
Λ	λ	"l"
M	μ	"m"
N	ν	"n"
Ξ	ξ	"ks"
O	o	"o"
Π	π	"p"
P	ρ	"r"
Σ	σ, ς	"s"
T	τ	"t"
Y	υ	"ee"
Φ	φ	"f"
X	χ	"kh"
Ψ	ψ	"ps"
Ω	ω	"o"

άδικα unfairly
αδίκημα (το) offence
αδικία (η) injustice
αδίστακτα without hesitation
αδυναμία (η) weakness
αδυνατίζω to slim
αέρας (ο) wind
αερογραμμές (οι) airways || **Βρετανικές Αερογραμμές** British Airways || **Ολυμπιακές Αερογραμμές** Olympic Airways
αεροδρόμιο (το), αερολιμένας, αερολιμήν (ο) airport
αεροπλάνο (το), aeroplane
αεροπορία (η) air force
αεροπορικό εισιτήριο (το) air ticket
αεροπορική αλληλογραφία (η) air mail
αεροπορικώς by air
αεροσκάφος (το) aircraft
αετός (ο) eagle
αζήτητος/η/ο unclaimed
αηδία (η) disgust
αηδόνι (το) nightingale
αθεράπευτος/η/ο incurable
Αθήνα (η) Athens
αθλητής/αθλήτρια athete
αθλητικό κέντρο sports centre
αθλητισμός (ο) sports
άθλιος/α/ο miserable
αθόρυβα quietly
αθώος/α/ο innocent
´Αθως Athos, the Holy Mountain
Αιγαίο (το) the Aegean Sea
Αίγινα (η) Aegina
αίθουσα (η) room || **αίθουσα αναμονής** waiting room || **αίθουσα αναχωρήσεων** departure lounge
αίμα (το) blood
αίνιγμα (το) riddle
αίσθημα (το) feeling
αισιοδοξία (η) optimism

Α	α	"a"
Β	β	"v"
Γ	γ	"gh" _or_ "y"
Δ	δ	"dh"
Ε	ε	"e"
Ζ	ζ	"z"
Η	η	"ee"
Θ	θ	"th"
Ι	ι	"ee"
Κ	κ	"k"
Λ	λ	"l"
Μ	μ	"m"
Ν	ν	"n"
Ξ	ξ	"ks"
Ο	ο	"o"
Π	π	"p"
Ρ	ρ	"r"
Σ	σ, ς	"s"
Τ	τ	"t"
Υ	υ	"ee"
Φ	φ	"f"
Χ	χ	"kh"
Ψ	ψ	"ps"
Ω	ω	"o"

αίτημα (το) demand
αίτηση (η) application
αιτία (η) reason, cause
αίτιος/α/ο responsible for
αιχμάλωτος (ο) captive
αιώνας (ο) century
ακαδημαϊκός (ο) academic
ακάθαρτος/η/ο dirty
ακαθόριστος/η/ο undefined
ακάλεστος/η/ο uninvited
ακαλλιέργητος/η/ο uncultivated
ακατάδεκτος/η/ο snobbish
ακουστικά (τα) earphones || **ακουστικά βαρυκοΐας** hearing aids
ακουστικό (το) receiver (*telephone*)
ακούω to hear
άκρη (η) edge
Ακρόπολη/ις (η) the Acropolis
ακτή (η) beach, shore
ακτινογραφία (η) X-ray
ακτινολόγος (ο/η) X-ray specialist
ακυρώνω to cancel
αλάτι (το) salt
αλέθω to grind
αλεύρι (το) flour
αλήθεια (η) truth
αλιεία (η) fishing || **είδη αλιείας** fishing tackle
αλκοολικός/ή/ό alcoholic
αλλά but
αλλαγή (η) change || **δεν γίνονται αλλαγές** goods cannot be exchanged || **δεν αλλάζονται** goods will not be exchanged
αλληλογραφία (η) correspondence
αλληλογραφώ to correspond
αλλοδαπός/ή foreign national || **αστυνομία αλλοδαπών** aliens' police
άλλος/η/ο other; next
άλλοτε formerly
αλλού elsewhere

Α	α	"a"
Β	β	"v"
Γ	γ	"gh" *or* "y"
Δ	δ	"dh"
Ε	ε	"e"
Ζ	ζ	"z"
Η	η	"ee"
Θ	θ	"th"
Ι	ι	"ee"
Κ	κ	"k"
Λ	λ	"l"
Μ	μ	"m"
Ν	ν	"n"
Ξ	ξ	"ks"
Ο	ο	"o"
Π	π	"p"
Ρ	ρ	"r"
Σ	σ, ς	"s"
Τ	τ	"t"
Υ	υ	"ee"
Φ	φ	"f"
Χ	χ	"kh"
Ψ	ψ	"ps"
Ω	ω	"o"

αλμυρός/ή/ό salty
άλογο (το) horse
αλτ! stop!
αλυσίδα (η) chain
αμάξωμα (το) body (*of car*)
αμαρτία (η) sin
αμαρτωλός/ή/ό sinful; sinner
άμβλωση (η) abortion
άμβωνας (ο) pulpit
αμελής/ής/ές negligent
αμερικάνικος/η/ο American (*thing*)
Αμερικανός/ίδα American (*man/woman*)
Αμερική (η) America
αμέσως at once
αμήν amen
αμηχανία (η) embarrassment
αμίαντος (ο) asbestos
αμίλητος/η/ο silent
άμιλλα (η) competition
άμμος (η) sand
αμμουδιά (η) sandy beach
αμοιβή (η) reward
αμόρφωτος/η/ο uneducated
αμπέλι (το) vineyard; vine
αμυγδαλιά (η) almond tree
αμύγδαλο (το) almond
άμυνα (η) defence
αμφιβάλλω to doubt
αμφιθέατρο (το) amphitheatre
αμφορέας (ο) jar
αν if
αναβάλλω to postpone
αναβολή (η) delay
ανάβω to switch on
αναγγελία (η) announcement
αναγέννηση (η) renaissance
αναγκάζω to compel
ανάγλυφο (το) relief sculpture
αναγνωρίζω to recognise
ανάγνωση (η) reading
αναζήτηση (η) search

A	α	"a"
B	β	"v"
Γ	γ	"gh" *or* "y"
Δ	δ	"dh"
E	ε	"e"
Z	ζ	"z"
H	η	"ee"
Θ	θ	"th"
I	ι	"ee"
K	κ	"k"
Λ	λ	"l"
M	μ	"m"
N	ν	"n"
Ξ	ξ	"ks"
O	ο	"o"
Π	π	"p"
P	ρ	"r"
Σ	σ, ς	"s"
T	τ	"t"
Y	υ	"ee"
Φ	φ	"f"
X	χ	"kh"
Ψ	ψ	"ps"
Ω	ω	"o"

αναθεώρηση (η) revision
αναίδεια (η) impudence
αναιμία (η) anaemia
ανακαλύπτω to discover
ανακαλώ to revoke
ανακήρυξη (η) declaration
ανακοινώνω to announce
ανάκριση (η) interrogation
ανάκτορα (τα) palace
ανακωχή (η) truce
αναλαμβάνω to undertake
ανάλυση (η) analysis
αναμένω to wait
ανάμεσα between, among
ανάμνηση (η) memory, recollection
αναμονή (η) waiting || **αίθουσα**
 αναμονής waiting room
ανανάς (o) pineapple
ανανεώνω to renew
ανάξιος/α/ο unworthy
αναπαύομαι to rest
ανάπηρος/η/ο handicapped, disabled
αναπληρώνω to replace
αναπνέω to breathe
αναπνοή (η) breath
αναποφάσιστος/η/ο irresolute
αναπόφευκτος/η/ο inevitable,
 unavoidable
αναπτήρας (o) cigarette lighter
αναπτυγμένος/η/ο developed
ανάρρωση (η) convalescence
αναρωτιέμαι to wonder
ανάσα (η) breath
ανασκαφή (η) excavation
αναστεναγμός (o) sigh
ανάστημα (το) stature, height
ανατινάζω to blow up
ανατολή (η) east
ανατολικός/ή/ό eastern
ανατομία (η) anatomy
ανατρέπω to overthrow

Α	α	"a"
Β	β	"v"
Γ	γ	"gh" or "y"
Δ	δ	"dh"
Ε	ε	"e"
Ζ	ζ	"z"
Η	η	"ee"
Θ	θ	"th"
Ι	ι	"ee"
Κ	κ	"k"
Λ	λ	"l"
Μ	μ	"m"
Ν	ν	"n"
Ξ	ξ	"ks"
Ο	ο	"o"
Π	π	"p"
Ρ	ρ	"r"
Σ	σ, ς	"s"
Τ	τ	"t"
Υ	υ	"ee"
Φ	φ	"f"
Χ	χ	"kh"
Ψ	ψ	"ps"
Ω	ω	"o"

ανατροφή (η) upbringing
αναφέρω to mention
αναχώρηση (η) departure
‖ αναχωρήσεις departures ‖ αίθουσα
αναχωρήσεων departure lounge
αναψυκτήριο (το) refreshments
αναψυκτικό (το) soft drink
αναψυχή (η) recreation
άνδρας (ο) man
ανδρική μόδα men's fashions
ανδρών Men (toilets)
ανεβαίνω to go up
ανελκυστήρας (ο) lift, elevator
ανεμιστήρας (ο) fan
άνεμος (ο) wind
ανεξαρτησία (η) independence
ανεξήγητος/η/ο inexplicable
ανεπίσημα unofficially
ανεργία (η) unemployment
άνετος/η/ο comfortable
ανήκω to belong
ανήλικος/η/ο under age
ανηψιά (η) niece
ανηψιός (ο) nephew
άνθη (τα) flowers
ανθοπωλείο (το) florist's
άνθρωπος (ο) man, human being,
person
αν και although
ανοίγω to open
ανοικτός/ή/ό open
άνοιξη (η) spring (season)
ανομβρία (η) drought
ανοξείδωτος/η/ο stainless
ανταλλαγή (η) exchange
ανταλλακτικά (τα) spare parts
‖ γνήσια ανταλλακτικά genuine spare
parts
αντί instead of
αντιβιωτικά (τα) antibiotics
αντίγραφο (το) copy, reproduction

Α	α	"a"
Β	β	"v"
Γ	γ	"gh" or "y"
Δ	δ	"dh"
Ε	ε	"e"
Ζ	ζ	"z"
Η	η	"ee"
Θ	θ	"th"
Ι	ι	"ee"
Κ	κ	"k"
Λ	λ	"l"
Μ	μ	"m"
Ν	ν	"n"
Ξ	ξ	"ks"
Ο	ο	"o"
Π	π	"p"
Ρ	ρ	"r"
Σ	σ, ς	"s"
Τ	τ	"t"
Υ	υ	"ee"
Φ	φ	"f"
Χ	χ	"kh"
Ψ	ψ	"ps"
Ω	ω	"o"

αντίκες (οι) antiques
αντικλεπτικά (τα) antitheft devices
αντίκρυ opposite
αντικρύζω to face
αντίο goodbye
αντιπάθεια (η) dislike
αντίπαλος (ο) adversary
αντιπηκτικό (το) antifreeze
αντίποινα (τα) reprisals
αντιπρόσωπος (ο) representative
αντλία (η) pump || **αντλία βενζίνης** petrol pump
αντρόγυνο (το) couple
ανυπομονησία (η) impatience
ανύποπτος/η/ο unsuspecting
ανώμαλος/η/ο uneven || **ανωμαλία οδοστρώματος** bad or uneven road surface
ανώνυμα anonymously
αξεσουάρ (τα) accessories || **αξεσουάρ αυτοκινήτων** car accessories
αξία (η) value || **αξία διαδρομής** fare
αξιοθέατα (τα) the sights
αξιοπρέπεια (η) dignity
άξονας (ο) axle
απαγορεύω to forbid || **απαγορεύεται η αναμονή** No waiting || **απαγορεύεται η διάβαση** Keep off || **απαγορεύεται η είσοδος** No entry || **απαγορεύεται το κάπνισμα** No smoking || **απαγορεύεται το προσπέρασμα** No overtaking || **απαγορεύεται η στάθμευση** No parking || **απαγορεύεται η τοιχοκόλληση** No posters, Post no bills || **απαγορεύεται η τοποθέτηση σκουπιδιών** No dumping (*of rubbish*) || **απαγορεύονται τα σκυλιά** No dogs || **απαγορευτική ένδειξη** No smoking; No parking
απαίτηση (η) claim
απαλλαγή ευθύνης collision damage

Α	α	"a"
Β	β	"v"
Γ	γ	"gh" *or* "y"
Δ	δ	"dh"
Ε	ε	"e"
Ζ	ζ	"z"
Η	η	"ee"
Θ	θ	"th"
Ι	ι	"ee"
Κ	κ	"k"
Λ	λ	"l"
Μ	μ	"m"
Ν	ν	"n"
Ξ	ξ	"ks"
Ο	ο	"o"
Π	π	"p"
Ρ	ρ	"r"
Σ	σ, ς	"s"
Τ	τ	"t"
Υ	υ	"ee"
Φ	φ	"f"
Χ	χ	"kh"
Ψ	ψ	"ps"
Ω	ω	"o"

waiver (*insurance*)

απάντηση (η) reply

απαντώ to reply

απέναντι opposite

απεργία (η) strike

από from

απογείωση (η) takeoff

απόγευμα (το) afternoon

απόδειξη (η) receipt

αποθήκη (η) warehouse

αποκλειστικός/ή/ό exclusive
|| **αποκλειστικός αντιπρόσωπος** sole representative

απόκριες (οι) carnival

απομνημονεύματα (τα) memoirs

απομονώνω to isolate

αποσκευές (οι) luggage

απόστημα (το) abscess

αποτέλεσμα (το) result

απόφαση (η) decision

απόχη (η) fishing/butterfly net

απόψε tonight

Απρίλιος (ο) April

Αργολίδα (η) Argolis

αργότερα later

Άρειος Πάγος Supreme Court

αρέσω to please || **μου αρέσει** I like

αριθμός (ο) number || **αριθμός διαβατηρίου** passport number || **αριθμός πτήσεως** flight number

αριστερά left (*side*)

άρνηση (η) refusal

αρνί (το) lamb

αρραβώνες (οι) engagement (*to be married*)

αρρώστια (η) illness

άρρωστος/η/ο ill || **άρρωστος/η** patient

αρτοποιία (η) bakery

αρχαιολογικός χώρος archaeological site

αρχαιολόγος (ο/η) archaeologist

A	α	"a"
B	β	"v"
Γ	γ	"gh" *or* "y"
Δ	δ	"dh"
E	ε	"e"
Z	ζ	"z"
H	η	"ee"
Θ	θ	"th"
I	ι	"ee"
K	κ	"k"
Λ	λ	"l"
M	μ	"m"
N	ν	"n"
Ξ	ξ	"ks"
O	ο	"o"
Π	π	"p"
P	ρ	"r"
Σ	σ, ς	"s"
T	τ	"t"
Y	υ	"ee"
Φ	φ	"f"
X	χ	"kh"
Ψ	ψ	"ps"
Ω	ω	"o"

αρχαίος/α/ο ancient
αρχή (η) beginning; authority
αρχιεπισκοπή (η) archbishopric
αρχιεπίσκοπος (ο) archbishop
αρχίζω to begin
άρωμα (το) perfume
ασανσέρ (το) lift, elevator
ασήμι (το) silver
ασημικά (τα) silverware
ασθενής (ο/η) patient
άσθμα (το) asthma
άσκοπος/η/ο improper; lacking in
purpose || **άσκοπη χρήση** improper use
ασπίδα (η) shield
ασπιρίνη (η) aspirin
άσπρος/η/ο white
αστακός (ο) lobster
αστικός νομισματοδέκτης coin-
operated telephone for local calls
άστρο (το) star
αστυνομία (η) police || **αστυνομία**
αλλοδαπών aliens' police
αστυνομική διάταξη police notice
αστυνομικός σταθμός police station
αστυφύλακας (ο) town policeman
ασφάλεια (η) insurance; fuse
|| **ασφάλεια έναντι κλοπής** insurance
against theft || **ασφάλεια έναντι**
πυρκαϊάς insurance against fire
|| **ασφάλεια έναντι τρίτων** third party
insurance || **ασφάλεια ζωής** life
insurance
ασφάλιση (η) insurance || **κοινωνικές**
ασφαλίσεις national insurance
|| **ασφάλιση οδηγού και επιβαινόντων**
personal accident insurance || **πλήρης**
ασφάλιση comprehensive insurance
άσχημος/η/ο ugly
ατμοπλοϊκό εισιτήριο boat ticket
ατμός (ο) steam
ατομικός/ή/ό personal

Α	α	"a"
Β	β	"v"
Γ	γ	"gh" or "y"
Δ	δ	"dh"
Ε	ε	"e"
Ζ	ζ	"z"
Η	η	"ee"
Θ	θ	"th"
Ι	ι	"ee"
Κ	κ	"k"
Λ	λ	"l"
Μ	μ	"m"
Ν	ν	"n"
Ξ	ξ	"ks"
Ο	ο	"o"
Π	π	"p"
Ρ	ρ	"r"
Σ	σ, ς	"s"
Τ	τ	"t"
Υ	υ	"ee"
Φ	φ	"f"
Χ	χ	"kh"
Ψ	ψ	"ps"
Ω	ω	"o"

αψίδα

άτομο (το) individual
Αττική (η) Attica
ατύχημα (το) accident
αυγό (το) egg || **αυγό βραστό** boiled egg || **αυγό μελάτο** soft boiled egg || **αυγό ποσέ** poached egg || **αυγό τηγανητό** fried egg || **αυγά ημέρας** newly laid eggs
αυγολέμονο σούπα soup containing rice, chicken stock, egg and lemon
Αύγουστος (ο) August
αύριο tomorrow
Αυστραλία (η) Australia
αυτή she; this
αυτί (το) ear
αυτοί they; these
αυτοκίνητο (το) car || **ενοικιάσεις αυτοκινήτων** car hire || **Ελληνική Λέσχη Αυτοκινήτου και Περιηγήσεων** Automobile and Touring Club of Greece || **στάθμευση αυτοκινήτων** car parking || **συνεργείο αυτοκινήτων** car repairs
αυτοκινητόδρομος (ο) motorway
αυτόματος/η/ο automatic || **αυτόματη μετάδοση** automatic transmission
αυτός/ή/ό he/she/it
αφαίρεση (η) substraction, deduction
άφιξη (η) arrival || **αφίξεις** arrivals || **δελτίο αφίξεως** arrival card
αφορολόγητα (τα) duty-free goods
Αφροδίτη Aphrodite; medium white wine from Cyprus
αφυδάτωση (η) dehydration
Αχάια Κλάους wine from Patras
αχθοφόρος (ο) porter
αχινός (ο) sea urchin
αχλάδι (το) pear
αχλαδιά (η) pear tree
άχρηστα (τα) waste
αψίδα (η) arch

Α	α	"a"
Β	β	"v"
Γ	γ	"gh" *or* "y"
Δ	δ	"dh"
Ε	ε	"e"
Ζ	ζ	"z"
Η	η	"ee"
Θ	θ	"th"
Ι	ι	"ee"
Κ	κ	"k"
Λ	λ	"l"
Μ	μ	"m"
Ν	ν	"n"
Ξ	ξ	"ks"
Ο	ο	"o"
Π	π	"p"
Ρ	ρ	"r"
Σ	σ, ς	"s"
Τ	τ	"t"
Υ	υ	"ee"
Φ	φ	"f"
Χ	χ	"kh"
Ψ	ψ	"ps"
Ω	ω	"o"

B, β

βαγόνι (το) carriage (*train*)
βάζω to put
βάθος (το) depth
βαλανιδιά (η) oak tree
βαλβίδα (η) valve
βαλίτσα (η) suitcase
βαμβακερός/ή/ό made of cotton
βαμβάκι (το) cotton; cotton wool
βαρέλι (το) barrel || μπύρα από βαρέλι
 draught beer
βάρκα (η) boat
βάρος (το) weight
βαρύς/ιά/ύ heavy
βάση (η) base
βασιλιάς (ο) king
βασίλισσα (η) queen
βατόμουρο (το) blackberry
βάτραχος (ο) frog
βαφή (η) paint, dye
βαφτίσια (τα) christening
βγάζω to take off
βγαίνω to go out
βέβαιος/η/ο certain, sure
βελόνα (η) needle
βενζίνη (η) petrol
βεράντα (η) veranda
βήχας (ο) cough
βία (η) violence
βιαστικά hastily
βιβλίο (το) book
βιβλιοθήκη (η) bookcase; library
 || Δημοτική Βιβλιοθήκη Public Library
 || Κεντρική Βιβλιοθήκη Central Library
βιβλιοπωλείο (το) bookshop
Βίβλος (η) the Bible
βίδα (η) screw

A	α	"a"
B	β	"v"
Γ	γ	"gh" *or* "y"
Δ	δ	"dh"
E	ε	"e"
Z	ζ	"z"
H	η	"ee"
Θ	θ	"th"
I	ι	"ee"
K	κ	"k"
Λ	λ	"l"
M	μ	"m"
N	ν	"n"
Ξ	ξ	"ks"
O	o	"o"
Π	π	"p"
P	ρ	"r"
Σ	σ, ς	"s"
T	τ	"t"
Y	υ	"ee"
Φ	φ	"f"
X	χ	"kh"
Ψ	ψ	"ps"
Ω	ω	"o"

βιομηχανία (η) industry
βιοτεχνία (η) handicraft
βιταμίνη (η) vitamin
βιτρίνα (η) shop window
βλάστηση (η) vegetation
βλέπω to see
βόδι (το) ox || **βοδινό κρέας** beef
βοήθεια (η) help || **Κέντρο Άμεσης
Βοήθειας** Centre for Emergency Aid
|| **οδική βοήθεια** breakdown service
|| **πρώτες βοήθειες** first aid
βοηθώ to help
βόμβα (η) bomb
βομβητής (o) buzzer
βορράς (o) north
βουλή (η) parliament
βουνό (το) mountain
βούρτσα (η) brush
βούτυρο (το) butter
βράδυ (το) evening
βραχιόλι (το) bracelet
βράχος (o) rock
Βρεττανία (η) Britain
βρετανικός/ή/ό British (*thing*)
|| **Βρετανικές Αερογραμμές** British
Airways
Βρετανός/ίδα British man/woman
βρίσκω to find
βροχερός/ή/ό rainy || **βροχερός καιρός**
wet weather
βροχή (η) rain
βρύση (η) tap, fountain
βωμός (o) altar

A	α	"a"
B	β	"v"
Γ	γ	"gh" *or* "y"
Δ	δ	"dh"
E	ε	"e"
Z	ζ	"z"
H	η	"ee"
Θ	θ	"th"
I	ι	"ee"
K	κ	"k"
Λ	λ	"l"
M	μ	"m"
N	ν	"n"
Ξ	ξ	"ks"
O	o	"o"
Π	π	"p"
P	ρ	"r"
Σ	σ, ς	"s"
T	τ	"t"
Y	υ	"ee"
Φ	φ	"f"
X	χ	"kh"
Ψ	ψ	"ps"
Ω	ω	"o"

Γ, γ

γάιδαρος (ο) donkey
γάλα (το) milk
γαλάζιος/α/ο blue
γαλακτοπωλείο (το) dairy products
Γαλλία (η) France
γαλλικός/ή/ό French (*thing*)
Γάλλος/ίδα Frenchman/-woman
γαλοπούλα (η) turkey
γάμος (ο) wedding, marriage
γαμπρός (ο) brother-in-law; son-in-law; bridegroom
γάντι (το) glove
γαρίδα (η) shrimp
γαρύφαλλο (το) carnation
γάτα (η) cat
γεια σου hello; goodbye
γείτονας/ισσα neighbour
γειτονιά (η) neighbourhood
γέλιο (το) laughter
γελώ to laugh
γεμάτος/η/ο full
γενέθλια (τα) birthday
γένια (τα) beard
γενιά (η) generation
γενικός/ή/ό general ‖ Γενικό Νοσοκομείο General Hospital
γέννηση (η) birth
γεράματα (τα) old age
Γερμανία (η) Germany
γερμανικός/ή/ό German (*thing*)
Γερμανός/ίδα German (*man/woman*)
γερός/ή/ό healthy, strong
γέρος (ο) old man
γεύμα (το) meal
γεύση (η) taste
γέφυρα (η) bridge

Α	α	"a"
Β	β	"v"
Γ	γ	"gh" *or* "y"
Δ	δ	"dh"
Ε	ε	"e"
Ζ	ζ	"z"
Η	η	"ee"
Θ	θ	"th"
Ι	ι	"ee"
Κ	κ	"k"
Λ	λ	"l"
Μ	μ	"m"
Ν	ν	"n"
Ξ	ξ	"ks"
Ο	ο	"o"
Π	π	"p"
Ρ	ρ	"r"
Σ	σ, ς	"s"
Τ	τ	"t"
Υ	υ	"ee"
Φ	φ	"f"
Χ	χ	"kh"
Ψ	ψ	"ps"
Ω	ω	"o"

γεωγραφία (η) geography
γεωργία (η) agriculture
γη (η) earth, ground, land
για for
γιαγιά (η) grandmother
γιακάς (ο) collar
γιαούρτι (το) yogurt
γιαπωνέζικος/η/ο Japanese (*thing*)
γιασεμί (το) jasmine
γιατί why; because
γιατρός (ο/η) doctor
γίδα (η) goat
γίνομαι to become || γίνονται δεκτές πιστωτικές κάρτες we accept credit cards
γιορτή (η) public holiday
γιος (ο) son
γιωτ (το) yacht
γκάζι (το) accelerator (*car*); gas
γκαράζ (το) garage
γκαρσόν, γκαρσόνι (το) waiter
γκρεμός (ο) precipice
γκρίζος/α/ο grey
γλάρος (ο) seagull
γλάστρα (η) flowerpot
γλέντι (το) feast
γλυκό (το), γλυκά (τα) sweet pastries and cakes, patisserie
γλυκό ταψιού pastries in syrup
γλυκός/ιά/ό sweet
γλύπτης (ο/η) sculptor
γλυπτική (η) sculpture
Γλυφάδα (η) sea resort of Glyfada
γλώσσα (η) tongue; language; sole (*fish*)
γνήσιος/α/ο genuine
γνωρίζω to know
γνώση (η) knowledge
γόνατο (το) knee
γονείς (οι) parents
γουιντσέρφινγκ (το) windsurfing

A	α	"a"
B	β	"v"
Γ	γ	"gh" *or* "y"
Δ	δ	"dh"
E	ε	"e"
Z	ζ	"z"
H	η	"ee"
Θ	θ	"th"
I	ι	"ee"
K	κ	"k"
Λ	λ	"l"
M	μ	"m"
N	ν	"n"
Ξ	ξ	"ks"
O	ο	"o"
Π	π	"p"
P	ρ	"r"
Σ	σ, ς	"s"
T	τ	"t"
Y	υ	"ee"
Φ	φ	"f"
X	χ	"kh"
Ψ	ψ	"ps"
Ω	ω	"o"

γούνα (η) fur
γουρούνι (το) pig
γραβάτα (η) tie
γράμμα (το) letter || **γράμμα επείγον** urgent *or* express letter || **γράμμα συστημένο** registered letter
γραμμάριο (το) gram
γραμματοκιβώτιο (το) letter box
γραμματόσημο (το) stamp || **αυτόματος πωλητής γραμματοσήμων** automatic stamp dispenser
γραφείο (το) office; desk || **Γραφείο Τουρισμού** Tourist Office
γράφω to write
γρήγορα quickly
γριά (η) old woman
γρίππη (η) influenza
γυαλί (το) glass || **γυαλιά (τα)** glasses || **γυαλιά του ηλίου** sunglasses
Γυμνάσιο (το) ≈ lower secondary school
γυμνός/ή/ό naked
γυναίκα (η) woman || **γυναικών** Ladies (*toilets*)
γυναικολόγος (ο/η) gynaecologist
γύρος (ο) doner kebab
γύρω round, about
γωνία (η) corner

Δ, δ

δάκρυ (το) tear
δακρύζω to shed tears
δακτύλιος (ο) ring, circle
δαμάσκηνο (το) plum
δανείζω to lend
δάνειο (το) loan
δαντέλα (η) lace
δάπεδο (το) floor

Α	α	"a"
Β	β	"v"
Γ	γ	"gh" *or* "y"
Δ	δ	"dh"
Ε	ε	"e"
Ζ	ζ	"z"
Η	η	"ee"
Θ	θ	"th"
Ι	ι	"ee"
Κ	κ	"k"
Λ	λ	"l"
Μ	μ	"m"
Ν	ν	"n"
Ξ	ξ	"ks"
Ο	ο	"o"
Π	π	"p"
Ρ	ρ	"r"
Σ	σ, ς	"s"
Τ	τ	"t"
Υ	υ	"ee"
Φ	φ	"f"
Χ	χ	"kh"
Ψ	ψ	"ps"
Ω	ω	"o"

δάσκαλος/α teacher
δασμός (ο) duty, tax
δάσος (το) forest, wood
δαχτυλίδι (το) ring (*for finger*)
δάχτυλο (το) finger
δείπνο (το) dinner
δέκα ten
δέκατος/η/ο tenth
δεκαέξη sixteen
δεκαεννέα nineteen
δεκαεπτά seventeen
δεκαοκτώ eighteen
δεκαπενθήμερο (το) fortnight
δεκαπέντε fifteen
δεκατέσσερα fourteen
δεκατρία thirteen
Δεκέμβριος (ο) December
δελτίο (το) card, coupon || δελτίο
  αφίξεως arrival card || δελτίο λιανικής
  πωλήσεως bill for retail sale
δελφίνι (το) dolphin || ιπτάμενο
  δελφίνι hydrofoil
Δελφοί (οι) Delphi
δέμα (το) parcel
Δεμέστιχα white wine from Southern
  Greece
δεν not || δεν γίνονται αλλαγές goods
  cannot be exchanged || δεν δίνει ρέστα
  no change given
δέντρο (το) tree
δένω to tie
δεξιά right (*side*)
δέρμα (το) skin; leather
δερματολόγος (ο/η) dermatologist
δέσιμο (το) tying
δεσποινίς/ίδα (η) Miss
Δευτέρα (η) Monday
δεύτερος/η/ο second
δηλητήριο (το) poison
Δήλος (η) Delos
δήλωση (η) announcement, statement

A	α	"a"
B	β	"v"
Γ	γ	"gh" *or* "y"
Δ	δ	"dh"
E	ε	"e"
Z	ζ	"z"
H	η	"ee"
Θ	θ	"th"
I	ι	"ee"
K	κ	"k"
Λ	λ	"l"
M	μ	"m"
N	ν	"n"
Ξ	ξ	"ks"
O	ο	"o"
Π	π	"p"
P	ρ	"r"
Σ	σ, ς	"s"
T	τ	"t"
Y	υ	"ee"
Φ	φ	"f"
X	χ	"kh"
Ψ	ψ	"ps"
Ω	ω	"o"

|| **δήλωση συναλλάγματος** currency declaration || **είδη προς δήλωση** goods to declare || **τίποτε προς δήλωση** nothing to declare

Δημαρχείο (το), Δημαρχιακό Μέγαρο Town Hall

δημοκρατία (η) democracy

δήμος (ο) municipality

δημόσιος/α/ο public || **δημόσια έργα** public works, road works || **δημόσιος κήπος** public gardens

δημοτικός/ή/ό public || **Δημοτική Αγορά** (public) market || **Δημοτική Βιβλιοθήκη** Public Library

διαβάζω to read

διάβαση πεζών pedestrian crossing || **υπόγεια διάβαση πεζών** underground pedestrian crossing

διαβατήριο (το) passport || **αριθμός διαβατηρίου** passport number || **έλεγχος διαβατηρίων** passport control

διαβήτης (ο) diabetes

διαδρομή (η) route

διάδρομος (ο) corridor

διαζύγιο (το) divorce

διαθήκη (η) will

διαίρεση (η) division

δίαιτα (η) diet

διακεκριμένος/η/ο distinguished || **διακεκριμένη θέση** business class

διακοπές (οι) holidays

διάλειμμα (το) interval, break

διάλεκτος (η) dialect

διάλεξη (η) lecture, talk

διάλυση (η) closing down

διαμάντι (το) diamond

διαμέρισμα (το) flat, apartment

διανομέας (ο) distributor (*car*)

διανυκτερεύει all-night (*chemist, restaurant etc*)

διάρκεια (η) duration || **κατά τη**

Α	α	"a"
Β	β	"v"
Γ	γ	"gh" *or* "y"
Δ	δ	"dh"
Ε	ε	"e"
Ζ	ζ	"z"
Η	η	"ee"
Θ	θ	"th"
Ι	ι	"ee"
Κ	κ	"k"
Λ	λ	"l"
Μ	μ	"m"
Ν	ν	"n"
Ξ	ξ	"ks"
Ο	ο	"o"
Π	π	"p"
Ρ	ρ	"r"
Σ	σ, ς	"s"
Τ	τ	"t"
Υ	υ	"ee"
Φ	φ	"f"
Χ	χ	"kh"
Ψ	ψ	"ps"
Ω	ω	"o"

διάρκεια της ημέρας during the day	A α	"a"
διασκέδαση (η) entertainment || **κέντρο διασκεδάσεως** night club	B β	"v"
διάστημα (το) interval, space	Γ γ	"gh" *or* "y"
διαταγή (η) order		
διατηρώ to preserve, keep || **διατηρείτε την πόλη καθαρή** keep the town clean	Δ δ	"dh"
διατροφή (η): πλήρης διατροφή full board	E ε	"e"
διαφέρω to differ	Z ζ	"z"
διαφήμιση (η) advertisement		
διαφορά (η) difference	H η	"ee"
δίδυμος/η twin	Θ θ	"th"
διεθνής/ής/ές international		
διερμηνέας (ο/η) interpreter	I ι	"ee"
διεύθυνση (η) address; management		
διευθυντής (ο/η) manager; head teacher	K κ	"k"
δικαστήριο (το) court	Λ λ	"l"
δικαστής (ο) judge		
δικηγόρος (ο) lawyer	M μ	"m"
δίνω to give	N ν	"n"
διορθώνω to correct		
διορίζω to appoint	Ξ ξ	"ks"
διότι because	O ο	"o"
δίπλα next to		
διπλός/ή/ό double || **διπλό δωμάτιο** double room || **διπλό κρεββάτι** double bed	Π π	"p"
διπλότυπος λογαριασμός duplicate bill	P ρ	"r"
δισκοθήκη (η) record collection	Σ σ, ς	"s"
δίσκος (ο) record		
διυλιστήρια (τα) refinery	T τ	"t"
δίφραγκο (το) 2-drachma piece		
δίχτυ (το) net	Y υ	"ee"
δίψα (η) thirst	Φ φ	"f"
διψώ to be thirsty		
διώκω to persecute || **διώκεται ποινικώς** will be prosecuted	X χ	"kh"
δολάριο (το) dollar	Ψ ψ	"ps"
δόλωμα (το) bait		
δόντι (το) tooth	Ω ω	"o"

δουλειά (η) work
δραχμή (η) drachma
δρομολόγιο (το) timetable; route
‖ **εξωτερικά δρομολόγια** international routes ‖ **εσωτερικά δρομολόγια** internal routes
δρόμος (ο) street, way
δύο two
δύση (η) west
δυσκοιλιότητα (η) constipation
δύσκολος/η/ο difficult
δυστύχημα (το) accident
δυστυχισμένος/η/ο unhappy
δυτικός/ή/ό western
δώδεκα twelve
δωδεκάδα (η) dozen
Δωδεκάνησα (τα) the Dodecanese
δωμάτιο (το) room
δωρεάν free of charge
δώρο (το) present, gift

Ε, ε

εάν if
εβδομάδα (η) week
εβδομήντα seventy
έβδομος/η/ο seventh
εγγονή granddaughter
εγγονός grandson
εγγραφή (η) registration
εγγύηση (η) deposit, guarantee
εγκαταλείπω to abandon
εγκατάλειψη πλοίου abandon ship
έγχρωμος/η/ο coloured ‖ **έγχρωμες φωτογραφίες** colour photographs
εγώ I
εδώ here
έθιμο (το) custom
εθνικός/ή/ό national ‖ **εθνικό θέατρο**

Α	α	"a"
Β	β	"v"
Γ	γ	"gh" *or* "y"
Δ	δ	"dh"
Ε	ε	"e"
Ζ	ζ	"z"
Η	η	"ee"
Θ	θ	"th"
Ι	ι	"ee"
Κ	κ	"k"
Λ	λ	"l"
Μ	μ	"m"
Ν	ν	"n"
Ξ	ξ	"ks"
Ο	ο	"o"
Π	π	"p"
Ρ	ρ	"r"
Σ	σ, ς	"s"
Τ	τ	"t"
Υ	υ	"ee"
Φ	φ	"f"
Χ	χ	"kh"
Ψ	ψ	"ps"
Ω	ω	"o"

national theatre || **εθνικοί οδοί** national highways || **εθνικός κήπος** public garden || **εθνικός ύμνος** national anthem

έθνος (το) nation

ειδικός/ή/ό specialist || **ειδικό τμήμα ...** special department for ...

είδος (το) kind, sort || **είδη** goods || **είδη αλιείας** fishing tackle || **είδη προς δήλωση** goods to declare || **είδη εξοχής** camping equipment || **είδη καπνιστού** tobacconist || **είδη κήπου** garden centre || **είδη υγιεινής** bathrooms

εικόνα (η) picture, icon

εικοσάρικο (το) 20-drachma piece

είκοσι twenty

είμαι I am

είμαστε we are

είναι it is

εισαγωγές (οι) imports

είσαι you are

εισιτήριο (το) ticket || **εισιτήριο απλής διαδρομής** single ticket || **εισιτήριο μετ´ επιστροφής** return ticket || **ατμοπλοϊκό εισιτήριο** boat ticket || **σιδηροδρομικό εισιτήριο** rail ticket || **φοιτητικό εισιτήριο** student ticket

είσοδος (η) entrance, entry

εισπράκτορας (ο) conductor (*on bus*) || **χωρίς εισπράκτορα** without conductor, one-man operated (*bus: exact fare needed*)

είστε you (*plural*) are

εκατό one hundred

εκδοτήριο (το) booking office, ticket office

εκεί there

εκείνος/η/ο he/she/it

έκθεση (η) exhibition

εκκλησία (η) church

Α	α	"a"
Β	β	"v"
Γ	γ	"gh" *or* "y"
Δ	δ	"dh"
Ε	ε	"e"
Ζ	ζ	"z"
Η	η	"ee"
Θ	θ	"th"
Ι	ι	"ee"
Κ	κ	"k"
Λ	λ	"l"
Μ	μ	"m"
Ν	ν	"n"
Ξ	ξ	"ks"
Ο	ο	"o"
Π	π	"p"
Ρ	ρ	"r"
Σ	σ, ς	"s"
Τ	τ	"t"
Υ	υ	"ee"
Φ	φ	"f"
Χ	χ	"kh"
Ψ	ψ	"ps"
Ω	ω	"o"

εκλέγω to chose, elect

εκλογές (οι) elections

έκπτωση (η) discount || εκπτώσεις sale

εκσκαφή (η) excavation

εκτελούνται έργα road works

έκτος/η/ο sixth

εκτός except, unless || εκτός
λειτουργίας out of order

έλα! come on!, come along!, come
here!

ελαστικό (το) tyre || σέρβις ελαστικών
tyre service

ελατήριο (το) spring (coil)

ελαττώνω to reduce || ελαττώσατε
ταχύτητα reduce speed

ελαφρός/ή/ό light (in weight)

ελάχιστος/η/ο minimal

έλεγχος (ο) control || έλεγχος
διαβατηρίων passport control || έλεγχος
εισιτηρίων check-in || έλεγχος
ελαστικών tyre check || έλεγχος
επιβατών και αποσκευών check-in
|| αγορανομικός έλεγχος price control
|| υγειονομικός έλεγχος health control

ελεύθερος/η/ο free; for hire

ελιά (η) olive; olive tree

έλκος (το) ulcer

Ελλάδα, Ελλάς (η) Greece

´Ελληνας/ίδα Greek (man/woman)

ελληνικά (τα) Greek (language)

ελληνικός/ή/ό Greek (thing)
|| Ελληνικά Ταχυδρομεία Greek Post
Office || Ελληνική Δημοκρατία
Republic of Greece || Ελληνική Λέσχη
Αυτοκινήτου και Περιηγήσεων
(ΕΛΠΑ) Automobile and Touring Club
of Greece || Ελληνικής κατασκευής
made in Greece || το Ελληνικό Athens
Airport || Ελληνικός Οργανισμός
Τουρισμού Greek Tourist Organisation
|| Ελληνικό προϊόν product of Greece

A	α	"a"
B	β	"v"
Γ	γ	"gh" or "y"
Δ	δ	"dh"
E	ε	"e"
Z	ζ	"z"
H	η	"ee"
Θ	θ	"th"
I	ι	"ee"
K	κ	"k"
Λ	λ	"l"
M	μ	"m"
N	ν	"n"
Ξ	ξ	"ks"
O	o	"o"
Π	π	"p"
P	ρ	"r"
Σ	σ, ς	"s"
T	τ	"t"
Y	υ	"ee"
Φ	φ	"f"
X	χ	"kh"
Ψ	ψ	"ps"
Ω	ω	"o"

ελπίδα (η) hope
ελπίζω to hope
εμβολιασμός (ο) vaccination
έμβολο (το) piston
εμείς we
εμετός (ο) vomit || έκανα εμετό I was sick
εμποδίζω to prevent
εμπόδιο (το) obstacle
εμπόρευμα (το) merchandise
εμπόριο (το) trade
έμπορος (ο) merchant, tradesman
εμπρός forward, in front
εμφανίζω to develop (film) || εμφάνιση παράδοση σε 1 ώρα films developed in 1 hour
εναντίον against
έναρξη (η) opening, beginning
ένας/μία/ένα one
ένατος/η/ο ninth
ένδυμα (το) article of clothing || έτοιμα ενδύματα ready-to-wear
ένεση (η) injection
ενέχυρα (τα) pawnshop
εννέα nine
ενοικιάζω to rent, hire || ενοικιάζεται to let
ενοικιάσεις for hire
ενοίκιο (το) rent
εντάξει all right, OK
έντεκα eleven
έντερα (τα) intestines
έντομο (το) insect
εντομοκτόνο (το) insecticide
έντυπο (το) form (to fill in)
ενώ while
εξετάζω to examine
έξη/ι six
εξηγώ to explain
εξήντα sixty
έξοδος (η) exit; gate (at airport)

A	α	"a"
B	β	"v"
Γ	γ	"gh" or "y"
Δ	δ	"dh"
E	ε	"e"
Z	ζ	"z"
H	η	"ee"
Θ	θ	"th"
I	ι	"ee"
K	κ	"k"
Λ	λ	"l"
M	μ	"m"
N	ν	"n"
Ξ	ξ	"ks"
O	ο	"o"
Π	π	"p"
P	ρ	"r"
Σ	σ, ς	"s"
T	τ	"t"
Y	υ	"ee"
Φ	φ	"f"
X	χ	"kh"
Ψ	ψ	"ps"
Ω	ω	"o"

εξοπλισμός (ο) equipment
εξοχή (η) countryside
εξυπηρέτηση (η) service
έξω out, outside
εξωλέμβιες (οι) boats with outboard motors
εξώστης (ο) circle, balcony (*in theatre*)
εξωτερικός/ή/ό external || **το εξωτερικό** foreign countries (*outside Greece*) || **εξωτερικού** letters - abroad (*on post boxes*) || **πτήσεις εξωτερικού** international flights
ΕΟΚ EEC
ΕΟΤ = Ελληνικός Οργανισμός Τουρισμού
επάγγελμα (το) occupation, profession
επαναλαμβάνω to repeat
επανάσταση (η) revolution
επάργυρος/η/ο silver-plated
έπαυλη (η) villa
επείγον, επείγουσα urgent, express
επειδή because
έπειτα then
επέτειος (η) anniversary
επιβάτης/τρια passenger || **διερχόμενοι επιβάτες** passengers in transit
επιβατικά (τα) private cars
επιβεβαιώνω to confirm
επιβίβαση (η) boarding || **κάρτα επιβιβάσεως** boarding card
Επίδαυρος (η) Epidavros
επιδόρπιο (το) dessert
επιθεώρηση (η) revue (*in theatre*)
επικίνδυνος/η/ο dangerous || **επικίνδυνη κατωφέρεια** dangerous incline
επιλογή (η) selection
επιμένω to insist
έπιπλο (το) piece of furniture
επίσης also
επισκευή (η) repair || **επισκευές** repairs

Α	α	"a"
Β	β	"v"
Γ	γ	"gh" *or* "y"
Δ	δ	"dh"
Ε	ε	"e"
Ζ	ζ	"z"
Η	η	"ee"
Θ	θ	"th"
Ι	ι	"ee"
Κ	κ	"k"
Λ	λ	"l"
Μ	μ	"m"
Ν	ν	"n"
Ξ	ξ	"ks"
Ο	ο	"o"
Π	π	"p"
Ρ	ρ	"r"
Σ	σ, ς	"s"
Τ	τ	"t"
Υ	υ	"ee"
Φ	φ	"f"
Χ	χ	"kh"
Ψ	ψ	"ps"
Ω	ω	"o"

επίσκεψη (η) visit || **ώρες επισκέψεως** visiting hours

επιστολή (η) letter || **επιστολή επείγουσα** urgent or express letter || **επιστολή συστημένη** registered letter

επιστροφή (η) return || **επιστροφή νομισμάτων** returned coins || **επιστροφές** returned goods

επιταγή (η) cheque || **ταχυδρομική επιταγή** postal order

επιτρέπω to permit

επιτυγχάνω to succeed

επιφάνεια (η) surface

επόμενος/η/ο next

εποχή (η) season

επτά seven

Επτάνησα (τα) Ionian Islands

επώνυμο (το) surname

έργα (τα) road works

εργαλείο (το) tool

εργασία (η) work

εργαστήριο (το) workshop

εργάτης (ο) worker

εργοστάσιο (το) factory

έρευνα (η) search, research

έρχομαι to come

ερώτηση (η) question

εσείς you (*plural*)

εστιατόριο (το) restaurant

εσύ you (*singular*)

εσώρουχα (τα) underwear

εσωτερικός/ή/ό internal || **εσωτερικού** letters – inland (*on post boxes*) || **πτήσεις εσωτερικού** internal flights

εταιρ(ε)ία (η) company, firm

ετήσιος/α/ο annual

έτοιμος/η/ο ready

έτος (το) year

έτσι so, like this || **έτσι κι έτσι** so-so, middling

ευθεία (η) straight line || **κατ´ ευθείαν**

A ˉ	α	"a"
B	β	"v"
Γ	γ	"gh" or "y"
Δ	δ	"dh"
E	ε	"e"
Z	ζ	"z"
H ˙	η	"ee"
Θ	θ	"th"
I	ι	"ee"
K	κ	"k"
Λ	λ	"l"
M	μ	"m"
N	ν	"n"
Ξ	ξ	"ks"
O	ο	"o"
Π	π	"p"
P	ρ	"r"
Σ	σ, ς	"s"
T	τ	"t"
Y	υ	"ee"
Φ	φ	"f"
X	χ	"kh"
Ψ	ψ	"ps"
Ω	ω	"o"

straight on
ευθυγράμμιση (η) wheel alignment
ευκαιρία (η) opportunity; bargain
ευκολία (η) ease, convenience
‖ **ευκολίες πληρωμής** credit terms
Ευρώπη (η) Europe
ευτυχισμένος/η/ο happy
ευχαριστώ thank you
εφημερίδα (η) newspaper
έχω to have

Z, ζ

Ζάκυνθος (η) Zante, Zakynthos
ζαλάδα (η) dizziness
ζαμπόν (το) ham
Ζάππειο (το) Zappio (public garden in
Athens)
ζάρια (τα) dice
ζάχαρη (η) sugar
ζαχαροπλαστείο (το) patisserie
ζεστός/ή/ό warm
ζέστη (η) heat ‖ **κάνει ζέστη** it's hot
ζευγάρι (το) couple, pair
ζήλεια (η) jealousy
ζηλεύω to be jealous
ζημιά (η) damage ‖ **κάθε ζημιά**
τιμωρείται anyone causing damage will
be prosecuted
ζητώ to ask; to seek
ζήτω! hurray!
ζούγκλα (η) jungle
ζυγαριά (η) scales (*for weighing*)
ζυγοστάθμιση (η) wheel balancing
ζυμαρικά (τα) pastries
ζω to live
ζωγραφίζω to draw, paint
ζωγραφική (η) painting (*art*)
ζωή (η) life

Α	α	"a"
Β	β	"v"
Γ	γ	"gh" *or* "y"
Δ	δ	"dh"
Ε	ε	"e"
Ζ	ζ	"z"
Η	η	"ee"
Θ	θ	"th"
Ι	ι	"ee"
Κ	κ	"k"
Λ	λ	"l"
Μ	μ	"m"
Ν	ν	"n"
Ξ	ξ	"ks"
Ο	ο	"o"
Π	π	"p"
Ρ	ρ	"r"
Σ	σ, ς	"s"
Τ	τ	"t"
Υ	υ	"ee"
Φ	φ	"f"
Χ	χ	"kh"
Ψ	ψ	"ps"
Ω	ω	"o"

ζώνη (η) belt ‖ ζώνη ασφαλείας safety belt
ζώο (το) animal
ζωολογικός κήπος zoo

Η, η

η the (*with feminine nouns*)
ή or
ηλεκτρισμός (ο) electricity
ηλεκτρονικός/ή/ό electronic ‖ ηλεκτρονική ζυγοστάθμιση electronic wheel balancing ‖ ηλεκτρονικός έλεγχος electronic check
ηλιακός/ή/ό solar
ηλίαση (η) sunstroke
ηλικία (η) age
ηλιοβασίλεμα (το) sunset
ηλιοθεραπεία (η) sunbathing
ήλιος (ο) sun
ημέρα (η) day
ημερήσιος/α/ο daily
ημερομηνία (η) date ‖ ημερομηνία αναχωρήσεως date of departure ‖ ημερομηνία αφίξεως date of arrival ‖ ημερομηνία γεννήσεως date of birth ‖ ημερομηνία λήξεως expiry date
ημιδιατροφή (η) half board
Ηνωμένο Βασίλειο United Kingdom
ΗΠΑ USA
Ήπειρος (η) Epirus
Ηράκλειο (το) Iraklion
ήρωας (ο) hero
ηρωίδα (η) heroine
ησυχία (η) calmness, quiet
ήταν was; were
ήχος (ο) sound
ηχώ to sound, echo
ηχώ (η) echo

Α	α	"a"
Β	β	"v"
Γ	γ	"gh" *or* "y"
Δ	δ	"dh"
Ε	ε	"e"
Ζ	ζ	"z"
Η	η	"ee"
Θ	θ	"th"
Ι	ι	"ee"
Κ	κ	"k"
Λ	λ	"l"
Μ	μ	"m"
Ν	ν	"n"
Ξ	ξ	"ks"
Ο	ο	"o"
Π	π	"p"
Ρ	ρ	"r"
Σ	σ, ς	"s"
Τ	τ	"t"
Υ	υ	"ee"
Φ	φ	"f"
Χ	χ	"kh"
Ψ	ψ	"ps"
Ω	ω	"o"

Θ, θ

θα shall, will
θαλαμηπόλος (ο) room steward on boat
θάλασσα (η) sea || **θαλάσσιο
αλεξίπτωτο** paragliding || **θαλάσσιο σκι**
water skiing || **θαλάσσιο σπορ** water
sports
θάνατος (ο) death
θάρρος (το) courage
Θάσος Thasos
θέα (η) view
θέατρο (το) theatre
θεία (η) aunt
θείος (ο) uncle
θέλω to want
θεός (ο) god
θεραπεία (η) treatment
θερινός/ή/ό summer || **θερινές διακοπές**
summer holidays
θερισμός (ο) harvest
θέρμανση (η) heating
θερμίδα (η) calorie
Θερμοπύλαι/ες (οι) Thermopylae
θερμοστάτης (ο) thermostat
θέση (η) place, seat || **θέση στάθμευσης
αυτοκινήτων** parking || **διακεκριμένη
θέση** business class || **κράτηση θέσης**
seat reservation || **οικονομική θέση**
economy class || **πρώτη θέση** first class
Θεσσαλία (η) Thessaly
Θεσσαλονίκη (η) Salonica
Θήβαι/α (η) Thebes
θηλυκός female, feminine
θόρυβος (ο) noise
Θράκη (η) Thrace
θρησκεία (η) religion
θρόνος (ο) throne

Α	α	"a"
Β	β	"v"
Γ	γ	"gh" *or* "y"
Δ	δ	"dh"
Ε	ε	"e"
Ζ	ζ	"z"
Η	η	"ee"
Θ	θ	"th"
Ι	ι	"ee"
Κ	κ	"k"
Λ	λ	"l"
Μ	μ	"m"
Ν	ν	"n"
Ξ	ξ	"ks"
Ο	ο	"o"
Π	π	"p"
Ρ	ρ	"r"
Σ	σ, ς	"s"
Τ	τ	"t"
Υ	υ	"ee"
Φ	φ	"f"
Χ	χ	"kh"
Ψ	ψ	"ps"
Ω	ω	"o"

θύελλα (η) storm
θυμάμαι to remember
θυμάρι (το) thyme
θυμώνω to get angry
θύρα (η) door; gate (*at airport*)
  || **πυροστεγής θύρα** fire door
θυρίδα, θυρίς (η) ticket window
  || **θυρίς καταθέσεων** deposits, night safe (*bank*)
θυροτηλέφωνο (το) emergency phone (*on train*)
θυρωρείο (το) porter
θώρακας (ο) chest

Ι, ι

Ιανουάριος (ο) January
Ιαπωνία Japan
ιαπωνικός/ή/ό Japanese (*thing*)
ιατρική περίθαλψη medical treatment
ιατρός (ο/η) doctor
ιδέα (η) idea
ιδιοκτήτης/τρια owner
ίδιος/α/ο same || **εγώ ο ίδιος** myself
ιδιωτικός/ή/ό private || **ιδιωτικός χώρος** private, keep off *or* out; no parking
ίδρυμα (το) institution
ιερέας (ο) priest
ιερό (το) sanctuary (*in church*)
ιθαγένεια (η) nationality
ικανοποίηση (η) satisfaction
ικανός/ή/ό able
ιματιοθήκη (η) cloakroom
Ιόνιο Πέλαγο Ionian sea
Ιόνιοι Νήσοι Ionian islands
ιός (ο) virus
Ιούλιος (ο) July
Ιούνιος (ο) June

Α	α	"a"
Β	β	"v"
Γ	γ	"gh" *or* "y"
Δ	δ	"dh"
Ε	ε	"e"
Ζ	ζ	"z"
Η	η	"ee"
Θ	θ	"th"
Ι	ι	"ee"
Κ	κ	"k"
Λ	λ	"l"
Μ	μ	"m"
Ν	ν	"n"
Ξ	ξ	"ks"
Ο	ο	"o"
Π	π	"p"
Ρ	ρ	"r"
Σ	σ, ς	"s"
Τ	τ	"t"
Υ	υ	"ee"
Φ	φ	"f"
Χ	χ	"kh"
Ψ	ψ	"ps"
Ω	ω	"o"

ιππασία (η) riding
ιπποδρομίες (οι) horse racing
ιππόδρομος (ο) race track
ιπτάμενος/η/ο flying || **ιπτάμενο δελφίνι** hydrofoil
Ιρλανδία (η) Ireland
ιρλανδικός/ή/ό Irish (*thing*)
Ιρλανδός/έζα Irishman/-woman
ισθμός (ο) canal || **ο Ισθμός της Κορίνθου** the Corinth canal
ίσκιος (ο) shadow
ισόγειο (το) ground floor
ίσος/η/ο equal to
Ισπανία (η) Spain
ισπανικός/ή/ό Spanish (*thing*)
Ισπανός/ίδα Spaniard (*man*/*woman*)
ιστιοπλοΐα (η) sailing
ιστορία (η) history; story
ίσως perhaps
Ιταλία (η) Italy
ιταλικός/ή/ό Italian (*thing*)
Ιταλός/ίδα Italian (*man*/*woman*)
ΙΧ private cars (*parking sign*)
ιχθυοπωλείο (το) fishmonger's
Ιωάννινα (τα) Ioannina

K, κ

κάβα (η) trolley *or* rack for drinks, off-licence
Κάβα-Καμπά dry rosé wine
κάβουρας (ο) crab
καζίνο (το) casino
καθαρίζω to clean
καθαριστήριο (το) dry cleaner's
καθαρίστρια (η) cleaner
καθαρός/ή/ό clean || **Καθαρά Δευτέρα** Ash Wednesday
κάθε every, each

Α	α	"a"
Β	β	"v"
Γ	γ	"gh" *or* "y"
Δ	δ	"dh"
Ε	ε	"e"
Ζ	ζ	"z"
Η	η	"ee"
Θ	θ	"th"
Ι	ι	"ee"
Κ	κ	"k"
Λ	λ	"l"
Μ	μ	"m"
Ν	ν	"n"
Ξ	ξ	"ks"
Ο	ο	"o"
Π	π	"p"
Ρ	ρ	"r"
Σ	σ, ς	"s"
Τ	τ	"t"
Υ	υ	"ee"
Φ	φ	"f"
Χ	χ	"kh"
Ψ	ψ	"ps"
Ω	ω	"o"

καθεδρικός ναός cathedral
καθημερινά daily || **καθημερινά δρομολόγια** daily departures
καθημερινή (η) weekday
κάθισμα (το) seat
καθολικός/ή/ό Catholic
καθόλου not at all
κάθομαι to sit
καθρέφτης (ο) mirror
καθυστέρηση (η) delay
και and
Καινή Διαθήκη (η) New Testament
καΐκι (το) boat
καινούριος/α/ο new
καιρός (ο) weather
καίω to burn
κακάο (το) drinking chocolate
κακία (η) malice, ill will
κακοκαιρία (η) bad weather
κακός/ιά/ό wicked
καλά well, all right
καλάθι (το) basket
καλαμάρι (το) squid
καλημέρα good morning
καληνύχτα good night
καλησπέρα good evening
καλλιέργεια (η) cultivation
καλλιστεία (τα) beauty contest
καλλυντικά (τα) cosmetics
καλόγερος (ο) monk
καλόγρια (η) nun
καλοκαίρι (το) summer
καλοριφέρ (το) central heating; radiator
κάλος corn (*on foot*)
καλός/ή/ό good
καλοψημένο well done (*meat*)
καλσόν (το) tights
κάλτσα (η) sock, stocking
καλύτερα better
καλώδιο (το) cable, lead
καμαριέρα (η) chambermaid

A	α	"a"
B	β	"v"
Γ	γ	"gh" *or* "y"
Δ	δ	"dh"
E	ε	"e"
Z	ζ	"z"
H	η	"ee"
Θ	θ	"th"
I	ι	"ee"
K	κ	"k"
Λ	λ	"l"
M	μ	"m"
N	ν	"n"
Ξ	ξ	"ks"
O	ο	"o"
Π	π	"p"
P	ρ	"r"
Σ	σ, ς	"s"
T	τ	"t"
Y	υ	"ee"
Φ	φ	"f"
X	χ	"kh"
Ψ	ψ	"ps"
Ω	ω	"o"

καμμιά anyone; no one (*feminine form*)

καμπάνα (η) bell (*church*)

καμπαρτίνα (η) raincoat

καμπή (η) bend (*in road*)

καμπίνα (η) cabin

Καναδάς (ο) Canada

Καναδός/έζα Canadian (*man/woman*)

κανάλι (το) canal; channel (*TV*)

κανάτα (η) jug

κανέλλα (η) cinnamon

κανένας/καμιά/κανένα anyone; no one

κανό (το) canoe

κανόνας (ο) rule

κάνω to do

καπέλο (το) hat

καπετάνιος (ο) captain (*of ship*)

καπνίζω to smoke || **μη καπνίζετε** No smoking

κάπνισμα (το) smoking || **απαγορεύεται το κάπνισμα** No smoking

καπνιστής (ο) smoker || **είδη καπνιστού** tobacconist's (*shop*)

καπνοπωλείο (το) tobacconist

καπνός (ο) smoke; tobacco

καπό (το) car bonnet

κάποιος/α/ο someone

κάποτε sometimes

κάπου somewhere

καράβι (το) boat, ship

καραμέλα (η) sweet(s)

καραντίνα (η) quarantine

κάρβουνο (το) coal || **στα κάρβουνα** charcoal-grilled

καρδιά (η) heart || **καρδιακή προσβολή** heart attack

καρδιολόγος (ο/η) heart specialist

καρέκλα (η) chair

καρμπιρατέρ (το) carburettor

καρναβάλι (το) carnival

καροτσάκι (το) pushchair

καρπός (ο) fruit

Α	α	"a"
Β	β	"v"
Γ	γ	"gh" *or* "y"
Δ	δ	"dh"
Ε	ε	"e"
Ζ	ζ	"z"
Η	η	"ee"
Θ	θ	"th"
Ι	ι	"ee"
Κ	κ	"k"
Λ	λ	"l"
Μ	μ	"m"
Ν	ν	"n"
Ξ	ξ	"ks"
Ο	ο	"o"
Π	π	"p"
Ρ	ρ	"r"
Σ	σ, ς	"s"
Τ	τ	"t"
Υ	υ	"ee"
Φ	φ	"f"
Χ	χ	"kh"
Ψ	ψ	"ps"
Ω	ω	"o"

καρπούζι (το) watermelon
κάρτα (η) card || **κάρτα απεριόριστων διαδρομών** rail card for unlimited travel || **κάρτα επιβιβάσεως** boarding card || **καρτ-ποστάλ** postcard || **επαγγελματική κάρτα** business card || **μόνο με κάρτα** cardholders only || **πιστωτικές κάρτες** credit cards
καρύδα (η) coconut
καρύδι (το) walnut
καρφί (το) nail
καρφίτσα (η) pin, brooch
καρχαρίας (ο) shark
κασέτα (η) tape (*for recording*)
κασετόφωνο (το) tape recorder
κάστανο (το) chestnut
Καστέλλι Μίνως medium dry red wine from Cyprus
κάστρο (το) castle, fortress
κατά against
καταδίκη (η) sentence (*of court*)
κατάθεση (η) deposit; statement to police
καταιγίδα (η) storm
καταλαβαίνω to understand
κατάλληλος/η/ο suitable
κατάλογος (ο) list; menu; directory || **τηλεφωνικός κατάλογος** telephone directory
καταπίνω to swallow
καταπραϋντικό (το) tranquilliser
καταρράκτης (ο) waterfall
κατασκευή (η): Ελληνικής κατασκευής made in Greece
κατασκήνωση (η) camping
κατάσκοπος (ο) spy
κατάσταση (η) condition, situation
κατάστημα (το) shop
κατάστρωμα (το) deck
καταψύκτης (ο) freezer
κατεβάζω to bring down, lower

A	α	"a"
B	β	"v"
Γ	γ	"gh" *or* "y"
Δ	δ	"dh"
E	ε	"e"
Z	ζ	"z"
H	η	"ee"
Θ	θ	"th"
I	ι	"ee"
K	κ	"k"
Λ	λ	"l"
M	μ	"m"
N	ν	"n"
Ξ	ξ	"ks"
O	ο	"o"
Π	π	"p"
P	ρ	"r"
Σ	σ, ς	"s"
T	τ	"t"
Y	υ	"ee"
Φ	φ	"f"
X	χ	"kh"
Ψ	ψ	"ps"
Ω	ω	"o"

κατεβαίνω to descend

καταΐφι (το) a sweet made of shredded pastry stuffed with almonds

κατεπείγον, κατεπείγουσα urgent, express

κατεψυγμένος/η/ο frozen

κατηγορία (η) class (*of hotel*); accusation

κατηγορώ to accuse

κάτι something

κατοικία (η) residence

κατόπιν later, after

κατσαβίδι (το) screwdriver

κατσαρίδα (η) cockroach

κατσαρόλα (η) saucepan

κατσίκα (η) goat

κάτω under; lower

κατώφλι (το) threshold

καυγάς (ο) quarrel

καύσιμα (τα) fuel

καφέ brown

καφενείο (το) coffee house

καφές (ο) coffee (*usually Turkish coffee*) || **καφές βαρύς γλυκός** very sweet coffee || **καφές γλυκός** sweet coffee || **καφές μέτριος** medium sweet coffee || **καφές σκέτος** coffee without sugar || **καφές στιγμιαίος** instant coffee || **καφές φραπέ** iced coffee

καφετέρια (η) cafeteria

κέδρος (ο) cedar tree *or* wood

κέικ (το) cake

κ.εκ. cubic capacity

κελλάρι (το) cellar

κελλί (το) cell

κενό (το) gap

κέντημα (το) embroidery

κεντρικός/ή/ό central || **κεντρική βιβλιοθήκη** central library

κέντρο (το) centre; café || **κέντρο αλλοδαπών** aliens' centre || **κέντρο**

Α	α	"a"
Β	β	"v"
Γ	γ	"gh" *or* "y"
Δ	δ	"dh"
Ε	ε	"e"
Ζ	ζ	"z"
Η	η	"ee"
Θ	θ	"th"
Ι	ι	"ee"
Κ	κ	"k"
Λ	λ	"l"
Μ	μ	"m"
Ν	ν	"n"
Ξ	ξ	"ks"
Ο	ο	"o"
Π	π	"p"
Ρ	ρ	"r"
Σ	σ, ς	"s"
Τ	τ	"t"
Υ	υ	"ee"
Φ	φ	"f"
Χ	χ	"kh"
Ψ	ψ	"ps"
Ω	ω	"o"

διασκεδάσεως nightclub || **κέντρο εισιτηρίων** ticket office || **κέντρο πληροφόρησης νεότητος** youth information centre || **αθλητικό κέντρο** sports centre || **εξοχικό κέντρο** country café || **τηλεφωνικό κέντρο** telephone exchange

Κεραμεικός (ο) the cemetery of Keramikos

κεράσι (το) cherry

κερασιά (η) cherry tree

κερδίζω to earn; to win

κερί (το) candle

Κέρκυρα (η) Corfu

κέρμα (το) coin

κερνώ to buy a drink

κεφάλι (το) head

κέφι (το) good humour

κεφτές (ο) meatball

κηδεία (η) funeral

κήπος (ο) garden || **δημόσιος κήπος** public garden || **είδη κήπου** garden centre || **ζωολογικός κήπος** zoo

κηπουρός (ο) gardener

κιβώτιο (το) box || **κιβώτιο ταχύτητων** gearbox

κιθάρα (η) guitar

κιλό (το) kilo

κιμάς (ο) minced meat

κίνδυνος (ο) danger || **κίνδυνος θάνατος** extreme danger || **κίνδυνος πυρκαγιάς στο δάσος** fire risk (*in forest*) || **κώδων κινδύνου** emergency signal

κινηματογράφηση (η) filming

κινηματογράφος (ο) cinema

κίνηση (η) movement; traffic

κινητήρας (ο) engine

κινώ to move

κιόλας already

κίτρινος/η/ο yellow

Κιτρό slightly sour white wine from

Α	α	"a"
Β	β	"v"
Γ	γ	"gh" *or* "y"
Δ	δ	"dh"
Ε	ε	"e"
Ζ	ζ	"z"
Η	η	"ee"
Θ	θ	"th"
Ι	ι	"ee"
Κ	κ	"k"
Λ	λ	"l"
Μ	μ	"m"
Ν	ν	"n"
Ξ	ξ	"ks"
Ο	ο	"o"
Π	π	"p"
Ρ	ρ	"r"
Σ	σ, ς	"s"
Τ	τ	"t"
Υ	υ	"ee"
Φ	φ	"f"
Χ	χ	"kh"
Ψ	ψ	"ps"
Ω	ω	"o"

Naxos
κλαδί (το) branch (*of tree*)
κλαίω to cry
κλάμα (το) crying
κλάξον (το) horn (*in car*)
κλασσικός/ή/ό classical
κλέβω to steal
κλειδαρότρυπα (η) keyhole
κλειδί (το) spanner; key
κλείνω to close
κλειστός/ή/ό closed
κλέφτης (ο) thief
κληρονομώ to inherit
κλήρος (ο) the clergy
κλήση (η) summons
κλίμα (το) climate
κλινική (η) clinic
κλωστή (η) thread, cotton
κλωτσώ to kick
Κνωσσός (η) Knossos
κόβω to cut
κογχύλι (το) sea shell
κοιλάδα (η) valley
κοιλιά (η) belly, abdomen
κοιμούμαι to sleep
κοινό (το) public
κοινοβούλιο (το) parliament
κοινωνία (η) society
κοινωνικός/ή/ό social ‖ **κοινωνικές**
ασφαλίσεις national insurance
κοιτάζω to look at
κόκκαλο (το) bone
κοκκινέλι sweet red wine
κόκκινος/η/ο red
κοκορέτσι (το) stuffed lamb entrails
roasted on the spit
κόλαση (η) hell
κολατσιό (το) snack
κολοκυθάκι (το) courgette
κολοκύθι (το) marrow
κόλπος (ο) gulf

A	α	"a"
B	β	"v"
Γ	γ	"gh" *or* "y"
Δ	δ	"dh"
E	ε	"e"
Z	ζ	"z"
H	η	"ee"
Θ	θ	"th"
I	ι	"ee"
K	κ	"k"
Λ	λ	"l"
M	μ	"m"
N	ν	"n"
Ξ	ξ	"ks"
O	o	"o"
Π	π	"p"
P	ρ	"r"
Σ	σ, ς	"s"
T	τ	"t"
Y	υ	"ee"
Φ	φ	"f"
X	χ	"kh"
Ψ	ψ	"ps"
Ω	ω	"o"

κολύμπι (το) swimming
κολυμπώ to swim
κολώνα (η) pillar
κόμμα (το) political party
κομμάτι (το) piece
κομμωτήριο (το) hairdresser's
κομμωτής/κομμώτρια hair stylist
κομπολόι (το) string of beads
κομπόστα (η) stewed fruit
κομψός/ή/ό smart
κονιάκ (το) brandy
κονσέρβα (η) tinned food
κονσέρτο (το) concert
κοντά near
κοντός/ή/ό short
κοπέλλα (η) young woman
κόπος (ο) trouble
κορδέλλα (η) ribbon
κόρη (η) daughter
Κόρινθος (η) Corinth
κορίτσι (το) young girl
κόσμημα (το) jewellery || **κοσμήματα** jeweller's
κόσμος (ο) people
κοστούμι (το) man's suit
κότα (η) hen
κοτολέτα (η) chop
κοτόπουλο (το) chicken
κουβαλώ to carry
κουβάς (ο) bucket
κουβέντα (η) chat
κουβέρτα (η) blanket
κουδούνι (το) bell
κουζίνα (η) kitchen
κουκουβάγια (η) owl
κουκούτσι (το) pip, stone (*fruit*)
κουμπί (το) button
κουμπότρυπα (η) buttonhole
κούνια (η) swing; crib
κουνέλι (το) rabbit
κουνούπι (το) mosquito

A	α	"a"
B	β	"v"
Γ	γ	"gh" *or* "y"
Δ	δ	"dh"
E	ε	"e"
Z	ζ	"z"
H	η	"ee"
Θ	θ	"th"
I	ι	"ee"
K	κ	"k"
Λ	λ	"l"
M	μ	"m"
N	ν	"n"
Ξ	ξ	"ks"
O	o	"o"
Π	π	"p"
P	ρ	"r"
Σ	σ, ς	"s"
T	τ	"t"
Y	υ	"ee"
Φ	φ	"f"
X	χ	"kh"
Ψ	ψ	"ps"
Ω	ω	"o"

κουνουπίδι (το) cauliflower
κουνώ to move, shake
κουπί (το) oar
κουράζομαι to get tired
κουρασμένος/η/ο tired
κουρείο (το) barber's shop
κουρτίνα (η) curtain || **κουρτινόξυλο**
(το) curtain rail
κουταλάκι (το) teaspoon
κουτάλι (το) spoon
κουτί (το) box
κουτός/ή/ό silly
κουφός/ή/ό deaf
κραγιόν (το) lipstick
κρασί (το) wine || **κρασί γλυκό** sweet
wine || **κρασί λευκό** white wine
|| **κρασί κόκκινο** red wine || **κρασί**
ξηρό dry wine || **κρασί ροζέ** rosé wine
κράτος (το) state
κρατώ to hold, book
κρατήσεις (οι) bookings, reservations
κράτηση (η): κράτηση θέσης booking a
seat || **κρατήσεις ξενοδοχείων** hotel
bookings || **υπό κράτηση** in custody
κρέας (το) meat || **κρέας αρνίσιο** lamb
κρεβάτι (το) bed
κρεβατοκάμαρα (η) bedroom
κρέμα (η) cream || **κρέμα σαντιγύ**
whipped cream
κρεμάστρα (η) coat hanger
κρεμμύδι (το) onion
κρεοπωλείο (το) butcher's shop
κρεοπώλης (ο) butcher
Κρήτη (η) Crete
κρίμα (το) pity
κρουαζιέρα (η) cruise
κρουασάν (το) croissant
κρύβω to hide
κρύος/α/ο cold || **κάνει κρύο** it's cold
κρύσταλλο (το) crystal
κρυφά secretly

Α	α	"a"
Β	β	"v"
Γ	γ	"gh" *or* "y"
Δ	δ	"dh"
Ε	ε	"e"
Ζ	ζ	"z"
Η	η	"ee"
Θ	θ	"th"
Ι	ι	"ee"
Κ	κ	"k"
Λ	λ	"l"
Μ	μ	"m"
Ν	ν	"n"
Ξ	ξ	"ks"
Ο	ο	"o"
Π	π	"p"
Ρ	ρ	"r"
Σ	σ, ς	"s"
Τ	τ	"t"
Υ	υ	"ee"
Φ	φ	"f"
Χ	χ	"kh"
Ψ	ψ	"ps"
Ω	ω	"o"

κρυώνω to feel cold
κτηνιατρείο (το) veterinary surgery
κτίζω to build
κτίριο (το) building
κτυπώ to strike
κυάλια (τα) binoculars
κυβέρνηση (η) government
κυβερνήτης (ο) captain (*of aircraft*)
κυβικά εκατοστά cubic capacity
κυδώνι (το) quince
Κυκλάδες (οι) Cyclades
κύκλος (ο) circle
κυκλοφορία (η) traffic; circulation
κυλικείο (το) cafeteria
κύλινδρος (ο) cylinder
κυλιόμενες σκάλες escalators
κύμα (το) wave
κυνήγι (το) game, shooting
κυνηγώ to hunt, chase
Κύπρος (η) Cyprus
κυρία (η) Mrs; lady
Κυριακή (η) Sunday
κύριος (ο) Mr; gentleman
κώδικας (ο) code ‖ **κώδικας οδικής κυκλοφορίας** highway code
 ‖ **ταχυδρομικός κώδικας** post code
 ‖ **τηλεφωνικός κώδικας** dialling code
κωμωδία (η) comedy
Κως (η) Kos

Λ, λ

λαγός (ο) hare
λάδι (το) oil
λάθος (το) mistake
λαθρεμπόριο (το) smuggling
λαϊκός/ή/ό of the people, popular
 ‖ **λαϊκή μουσική** popular music
 ‖ **λαϊκή τέχνη** folk art

A	α	"a"
B	β	"v"
Γ	γ	"gh" *or* "y"
Δ	δ	"dh"
E	ε	"e"
Z	ζ	"z"
H	η	"ee"
Θ	θ	"th"
I	ι	"ee"
K	κ	"k"
Λ	λ	"l"
M	μ	"m"
N	ν	"n"
Ξ	ξ	"ks"
O	ο	"o"
Π	π	"p"
P	ρ	"r"
Σ	σ, ς	"s"
T	τ	"t"
Y	υ	"ee"
Φ	φ	"f"
X	χ	"kh"
Ψ	ψ	"ps"
Ω	ω	"o"

λαιμός (ο) throat
λαός (ο) the people
Λάρισα (η) Larisa
λάσπη (η) mud
λαστιχάκι (το) elastic band
λάστιχο (το) tyre; rubber; elastic
λατέρνα (η) barrel organ
λαχανικά (τα) vegetables
λαχείο (το) lottery || **κρατικό λαχείο**
state lottery
λειβάδι (το) meadow
λείπω to be absent
λειτουργία (η) function; mass (*in church*)
λειτουργώ to function, operate
λεκές (ο) stain
λέμβος (η) lifeboat
λεμονάδα (η) lemon squash
λεμόνι (το) lemon || **χυμός λεμονιού**
lemon juice
λεμονιά (η) lemon tree
λέξη (η) word
λεξικό (το) dictionary
λεπτό (το) minute
λεπτός/ή/ό thin, fine
Λέσβος (η) Lesbos
λέσχη (η) club || **Ελληνική Λέσχη
Αυτοκινήτου και Περιηγήσεων**
Automobile and Touring Club of
Greece
λευκός/ή/ό white || **λευκά είδη**
household linen
λεφτά (τα) money
λέω to say
λεωφορείο (το) bus
λεωφόρος (η) avenue
Λήμνος (η) Lemnos
λήξη (η) expiry
λησμονώ to forget
ληστεία (η) robbery
λιακάδα (η) sunshine

Α	α	"a"
Β	β	"v"
Γ	γ	"gh" *or* "y"
Δ	δ	"dh"
Ε	ε	"e"
Ζ	ζ	"z"
Η	η	"ee"
Θ	θ	"th"
Ι	ι	"ee"
Κ	κ	"k"
Λ	λ	"l"
Μ	μ	"m"
Ν	ν	"n"
Ξ	ξ	"ks"
Ο	ο	"o"
Π	π	"p"
Ρ	ρ	"r"
Σ	σ, ς	"s"
Τ	τ	"t"
Υ	υ	"ee"
Φ	φ	"f"
Χ	χ	"kh"
Ψ	ψ	"ps"
Ω	ω	"o"

λιανικός/ή/ό retail || λιανική πώληση retail sale

λίγος/η/ο a few, a little || λίγο ψημένο rare (*meat*)

λιθρίνι (το) grey mullet

λικέρ (το) liqueur

λιμάνι (το) port, harbour

Λιμενικό Σώμα coastguard

λιμήν (ο) port

λίμνη (η) lake

λίπανση (η) lubrication service

λιποθυμία (η) faint(ing)

λίρα (η) pound || Αγγλική λίρα pound sterling

λίτρο (το) litre

λογαριασμός (ο) bill

λογιστής (ο) accountant

λουκάνικο (το) sausage

λουκανόπιτα (η) sausage pie

λουκούμι (το) Turkish delight

λουλούδι (το) flower

λουτρό (το) bathroom; bath

λύνω to solve; to undo

λυόμενα (τα) prefabricated buildings

λύπη (η) sorrow

λυπούμαι to be sorry

λύσσα (η) rabies

Μ, μ

μα but

μαγαζί (το) shop

μαγειρεύω to cook

μαγιό (το) swimsuit

μαγνητόφωνο (το) tape recorder

μάγουλο (το) cheek

μαέστρος (ο) conductor (*of an orchestra*)

μαζεύω to gather

μαζί together

Α	α	"a"
Β	β	"v"
Γ	γ	"gh" *or* "y"
Δ	δ	"dh"
Ε	ε	"e"
Ζ	ζ	"z"
Η	η	"ee"
Θ	θ	"th"
Ι	ι	"ee"
Κ	κ	"k"
Λ	λ	"l"
Μ	μ	"m"
Ν	ν	"n"
Ξ	ξ	"ks"
Ο	ο	"o"
Π	π	"p"
Ρ	ρ	"r"
Σ	σ, ς	"s"
Τ	τ	"t"
Υ	υ	"ee"
Φ	φ	"f"
Χ	χ	"kh"
Ψ	ψ	"ps"
Ω	ω	"o"

μαθαίνω to learn
μάθημα (το) lesson
μαθητής/μαθή τρια pupil
Μάιος (ο) May
μαϊντανός (ο) parsley
μακαρόνια (τα) macaroni || **μακαρόνια παστίτσιο** macaroni with minced meat and white sauce
μακριά far away
Μαλβοίσια red wine from Sparta
μάλιστα yes
μαλλί (το) wool
μαλλιά (τα) hair
μάλλινος/η/ο woollen
μαμά (η) mum
μανίκι (το) sleeve
μανιτάρι (το) mushroom
μανταρίνι (το) tangerine
μαντήλι (το) handkerchief
Μαντηνία medium dry white wine
μαξιλάρι (το) pillow, cushion
Μαραθών/νας (ο) Marathon
μαργαρίνη (η) margarine
μαργαριτάρι (το) pearl
μαρέγγα (η) meringue
μάρκα (η) make (*of product*)
μάρμαρο (το) marble
μαρμελάδα (η) marmalade
μαρούλι (το) lettuce
Μάρτιος (ο) March
μάτι (το) eye
ματώνω to bleed
Μαυροδάφνη sweet red dessert wine
μαύρος/η/ο black
μαχαίρι (το) knife
μαχαιροπήρουνα (τα) cutlery
μάχη (η) battle, fight
με with
μεγάλος/η/ο large, big
μεγαλώνω to grow up; to bring up
μέγαρο (το) palace; *large building*

Α	α	"a"
Β	β	"v"
Γ	γ	"gh" *or* "y"
Δ	δ	"dh"
Ε	ε	"e"
Ζ	ζ	"z"
Η	η	"ee"
Θ	θ	"th"
Ι	ι	"ee"
Κ	κ	"k"
Λ	λ	"l"
Μ	μ	"m"
Ν	ν	"n"
Ξ	ξ	"ks"
Ο	ο	"o"
Π	π	"p"
Ρ	ρ	"r"
Σ	σ, ς	"s"
Τ	τ	"t"
Υ	υ	"ee"
Φ	φ	"f"
Χ	χ	"kh"
Ψ	ψ	"ps"
Ω	ω	"o"

containing apartments and flats
μέγεθος (το) size
μεζεδάκια (τα) selection of appetisers and salads served as starter
μεθαύριο the day after tomorrow
μεθύσι (το) drunkenness
μεθυσμένος/η/ο drunk
μέλι (το) honey
μέλισσα (η) bee
μελιτζάνα (η) aubergine
μέλος (το) member || **τα μέλη του πληρώματος** crew members
μενού (το) menu
μέρα (η) day
μερίδα (η) portion
μέσα in inside
μεσάνυχτα (τα) midnight
μεσημέρι (το) midday
Μεσόγειος (η) Mediterranean Sea
Μεσολόγγι (το) Messolongi
μέσω via
μετά after
μετακόμιση (η) moving house
μεταλλικός/ή/ό iron
μέταλλο (το) metal
μετάξι (το) silk
μεταξύ between, among || **εν τω μεταξύ** meanwhile
μετασχηματιστής (ο) adaptor
μεταφέρω to transport
μεταφράζω to translate
μεταχειρισμένος/η/ο used, second-hand || **μεταχειρισμένα αυτοκίνητα** second-hand cars
Μετέωρα (τα) the monasteries of Meteora
μετεωρολογικός σταθμός weather centre
μετρητά (τα) cash
μέτριος/α/ο medium
μετρό (το) underground (*railway*)

Α	α	"a"
Β	β	"v"
Γ	γ	"gh" *or* "y"
Δ	δ	"dh"
Ε	ε	"e"
Ζ	ζ	"z"
Η	η	"ee"
Θ	θ	"th"
Ι	ι	"ee"
Κ	κ	"k"
Λ	λ	"l"
Μ	μ	"m"
Ν	ν	"n"
Ξ	ξ	"ks"
Ο	ο	"o"
Π	π	"p"
Ρ	ρ	"r"
Σ	σ, ς	"s"
Τ	τ	"t"
Υ	υ	"ee"
Φ	φ	"f"
Χ	χ	"kh"
Ψ	ψ	"ps"
Ω	ω	"o"

μετρώ to count
μέτωπο (το) forehead
μέχρι until
μη do not || μη καπνίζετε no smoking
|| μη κόπτετε άνθη do not pick flowers
|| μη πατάτε το πράσινο keep off the
grass || μη ρίπτετε σκουπίδια no
dumping (*of rubbish*) || μη σταθμεύετε
no parking || μη στηρίζεστε στην
πόρτα do not lean against the door
μηδέν zero
μηλιά (η) apple tree
μήλο (το) apple
μηλόπιτα (η) apple pie
Μήλος (η) Melos
μήνας (ο) month || μήνας του μέλιτος
honeymoon
μητέρα (η) mother
μητριά (η) stepmother
μηχανή (η) machine; engine || φορητή
μηχανή portable camera
μηχανικός (ο) mechanic, engineer
μια a, an; one (*with feminine nouns*)
μίζα (η) starter (*in car*)
μικρός/ή/ό small, little
μιλώ to speak
μισθός (ο) wage
μισός/ή/ό half
μίσος (το) hatred
μνήμα (το) grave
μόδα (η) fashion || ανδρική μόδα
fashions for men
μοιράζω to share
μολύβι (το) pencil
μόλυνση (η) infection
μοναστήρι (το) monastery
μονόδρομος (ο) one-way street
μονοπάτι (το) path
μόνος/η/ο alone, only || μόνο είσοδος/
έξοδος entrance/exit only
μονός/ή/ό single

Α	α	"a"
Β	β	"v"
Γ	γ	"gh" *or* "y"
Δ	δ	"dh"
Ε	ε	"e"
Ζ	ζ	"z"
Η	η	"ee"
Θ	θ	"th"
Ι	ι	"ee"
Κ	κ	"k"
Λ	λ	"l"
Μ	μ	"m"
Ν	ν	"n"
Ξ	ξ	"ks"
Ο	ο	"o"
Π	π	"p"
Ρ	ρ	"r"
Σ	σ, ς	"s"
Τ	τ	"t"
Υ	υ	"ee"
Φ	φ	"f"
Χ	χ	"kh"
Ψ	ψ	"ps"
Ω	ω	"o"

Μόντε Χρήστος sweet red Cyprus wine

μοσχάρι (το) calf; veal || **μοσχάρι κρασάτο** veal cooked in wine || **μοσχάρι ψητό** roast veal

μοσχάτο dark red dessert wine with a muscatel flavour

μοτοσυκλέτα (η) motorcycle

μου my || **το παλτό μου** my coat

μουσείο (το) museum || **Αρχαιολογικό Μουσείο** Archaeological Museum || **Μουσείο Λαϊκής Τέχνης** Folk Museum

μουσική (η) music || **μουσικά όργανα** musical instruments

μουσκεύω to get wet

μουστάκι (το) moustache

μουστάρδα (η) mustard

μπαίνω to enter

μπακάλης (ο) grocer

μπακλαβάς (ο) a sweet made of flaky pastry stuffed with almonds and syrup

μπαλκόνι (το) balcony

μπάμια (η) okra

μπαμπάς (ο) dad

μπανάνα (η) banana

μπάνιο (το) bathroom; bath

μπαρμπούνι (το) red mullet

μπαταρία (η) battery

μπαχαρικά (τα) spices

μπέικον (το) bacon

μπιζού (τα) jewellery

μπιζέλι (το) pea

μπισκότο (το) biscuit

μπιφτέκι (το) steak

μπλε blue

μπλούζα (η) blouse

μπόρα (η) shower (*of rain*)

μπορώ to be able to

μπουζούκι (το) bouzouki

μπουκάλα (η) bottle || **μπουκάλα μεγάλη** large bottle || **μικρή μπουκάλα**

Α	α	"a"
Β	β	"v"
Γ	γ	"gh" *or* "y"
Δ	δ	"dh"
Ε	ε	"e"
Ζ	ζ	"z"
Η	η	"ee"
Θ	θ	"th"
Ι	ι	"ee"
Κ	κ	"k"
Λ	λ	"l"
Μ	μ	"m"
Ν	ν	"n"
Ξ	ξ	"ks"
Ο	ο	"o"
Π	π	"p"
Ρ	ρ	"r"
Σ	σ, ς	"s"
Τ	τ	"t"
Υ	υ	"ee"
Φ	φ	"f"
Χ	χ	"kh"
Ψ	ψ	"ps"
Ω	ω	"o"

half bottle
μπουρνούζι (το) bathrobe
Μπουτάρη dry red wine from Naoussa
μπράβο well done
μπριζόλα (η) steak
μπροστά in front
μπρούντζος (ο) brass
μπρούσικο dry red wine from Southern
  Greece
μπύρα (η) beer
μυαλό (το) brain
μύγα (η) fly (*insect*)
μυθολογία (η) mythology
μύθος (ο) myth
Μυκήναι/ες (οι) Mycenae
Μύκονος (η) Mykonos
μυρμήγκι (το) ant
μυστικό (το) secret
Μυστράς (ο) Mistras
μύτη (η) nose
Μυτιλήνη (η) Mytilini
μωρό (το) baby || **για μωρά** for babies
μωσαϊκό (το) mosaic

Ν, ν

να to, in order to
ναι yes
Νάξος (η) Naxos
ναός (ο) temple, church || **καθεδρικός
ναός** cathedral
ναρκωτικά (τα) drugs
ναύλα (τα) fare
νάυλον nylon
ναυλωμένος/η/ο chartered || **ναυλωμένη
πτήση** charter flight
ναύτης (ο) sailor
ναυτία (η) travel sickness
ναυτικός όμιλος sailing club

A	α	"a"
B	β	"v"
Γ	γ	"gh" *or* "y"
Δ	δ	"dh"
E	ε	"e"
Z	ζ	"z"
H	η	"ee"
Θ	θ	"th"
I	ι	"ee"
K	κ	"k"
Λ	λ	"l"
M	μ	"m"
N	ν	"n"
Ξ	ξ	"ks"
O	ο	"o"
Π	π	"p"
P	ρ	"r"
Σ	σ, ς	"s"
T	τ	"t"
Y	υ	"ee"
Φ	φ	"f"
X	χ	"kh"
Ψ	ψ	"ps"
Ω	ω	"o"

ναυτιλιακά yacht chandler
νεκρός/ή/ό dead
νεκροταφείο (το) cemetery
νεοελληνικά (τα) Modern Greek
νεολαία (η) youth
νέος/α/ο new; young
νερό (το) water ‖ **επιτραπέζιο νερό** still mineral water ‖ **μεταλλικό νερό** mineral water ‖ **πόσιμο νερό** drinking water
νεσκαφέ (το) instant coffee
νευρικό σύστημα nervous system
νεύρο (το) nerve
νέφος (το) cloud
νεφρό (το) kidney
νεωτερισμός (ο) improvement; novelty ‖ **κατάστημα νεωτερισμών** novelties; fashions
νηπιαγωγείο (το) nursery school
νησί (το) island
νησίδα (η) traffic island, central reservation
νίκη (η) victory
Νοέμβριος (ο) November
νοίκι (το) rent
νομαρχία (η) administration offices of a nomos
νομίζω to think
νόμιμος/η/ο legal
νόμισμα (το) coin ‖ **επιστροφή νομισμάτων** returned coins
νομισματοδέκτης (ο) coin-operated telephone ‖ **αστικός νομισματοδέκτης** coin-operated phone for local calls ‖ **υπεραστικός νομισματοδέκτης** coin-operated phone for long-distance calls
νόμος (ο) law
νομός (ο) nomos, Greek administrative unit
νονός/ά godfather/godmother
νοσοκομείο (το) hospital

Α	α	"a"
Β	β	"v"
Γ	γ	"gh" or "y"
Δ	δ	"dh"
Ε	ε	"e"
Ζ	ζ	"z"
Η	η	"ee"
Θ	θ	"th"
Ι	ι	"ee"
Κ	κ	"k"
Λ	λ	"l"
Μ	μ	"m"
Ν	ν	"n"
Ξ	ξ	"ks"
Ο	ο	"o"
Π	π	"p"
Ρ	ρ	"r"
Σ	σ, ς	"s"
Τ	τ	"t"
Υ	υ	"ee"
Φ	φ	"f"
Χ	χ	"kh"
Ψ	ψ	"ps"
Ω	ω	"o"

νοσοκόμος/α nurse
νόστιμος/η/ο tasty, attractive
νότιος/α/ο southern
νότος (ο) south
νους (ο) mind
ντολμαδάκια (τα) stuffed vine leaves
ντομάτα (η) tomato
ντουζίνα (η) dozen
ντουλάπα (η) wardrobe
ντουλάπι (το) cupboard
ντους (το) shower (*in bath*)
νωρίς (το) early
νωρίτερα earlier
ντρέπομαι to be shy; to be ashamed
ντυμένος/η/ο dressed
νυστάζω to feel sleepy
νύφη (η) sister-in-law; bride; daughter-in-law
νύχι (το) nail (*on finger*)
νύχτα (η) night
νυχτερίδα (η) bat (*animal*)
νυχτερινός/ή/ό all-night (*chemist's etc*)
νυχτικό (το) nightdress

Ξ, ξ

ξάδερφος/η cousin
ξανά again
ξαναλέω to repeat
ξανθός/ή/ό blond
ξαπλώνω to lie down
ξαφνικά suddenly
ξεγελώ to deceive
ξεκινώ to start, set off
ξεναγός (ο/η) guide
ξενοδοχείο (το) hotel || **κρατήσεις ξενοδοχείων** hotel reservations
ξένος/η/ο strange, foreign || **ξένος/η** stranger, foreigner; visitor

Α	α	"a"
Β	β	"v"
Γ	γ	"gh" *or* "y"
Δ	δ	"dh"
Ε	ε	"e"
Ζ	ζ	"z"
Η	η	"ee"
Θ	θ	"th"
Ι	ι	"ee"
Κ	κ	"k"
Λ	λ	"l"
Μ	μ	"m"
Ν	ν	"n"
Ξ	ξ	"ks"
Ο	ο	"o"
Π	π	"p"
Ρ	ρ	"r"
Σ	σ, ς	"s"
Τ	τ	"t"
Υ	υ	"ee"
Φ	φ	"f"
Χ	χ	"kh"
Ψ	ψ	"ps"
Ω	ω	"o"

ξενώνας (ο) guest house
ξεπερνώ to surpass
ξέρω to know
ξεσκεπάζω to uncover
ξεχνώ to forget
ξεχωρίζω to separate
ξηρά (η) dry land
ξηρός/ή/ό dry ‖ ξηροί καρποί dried
 fruits
ξινός/ή/ό sour
ξιφίας (ο) swordfish
ξύδι (το) vinegar
ξύλο (το) wood
ξυπνητήρι (το) alarm clock
ξυπνώ to wake up, rouse
ξύρισμα (το) shaving
ξυριστική μηχανή (η) shaver

Ο, ο

ο the (*with masculine nouns*)
ογδόντα eighty
όγδοος/η/ο eighth
οδηγία (η) instruction ‖ οδηγίες
 χρήσεως instructions for use
οδηγός (ο) driver; guidebook ‖ σήμα
 στον οδηγό signal to the driver (*"stop"
 button in bus*)
οδηγώ to drive
οδική βοήθεια breakdown service
οδοντιατρείο (το) dental surgery
οδοντίατρος, οδοντογιατρός (ο/η)
 dentist
οδοντόκρεμα (η) toothpaste
οδοντοστοιχία (η) denture(s)
οδός (η) road, street
Oθέλλος medium dry red wine from
 Cyprus
οθόνη (η) screen

Α	α	"a"
Β	β	"v"
Γ	γ	"gh" *or* "y"
Δ	δ	"dh"
Ε	ε	"e"
Ζ	ζ	"z"
Η	η	"ee"
Θ	θ	"th"
Ι	ι	"ee"
Κ	κ	"k"
Λ	λ	"l"
Μ	μ	"m"
Ν	ν	"n"
Ξ	ξ	"ks"
Ο	ο	"o"
Π	π	"p"
Ρ	ρ	"r"
Σ	σ, ς	"s"
Τ	τ	"t"
Υ	υ	"ee"
Φ	φ	"f"
Χ	χ	"kh"
Ψ	ψ	"ps"
Ω	ω	"o"

οικογένεια (η) family
οικονομική θέση economy class
οικόπεδο (το) plot of land
οίκος (ο) house || **οίκος μόδας** fashion
house
οινομαγειρείο (το) licensed restaurant
οινοπνευματώδη ποτά spirits
οίνος (ο) wine
οκτώ eight
Οκτώβριος (ο) October
όλα everything
ολισθηρό οδόστρωμα slippery road
surface
όλος/η/ο all of, the whole of
Ολυμπία (η) Olympia
Ολυμπιακή (η), Ολυμπιακές
Αερογραμμές Olympic Airways
Ολυμπιακό Στάδιο Olympic stadium
Ολυμπιακοί Αγώνες Olympic games
Όλυμπος (ο) Mount Olympus
ομάδα (η) team, group
ομελέτα (η) omelette
ομιλία (η) talk, speech
όμιλος (ο) club || **ναυτικός όμιλος**
sailing club
ομίχλη (η) fog
ομολογώ to admit, confess
Ομόνοια (η) Omonia Square (*in Athens*)
ομορφιά (η) beauty
ομπρέλλα (η) umbrella
όμως but
όνειρο (το) dream
όνομα (το) name
ονοματεπώνυμο (το) full name
όπερα (η) opera
οπτικά optician
όπως like, as
οπωσδήποτε definitely
οργανισμός (ο) organisation
 || **Οργανισμός Σιδηροδρόμων Ελλάδος**
Greek Railways || **Οργανισμός**

Α	α	"a"
Β	β	"v"
Γ	γ	"gh" *or* "y"
Δ	δ	"dh"
Ε	ε	"e"
Ζ	ζ	"z"
Η	η	"ee"
Θ	θ	"th"
Ι	ι	"ee"
Κ	κ	"k"
Λ	λ	"l"
Μ	μ	"m"
Ν	ν	"n"
Ξ	ξ	"ks"
Ο	ο	"o"
Π	π	"p"
Ρ	ρ	"r"
Σ	σ, ς	"s"
Τ	τ	"t"
Υ	υ	"ee"
Φ	φ	"f"
Χ	χ	"kh"
Ψ	ψ	"ps"
Ω	ω	"o"

Τηλεπικοινωνιών Ελλάδος Greek Telecommunications
οργανώνω to organise
οργανωμένος/η/ο organised
ορεκτικό (το) starter, appetiser
όρεξη (η) appetite || **καλή όρεξη** enjoy your meal!
ορθόδοξος/η/ο orthodox
ορκίζομαι to swear
όρκος (ο) oath
όρος (ο) condition || **όροι ενοικιάσεως** conditions of hire
όρος (το) mountain
όροφος (ο) floor, storey
οσο as
όταν when
OTE = Οργανισμός Τηλεπικοινωνιών Ελλάδος
Ουαλία (η) Wales
ούζο (το) ouzo, aniseed-flavoured spirit
ουρά (η) tail; queue
ουρανός (ο) sky
ουρολόγος (ο) urologist
οφθαλμίατρος (ο/η) eye specialist
όχημα (το) vehicle
όχθη (η) bank (*of river*)
όχι no

Π, π

παγάκι (το) ice cube
παγίδα (η) trap
παϊδάκια (τα) lamb chops
πάγκος (ο) bench
πάγος (ο) ice
παγωμένος/η/ο frozen || **μία μπύρα παγωμένη** one cold beer
παγωτό (το) ice cream
παζαρεύω to haggle

A	α	"a"
B	β	"v"
Γ	γ	"gh" *or* "y"
Δ	δ	"dh"
E	ε	"e"
Z	ζ	"z"
H	η	"ee"
Θ	θ	"th"
I	ι	"ee"
K	κ	"k"
Λ	λ	"l"
M	μ	"m"
N	ν	"n"
Ξ	ξ	"ks"
O	ο	"o"
Π	π	"p"
P	ρ	"r"
Σ	σ, ς	"s"
T	τ	"t"
Y	υ	"ee"
Φ	φ	"f"
X	χ	"kh"
Ψ	ψ	"ps"
Ω	ω	"o"

παιδί (το) child
παιδίατρος (ο/η) paediatrician
παιδικός/ή/ό for children || παιδικά
children's wear || παιδικός σταθμός
crèche || παιδικά σωσίβια children's
life jackets
παίζω to play
παιχνίδι (το) game, toy
πακέτο (το) parcel, packet
παλάτι (το) palace
πάλι again
παλιός/ά/ό old
Παλλήνη white wine from Attica
παλτό (το) coat
πάνα (η) nappy
Παναγία (η) the Virgin Mary
πανδοχείο (το) inn
πανεπιστήμιο (το) university
πανήγυρις (η) festivity, fair
πανσιόν (η) guesthouse
πάντα always
παντελόνι (το) trousers
παντοπωλείο (το) grocer's
πάντοτε always
παντού everywhere
παντόφλες (οι) slippers
πάνω on, upper
παξιμάδι (το) nut (for bolt)
παπάς (ο) priest
Πάπας (ο) Pope
πάπια (η) duck
παπάκι (το) duckling
πάπλωμα (το) duvet
παπούτσι (το) shoe
παππούς (ο) grandfather
παραβιάζω to violate, break (law)
παραγγελία (η) order, message
παραγωγή (η) production || Ελληνικής
παραγωγής produce of Greece
παράδειγμα (το) example
παράδεισος (ο) heaven

Α	α	"a"
Β	β	"v"
Γ	γ	"gh" *or* "y"
Δ	δ	"dh"
Ε	ε	"e"
Ζ	ζ	"z"
Η	η	"ee"
Θ	θ	"th"
Ι	ι	"ee"
Κ	κ	"k"
Λ	λ	"l"
Μ	μ	"m"
Ν	ν	"n"
Ξ	ξ	"ks"
Ο	ο	"o"
Π	π	"p"
Ρ	ρ	"r"
Σ	σ, ς	"s"
Τ	τ	"t"
Υ	υ	"ee"
Φ	φ	"f"
Χ	χ	"kh"
Ψ	ψ	"ps"
Ω	ω	"o"

παράδοση (η) delivery; tradition
παραθαλάσσιος/α/ο by the sea, coastal
παράθυρο (το) window
παραίτηση (η) resignation
παρακαλώ please
παρακαμπτήριος diversion
παραλαβή (η) collection
παραλία (η) seashore
παραμάνα (η) safety pin
παραμελώ to neglect
παράνομος/η/ο illegal
παράξενα strangely
παράπονο (το) complaint
Παρασκευή (η) Friday
παράσταση (η) performance
παράταση (η) extension
παρατηρώ to observe
παρέα (η) company
παρεξήγηση (η) misunderstanding
παρηγοριά (η) comfort, consolation
Παρθένος (η) the Virgin Mary
Παρθενών/ώνας (ο) the Parthenon
πάρκο (το) park
παρμπρίζ (το) windscreen
Παρνασσός (ο) Mount Parnassus
παρόμοιος/α/ο similar
Πάρος (η) Paros
παρουσία (η) presence
παρουσιάζω to present
πάστα (η) pastry
παστέλι (το) honey and sesame seed
  bar
Πάσχα (το) Easter
πατάτα (η) potato || πατάτες πουρέ
  mashed potatoes || πατάτες πηγανιτές
  chips || πατάτες φούρνου roast potatoes
πατέρας (ο) father
Πάτμος (η) Patmos
Πάτρα (η) Patras
πατώ to step || μη πατάτε το πράσινο
  keep off the grass

A	α	"a"
B	β	"v"
Γ	γ	"gh" *or* "y"
Δ	δ	"dh"
E	ε	"e"
Z	ζ	"z"
H	η	"ee"
Θ	θ	"th"
I	ι	"ee"
K	κ	"k"
Λ	λ	"l"
M	μ	"m"
N	ν	"n"
Ξ	ξ	"ks"
O	o	"o"
Π	π	"p"
P	ρ	"r"
Σ	σ, ς	"s"
T	τ	"t"
Y	υ	"ee"
Φ	φ	"f"
X	χ	"kh"
Ψ	ψ	"ps"
Ω	ω	"o"

πάτωμα (το) floor
παυσίπονο (το) painkiller
πάω to go
πεδιάδα (η) plain
πέδιλα (τα) sandals
πεζοδρόμιο (το) pavement
πεζόδρομος (ο) pedestrian area
πεζός (ο) pedestrian
πεθερά (η) mother-in-law
πεθερός (ο) father-in-law
πείνα (η) hunger
πεινώ to be hungry
πείρα (η) experience
πείραμα (το) experiment
Πειραιάς, Πειραιεύς (ο) Piraeus
πείσμα (το) obstinacy
πελάτης/τισσα customer
Πελοπόννησος (η) Peloponnese
Πέμπτη (η) Thursday
πέμπτος/η/ο fifth
πέννα (η) pen
πενήντα fifty
πέντε five
Πεντέλη medium dry red wine
πεπόνι (το) melon
πέρδικα (η) partridge
περηφάνεια (η) pride
περιβόλι (το) orchard
περιγιάλι (το) seashore
περιγραφή (η) description
περιέργεια (η) curiosity
περιεχόμενο (το) content(s)
περιμένω to wait
περιοδικό (το) magazine
περίοδος (η) period
περιουσία (η) property
περιοχή (η) area
περίπατος (ο) walk
περιποίηση (η) looking after, care
περίπου nearly, almost
περίπτερο (το) kiosk

A	α	"a"
B	β	"v"
Γ	γ	"gh" or "y"
Δ	δ	"dh"
E	ε	"e"
Z	ζ	"z"
H	η	"ee"
Θ	θ	"th"
I	ι	"ee"
K	κ	"k"
Λ	λ	"l"
M	μ	"m"
N	ν	"n"
Ξ	ξ	"ks"
O	ο	"o"
Π	π	"p"
P	ρ	"r"
Σ	σ, ς	"s"
T	τ	"t"
Y	υ	"ee"
Φ	φ	"f"
X	χ	"kh"
Ψ	ψ	"ps"
Ω	ω	"o"

περισσότερο more
περιστέρι (το) pigeon, dove
περιφρονώ to despise
περνώ to pass; to cross the road
περπατώ to walk
πέρ(υ)σι last year
πεταλούδα (η) butterfly
πετονιά (η) fishing line
πέτρα (η) stone
πετρέλαιο (το) oil, diesel fuel
πετσέτα (η) napkin, towel
πετώ to fly; to throw out
πεύκο (το) pine tree
πέφτω to fall
πηγάδι (το) well (*for water*)
πηγαίνω to go
πηγούνι (το) chin
πηδώ to jump
πήλινος/η/ο (of) clay
πηρούνι (το) fork
πιάτο (το) plate
πιέζω to press || **πιέσατε** push
πίεση (η) pressure
πικρός/ή/ό bitter
πιλάφι (το) pilau
πιλότος (ο) pilot
πινακίδα (η) sign; name/number plate
πινακοθήκη (η) art gallery
Πίνδος (η) Pindos
πίνω to drink
πίπα (η) pipe
πιπέρι (το) pepper || **πιπεριές γεμιστές**
  stuffed peppers
πισίνα (η) swimming pool
πιστεύω to believe
πιστολάκι (το) (small, hand-held)
  hairdrier
πιστοποιητικό (το) certificate
  || **πιστοποιητικό εμβολιασμού**
  vaccination certificate
πίστωση (η) credit

A	α	"a"
B	β	"v"
Γ	γ	"gh" *or* "y"
Δ	δ	"dh"
E	ε	"e"
Z	ζ	"z"
H	η	"ee"
Θ	θ	"th"
I	ι	"ee"
K	κ	"k"
Λ	λ	"l"
M	μ	"m"
N	ν	"n"
Ξ	ξ	"ks"
O	ο	"o"
Π	π	"p"
P	ρ	"r"
Σ	σ, ς	"s"
T	τ	"t"
Y	υ	"ee"
Φ	φ	"f"
X	χ	"kh"
Ψ	ψ	"ps"
Ω	ω	"o"

πιστωτικές κάρτες credit cards
πίσω behind; back
πίτα (η) pie
πίτσα (η) pizza
πιτσαρία (η) pizzeria
πλάι next to
πλαγιά (η) hillside
πλαγιάζω to lie down
πλαζ (η) beach
Πλάκα (η) Plaka, area at the foot of the Acropolis
πλαστικός/ή/ό plastic
πλατεία (η) square
πλάτη (η) back
πλατίνα (η) platinum
πλατίνες (οι) points (*in car*)
πλατύ/ιά/ύ wide, broad
πλεκτά (τα) knitwear
πλένω to wash
πληγή (η) wound
πλήθος (το) crowd
πληροφορίες (οι information
 || **πληροφορίες δρομολογίων** travel information
πλήρωμα (το) crew || **τα μέλη του πληρώματος** members of the crew
πληρωμή (η) payment || **ευκολίες πληρωμής** credit facilities
πλησιάζω to approach
πληρώνω to pay
πλοίο (το) ship
πλούσιος/α/ο rich
πλυντήριο (το) washing machine || **πλυντήριο αυτοκινήτων** car wash
πλύσιμο wash(ing) || **πλύσιμο αυτοκινήτων** car wash
πνεύμονας (ο) lung
πνίγω to suffocate
ποδήλατο (το) bicycle
ποδηλάτης (ο) cyclist
πόδι (το) foot

A	α	"a"
B	β	"v"
Γ	γ	"gh" *or* "y"
Δ	δ	"dh"
E	ε	"e"
Z	ζ	"z"
H	η	"ee"
Θ	θ	"th"
I	ι	"ee"
K	κ	"k"
Λ	λ	"l"
M	μ	"m"
N	ν	"n"
Ξ	ξ	"ks"
O	ο	"o"
Π	π	"p"
P	ρ	"r"
Σ	σ, ς	"s"
T	τ	"t"
Y	υ	"ee"
Φ	φ	"f"
X	χ	"kh"
Ψ	ψ	"ps"
Ω	ω	"o"

ποδόσφαιρο (το) football
ποιος/α/ο who
ποιότητα (η) quality
πόλεμος (ο) war
πόλη/ις (η) town
πολιτισμός (ο) civilisation
πολλοί many
πολυκατάστημα (το) department store
πολυκατοικία (η) block of flats
πολυκλινική (η) privately-run general clinic
πολύς/πολλή/πολύ many; much
πολλοί many
πολυτεχνείο (το) polytechnic
πονόδοντος (ο) toothache
πονοκέφαλος (ο) headache
πονόλαιμος (ο) sore throat
πόνος (ο) pain
πονώ to hurt
Πόρος (ο) Poros
πόρτα (η) door
πορτοκαλάδα (η) orange squash
πορτοκάλι (το) orange || χυμός πορτοκάλι orange juice
πορτοκαλί orange (*colour*)
πορτοκαλιά (η) orange tree
πορτοφόλι (το) wallet
πόσα how many
πόσο; how much? || πόσο κάνει; how much is it?
ποσοστό (το) rate, percentage || ποσοστό υπηρεσίας service charge
ποσότητα (η) quantity
ποτάμι (το) river
πότε; when?
ποτέ never
ποτήρι (το) glass (*for drinking*)
ποτό (το) drink
πού; where? || πού είναι; where is it?
πουκάμισο (το) shirt
πουλί (το) bird

Α	α	"a"
Β	β	"v"
Γ	γ	"gh" *or* "y"
Δ	δ	"dh"
Ε	ε	"e"
Ζ	ζ	"z"
Η	η	"ee"
Θ	θ	"th"
Ι	ι	"ee"
Κ	κ	"k"
Λ	λ	"l"
Μ	μ	"m"
Ν	ν	"n"
Ξ	ξ	"ks"
Ο	ο	"o"
Π	π	"p"
Ρ	ρ	"r"
Σ	σ, ς	"s"
Τ	τ	"t"
Υ	υ	"ee"
Φ	φ	"f"
Χ	χ	"kh"
Ψ	ψ	"ps"
Ω	ω	"o"

πούλμαν (το) coach
πουλώ to sell
πουρμπουάρ (το) tip (*to waiter etc*)
πούρο (το) cigar
πράγμα (το) thing
πράκτορας (ο) agent
πρακτορείο (το) agency
πραξικόπημα (το) coup
πράσινος/η/ο green
πρατήριο (το) specialist shop
  || πρατήριο βενζίνης petrol station
  || πρατήριο άρτου baker's
Πρέβεζα (η) Preveza
πρέπει it is necessary
πρεσβεία (η) embassy
πρεσβευτής (ο) ambassador
πρίζα (η) plug; socket
πριν before
προάστειο (το) suburb
πρόγευμα (το) breakfast
πρόγραμμα (το) programme
πρόεδρος (ο) president || προεδρικό
  μέγαρο presidential palace
προειδοποίηση (η) warning
προετοιμάζω to prepare
πρόθυμος/η/ο willing
προίκα (η) dowry
προϊόν (το) product || Ελληνικό προϊόν
  Greek product
προϊστάμενος (ο) manager, boss
προκαταβολή (η) deposit
προξενείο (το) consulate
πρόξενος (ο) consul
πρόοδος (η) progress
προορισμός (ο) destination
προπληρώνω to pay in advance
Προ-πο Greek football pools
προσγείωση (η) landing
προσδεθείτε fasten your safety belts
προσεκτικός/ή/ό careful
πρόσκληση (η) invitation

A	α	"a"
B	β	"v"
Γ	γ	"gh" *or* "y"
Δ	δ	"dh"
E	ε	"e"
Z	ζ	"z"
H	η	"ee"
Θ	θ	"th"
I	ι	"ee"
K	κ	"k"
Λ	λ	"l"
M	μ	"m"
N	ν	"n"
Ξ	ξ	"ks"
O	ο	"o"
Π	π	"p"
P	ρ	"r"
Σ	σ, ς	"s"
T	τ	"t"
Y	υ	"ee"
Φ	φ	"f"
X	χ	"kh"
Ψ	ψ	"ps"
Ω	ω	"o"

προσοχή (η) attention
προσπαθώ to try
προστατεύω to protect
πρόστιμο (το) fine
πρόσωπο (το) face
προσωρινός/ή/ό temporary
προτιμώ to prefer
προφυλακτήρας (ο) bumper (*of car*)
πρόχειρος/η/ο handy; impromptu
|| **πρόχειρο φαγητό** snacks
προχθές the day before yesterday
πρωθυπουργός prime minister
πρωί (το) morning
πρωινός/ή/ό of the morning || **το
πρωινό** breakfast
πρωτεύουσα (η) capital city
πρωτομαγιά May Day
πρώτος/η/ο first || **πρώτες βοήθειες** first
aid || **πρώτη θέση** first class
πρωτοχρονιά (η) New Year's Day
πτήση (η) flight || **πτήσεις εξωτερικού**
international flights || **πτήσεις
εσωτερικού** domestic flights || **αριθμός
πτήσης** flight number || **ναυλωμένη
πτήση** charter flight || **τακτικές πτήσεις**
scheduled flights
πυζάμες (υι) pyjamas
πυκνός/ή/ό thick, dense
πύλη (η) gate
πύργος (ο) castle, tower
πυρετός (ο) fever
πυρκαγιά (η) fire
πυροσβεστήρας (ο) fire extinguisher
πυροσβέστης (ο) fireman
πυροσβεστική (η) fire brigade
|| **πυροσβεστική υπηρεσία** fire brigade
|| **πυροσβεστική φωλεά** *case where fire-
fighting equipment is kept*
|| **πυροσβεστικός σταθμός** fire station
πώληση (η) sale || **λιανική πώληση**
retail sale || **χονδρική πώληση**

A	α	"a"
B	β	"v"
Γ	γ	"gh" *or* "y"
Δ	δ	"dh"
E	ε	"e"
Z	ζ	"z"
H	η	"ee"
Θ	θ	"th"
I	ι	"ee"
K	κ	"k"
Λ	λ	"l"
M	μ	"m"
N	ν	"n"
Ξ	ξ	"ks"
O	ο	"o"
Π	π	"p"
P	ρ	"r"
Σ	σ, ς	"s"
T	τ	"t"
Y	υ	"ee"
Φ	φ	"f"
X	χ	"kh"
Ψ	ψ	"ps"
Ω	ω	"o"

wholesale
πωλητής/πωλήτρια sales assistant
|| **αυτόματος πωλητής γραμματοσήμων**
stamp machine
πωλώ to sell || **πωλείται, πωλούνται**
for sale
πως that
πώς; how?

Ρ, ρ

ράβω to sew
ραδιενέργεια (η) radioactivity
ραδιόφωνο (το) radio
ραντάρ (το) radar
ραντεβού (το) appointment, date
ράφτης (ο) tailor
ρεζέρβα (η) spare wheel
Ρέθυμνο (το) Rethymno
ρέστα (τα) change (*money*)
ρετσίνα (η) retsina (*resinated white
wine*)
ρεύμα (το) current
ρευματισμοί (οι) rheumatism
ρήτορας (ο) orator
ρόδα (η) wheel
ροδάκινο (το) peach
ρόδι (το) pomegranate
ροδίτικο red wine from Rhodes
Ρόδος (η) Rhodes
ροζ pink
ρολόι (το) watch, clock
Ρομπόλα dry white wine from
Kefallinia
ρούμι (το) rum
ρουμπίνι (το) ruby
ρούχα (τα) clothes
ρύζι (το) rice
ρυζόγαλο (το) rice pudding

Α	α	"a"
Β	β	"v"
Γ	γ	"gh" *or* "y"
Δ	δ	"dh"
Ε	ε	"e"
Ζ	ζ	"z"
Η	η	"ee"
Θ	θ	"th"
Ι	ι	"ee"
Κ	κ	"k"
Λ	λ	"l"
Μ	μ	"m"
Ν	ν	"n"
Ξ	ξ	"ks"
Ο	ο	"o"
Π	π	"p"
Ρ	ρ	"r"
Σ	σ, ς	"s"
Τ	τ	"t"
Υ	υ	"ee"
Φ	φ	"f"
Χ	χ	"kh"
Ψ	ψ	"ps"
Ω	ω	"o"

ρυθμίζω to adjust
ρυμουλκώ to tow away
ρύπανση (η) pollution
ρυτίδα (η) wrinkle
ρωτώ to ask

Σ, σ, ς

Σάββατο (το) Saturday
Σαββατοκύριακο (το) weekend
σαγόνι (το) jaw
σακκάκι (το) jacket
σακκούλα (η) bag (*paper or plastic*)
σαλάμι (το) salami
Σαλαμίνα (η) Salamis
σαλάτα (η) salad
σαλιγκάρι (το) snail
σαλόνι (το) sitting room
σάλτσα (η) sauce
Σαμοθράκη (η) Samothrace
Σάμος (η) Samos
σαμπάνια (η) champagne
σαμπουάν (το) shampoo
Σαντορίνη (η) Santorini
σάντουιτς (το) sandwich
σαπούνι (το) soap
σαράντα forty
Σαρωνικός (ο) Saronic gulf
σας your (*plural*) || **το σπίτι σας** your house
σάτυρα (η) satire
σάτυρος (ο) satyr
σαύρα (η) lizard
σβήνω to extinguish, switch off || **σβήστε τα τσιγάρα σας** put out your cigarettes
σεβασμός (ο) respect
σειρά (η) turn; row; series
σεισμός (ο) earthquake

Α	α	"a"
Β	β	"v"
Γ	γ	"gh" *or* "y"
Δ	δ	"dh"
Ε	ε	"e"
Ζ	ζ	"z"
Η	η	"ee"
Θ	θ	"th"
Ι	ι	"ee"
Κ	κ	"k"
Λ	λ	"l"
Μ	μ	"m"
Ν	ν	"n"
Ξ	ξ	"ks"
Ο	ο	"o"
Π	π	"p"
Ρ	ρ	"r"
Σ	σ, ς	"s"
Τ	τ	"t"
Υ	υ	"ee"
Φ	φ	"f"
Χ	χ	"kh"
Ψ	ψ	"ps"
Ω	ω	"o"

σελίδα (η) page
σεντόνι (το) sheet
σεξ (το) sex
Σεπτέμβριος (ο) September
σερβίρω to serve
σέρβις (το) service
σεφ (ο) chef
σεφταλιά (η) spicy minced meat kebab
σηκώνομαι to get up
σηκώνω to raise, lift
σήμα (το) sign, signal || σήμα
κατατεθέν trade mark || σήμα κινδύνου
emergency signal || σήμα στον οδηγό
signal to the driver (*to stop*)
σημαία (η) flag
σημαίνω to mean || τι σημαίνει; what
does it mean?
σημείωμα (το) note
σήμερα today
σιγά slowly
σίγουρος/η/ο certain, safe
σίδερο (το) iron
σιδερώνω to iron
σιδηρόδρομος (ο) train; railway
|| σιδηροδρομικός σταθμός railway
station || σιδηροδρομικώς by rail
σιτάρι (το) wheat
σιωπή (η) silence
σκάβω to dig
σκάλα (η) ladder, staircase
σκαλί (το) step
σκάφος (το) vessel || στο σκάφος on
board || σκάφη ανοιχτής θαλάσσης
open sea vessels || φουσκωτά σκάφη
inflatable boats
σκελετός (ο) skeleton
σκεπάζω to cover
σκέτος/η/ο plain || ένας καφές σκέτος
coffee without sugar || ένα σκέτο
ουίσκυ a neat whisky
σκέφτομαι to think

Α	α	"a"
Β	β	"v"
Γ	γ	"gh" *or* "y"
Δ	δ	"dh"
Ε	ε	"e"
Ζ	ζ	"z"
Η	η	"ee"
Θ	θ	"th"
Ι	ι	"ee"
Κ	κ	"k"
Λ	λ	"l"
Μ	μ	"m"
Ν	ν	"n"
Ξ	ξ	"ks"
Ο	ο	"o"
Π	π	"p"
Ρ	ρ	"r"
Σ	σ, ς	"s"
Τ	τ	"t"
Υ	υ	"ee"
Φ	φ	"f"
Χ	χ	"kh"
Ψ	ψ	"ps"
Ω	ω	"o"

σκηνή (η) tent; stage
σκι ski ‖ σαλάσσιο σκι water ski(ing)
σκιά (η) shadow, shade
σκίζω to tear
Σκιάθος (η) Skiathos
σκληρός/ή/ό hard
σκοινί (το) rope
σκόνη (η) dust
σκοπός (ο) purpose
σκορδαλιά (η) garlic sauce
σκόρδο (το) garlic
σκοτάδι (το) darkness
σκοτώνω to kill
σκούπα (η) broom
σκουπίδι (το) rubbish, refuse
σκουπίζω to sweep
σκύβω to bend down
σκυλί (το) dog
Σκωτία (η) Scotland
σμαράγδι (το) emerald
σοβαρός/ή/ό serious
σόδα (η) soda
σοκάκι (το) narrow street
σοκολάτα (η) chocolate
σόλα (η) sole (of shoe)
σολομός (ο) salmon
σόμπα (η) heater
σου your ‖ το βιβλίο σου your book
σούβλα (η) skewer; lamb cooked on a skewer over charcoal
σουβλάκι (το) kebab
σουγιάς (ο) penknife
Σούνιο (το) Sounio
σούπα (η) soup
σουπερμάρκετ (το) supermarket
σουτιέν (το) bra
σπάγγος (ο) string
σπάζω to break
σπανάκι (το) spinach
σπανακόπιτα (η) spinach pie
σπάνιος/α/ο rare

A	α	"a"
B	β	"v"
Γ	γ	"gh" or "y"
Δ	δ	"dh"
E	ε	"e"
Z	ζ	"z"
H	η	"ee"
Θ	θ	"th"
I	ι	"ee"
K	κ	"k"
Λ	λ	"l"
M	μ	"m"
N	ν	"n"
Ξ	ξ	"ks"
O	ο	"o"
Π	π	"p"
P	ρ	"r"
Σ	σ, ς	"s"
T	τ	"t"
Y	υ	"ee"
Φ	φ	"f"
X	χ	"kh"
Ψ	ψ	"ps"
Ω	ω	"o"

σπαράγγι (το) asparagus
Σπάρτη (η) Sparta
σπεσιαλιτέ today's special dish
Σπέτσαι/ες (οι) Spetses
σπηλιά (η) cave
σπίρτο (το) match
σπίτι (το) house
σπονδυλική στήλη spine
σπορ (τα) sports
Σποράδες (οι) Sporades
σπουδάζω to study
σπρώχνω to push
σπυρί (το) boil (*abscess*)
σταγόνα (η) drop
στάδιο (το) stadium
σταθμαρχείο (το) stationmaster
στάθμευση/σις (η) parking
 ‖ στάθμευση αυτοκινήτων car parking
 ‖ ανώτατος χρόνος σταθμεύσεως
maximum parking time ‖ απαγορεύεται
η στάθμευση no parking ‖ μη
σταθμεύετε no parking ‖ χώρος
σταθμεύσεως parking area
σταθμός (ο) station ‖ μετεωρολογικός
σταθμός weather centre
 ‖ πυροσβεστικός σταθμός fire station
 ‖ σιδηροδρομικός σταθμός railway
station
σταματώ to stop
στάση/σις (η) stop ‖ στάση εργασίας
strike, stoppage ‖ στάση ΗΛΠΑΠ
trolley bus stop ‖ στάση λεωφορείου
bus stop
σταύλος (ο) stable
σταυροδρόμι (το) crossroads
σταυρόλεξο (το) crossword puzzle
σταυρός (ο) cross
σταφίδα (η) raisin
σταφύλι (το) grapes
στέγη (η) roof
στεγνοκαθαριστήριο (το) dry cleaner's

A	α	"a"
B	β	"v"
Γ	γ	"gh" *or* "y"
Δ	δ	"dh"
E	ε	"e"
Z	ζ	"z"
H	η	"ee"
Θ	θ	"th"
I	ι	"ee"
K	κ	"k"
Λ	λ	"l"
M	μ	"m"
N	ν	"n"
Ξ	ξ	"ks"
O	ο	"o"
Π	π	"p"
P	ρ	"r"
Σ	σ, ς	"s"
T	τ	"t"
Y	υ	"ee"
Φ	φ	"f"
X	χ	"kh"
Ψ	ψ	"ps"
Ω	ω	"o"

στεγνώνω to dry
στέκομαι to stand up; to stand still
στέλνω to send
στενάζω to sigh
στενός/ή/ό narrow
στέρεος/α/ο firm
στήθος (το) breast, chest
στηρίζομαι to lean against
στιγμή (η) moment || **μια στιγμή** just a
  moment
στιφάδο (το) beef stew with onions
στοά (η) arcade
στολίζω to decorate
στόλος (ο) fleet
στόμα (το) mouth
στομάχι (το) stomach
στρατιώτης (ο) soldier
στρείδι (το) oyster
στρίφωμα (το) hem (*of dress etc*)
στρογγυλός/ή/ό round
στροφή (η) turn
στρώμα (το) mattress
συγγενής (ο/η) relative
συγγνώμη sorry
συγκοινωνία (η) transport
συγχαρητήρια congratulations
συγχωρώ: με συγχωρείτε excuse me
σύζυγος (ο/η) husband/wife
συκιά (η) fig tree
σύκο (το) fig
συκώτι (το) liver
συλλέκτης (ο) collector
συλλογή (η) collection
συμβουλεύω to advise
συμβουλή (η) advice
συμπεριλαμβάνω to include
συμπεριφορά (η) behaviour
συμπλέκτης (ο) clutch (*of car*)
συμπληρώνω to fill in
σύμπτωμα (το) symptom
συμφωνία (η) agreement

A	α	"a"
B	β	"v"
Γ	γ	"gh" *or* "y"
Δ	δ	"dh"
E	ε	"e"
Z	ζ	"z"
H	η	"ee"
Θ	θ	"th"
I	ι	"ee"
K	κ	"k"
Λ	λ	"l"
M	μ	"m"
N	ν	"n"
Ξ	ξ	"ks"
O	ο	"o"
Π	π	"p"
P	ρ	"r"
Σ	σ, ς	"s"
T	τ	"t"
Y	υ	"ee"
Φ	φ	"f"
X	χ	"kh"
Ψ	ψ	"ps"
Ω	ω	"o"

συμφωνώ to agree

συνάλλαγμα (το) foreign exchange || **δήλωση συναλλάγματος** currency declaration || **τιμή συναλλάγματος** rate of foreign exchange

συνάντηση (η) meeting

συναυλία (η) concert

συνεργείο (το) workshop || **συνεργείο αυτοκινήτων** car repairs

συνεχίζω to continue

συνήθεια (η) habit

συνήθως usually

συνθήκες (οι) conditions

σύννεφο (το) cloud

σύνολο (το) total

σύνορα (τα) border, frontier

συνταγή (η) doctor's prescription; recipe

σύνταγμα (το) constitution || **Πλατεία Συντάγματος** Constitution Square (*in Athens*)

σύνταξη (η) pension

συντηρητικά (τα) preservatives

σύντομα soon

συντροφιά (η) company; companionship

σύρατε pull

σύρμα (το) wire

Σύρος (η) Syros

συρτάρι (το) drawer

συσκευασία (η) packing

σύστημα κλιματισμού air conditioning

συστημένη επιστολή registered letter

συχνά often

σφίγγω to squeeze

σφουγγάρι (το) sponge

σφράγισμα (το) filling (*in tooth*)

σφυγμός (ο) pulse

σχεδιάζω to plan

σχεδόν nearly

σχήμα (το) form, shape

σχηματίζω to form || **σχηματίστε τον**

Α	α	"a"
Β	β	"v"
Γ	γ	"gh" *or* "y"
Δ	δ	"dh"
Ε	ε	"e"
Ζ	ζ	"z"
Η	η	"ee"
Θ	θ	"th"
Ι	ι	"ee"
Κ	κ	"k"
Λ	λ	"l"
Μ	μ	"m"
Ν	ν	"n"
Ξ	ξ	"ks"
Ο	ο	"o"
Π	π	"p"
Ρ	ρ	"r"
Σ	σ, ς	"s"
Τ	τ	"t"
Υ	υ	"ee"
Φ	φ	"f"
Χ	χ	"kh"
Ψ	ψ	"ps"
Ω	ω	"o"

αριθμό dial the number
σχοινί (το) rope
σχολείο (το) school
σχολή (η) school || **σχολή οδηγών**
driving school
σώμα (το) body
σωσίβιο (το) life jacket || **ατομικό**
σωσίβιο personal life jacket || **παιδικά**
σωσίβια children's life jackets
σωστά correctly
σωφέρ (ο) chauffeur

Τ, τ

ταβέρνα (η) tavern
τάβλι (το) backgammon
ταγιέρ (το) woman's suit
ταινία (η) film; strip; tape
τακούνι (το) heel (*of shoe*)
τακτικά frequently
τακτοποιώ to arrange
ταλαιπωρία (η) difficulty, trouble
ταμείο (το) cashier's desk, till
ταμίας (ο/η) cashier
ταμιευτήριο (το) savings bank
ταξί (το) taxi || **αγοραίο ταξί** taxi
without a meter, fare to be agreed ||
γραφείο ταξί taxi office
ταξίδι (το) journey, tour || **ταξιδιωτικό**
γραφείο travel agent || **οργανωμένα**
ταξίδια organised tours || **πρακτορείο**
ταξιδίων travel agent
ταξιθέτης/τρια theatre attendant
ταπεινός/ή/ό humble
ταπέτο (το) rug
ταπετσαρία (η) upholstery
ταραμοσαλάτα (η) taramosalata (*dish*
containing roe, often served as a starter)
ταράτσα (η) roof

A	α	"a"
B	β	"v"
Γ	γ	"gh" *or* "y"
Δ	δ	"dh"
E	ε	"e"
Z	ζ	"z"
H	η	"ee"
Θ	θ	"th"
I	ι	"ee"
K	κ	"k"
Λ	λ	"l"
M	μ	"m"
N	ν	"n"
Ξ	ξ	"ks"
O	o	"o"
Π	π	"p"
P	ρ	"r"
Σ	σ, ς	"s"
T	τ	"t"
Y	υ	"ee"
Φ	φ	"f"
X	χ	"kh"
Ψ	ψ	"ps"
Ω	ω	"o"

ταραχή (η) disturbance
τασάκι (το) ashtray
Ταΰγετος (ο) Taygetos
ταύρος (ο) bull
ταυτότητα (η) identity card
τάφος (ο) grave
ταχεία (η) express train
ταχυδρομείο (το) post office
‖ **Ελληνικά ταχυδρομεία** Greek post office ‖ **ταχυδρομικά (τέλη)** postage
‖ **ταχυδρομικές επιταγές** postal orders
‖ **ταχυδρομικός κώδικας** post code
‖ **ταχυδρομικώς** by post
ταχύμετρο (το) speedometer
ταχύτητα, ταχύτης (η) speed ‖ **η ταχύτης ελέγχεται με ραντάρ** radar speed check ‖ **κιβώτιο ταχυτήτων** gearbox
τελειώνω to finish
τελετή (η) ceremony
τελευταίος/α/ο last
τελικά finally
τέλος (το) end; tax, duty ‖ **ταχυδρομικά τέλη** postage
τελωνείο (το) customs
τεμπέλης/α lazy
τέννις (το) tennis
τέντα (η) tent
τέρας (το) monster
τεράστιος/α/ο huge
τέρμα (το) terminus
τέσσερα four (*with neuter nouns*)
τέσσερες four (*with masculine and feminine nouns*)
Τετάρτη Wednesday
τέταρτος/η/ο fourth
τετράδιο (το) exercise book
τεύχος (το) issue
τέχνασμα (το) trick
τέχνη (η) art ‖ **λαϊκή τέχνη** folk art
τεχνητώς κεχρωσμένο contains

Α	α	"a"
Β	β	"v"
Γ	γ	"gh" *or* "y"
Δ	δ	"dh"
Ε	ε	"e"
Ζ	ζ	"z"
Η	η	"ee"
Θ	θ	"th"
Ι	ι	"ee"
Κ	κ	"k"
Λ	λ	"l"
Μ	μ	"m"
Ν	ν	"n"
Ξ	ξ	"ks"
Ο	ο	"o"
Π	π	"p"
Ρ	ρ	"r"
Σ	σ, ς	"s"
Τ	τ	"t"
Υ	υ	"ee"
Φ	φ	"f"
Χ	χ	"kh"
Ψ	ψ	"ps"
Ω	ω	"o"

artificial colourings
τεχνολογία (η) technology
τζάκι (το) fireplace
τζάμι (το) window pane
τζαμί (το) mosque
τζατζίκι (το) tsatsiki (*starter containing
yogurt, cucumber and garlic*)
τζόκεϋ (ο) jockey
τηγάνι (το) frying pan
τηγανίζω to fry
τηγανίτα (η) pancake
τηλεγράφημα (το) telegram
τηλεόραση (η) television
τηλεπικοινωνίες (οι) tele-
communications || **Οργανισμός
Τηλεπικοινωνιών Ελλάδος** Greek
Telecommunications
τηλεφώνημα (το) telephone call
τηλέφωνο (το) telephone
|| **τηλεφωνικός κατάλογος** telephone
directory || **τηλεφωνικός κώδικας**
dialling code || **υπεραστικά τηλέφωνα**
long distance calls
Τήλος (η) Tilos
Τήνος (η) Tinos
της her || **τα μαλλιά της** her hair
τι; what? || **τι είναι;** what is it?
τιμάριθμος (ο) cost of living
τιμή (η) price; honour || **τιμή
εισιτηρίου** price of a ticket, fare
τίμιος/α/ο honest
τιμοκατάλογος (ο) price list
τιμολόγιο (το) invoice
τιμόνι (το) steering wheel
τιμωρία (η) punishment
τιμωρώ to punish
τινάζω to shake
τίποτα nothing
τίτλος (ο) title
τμήμα (το) department; police station
το it; the (*with neuter nouns*)

Α	α	"a"
Β	β	"v"
Γ	γ	"gh" *or* "y"
Δ	δ	"dh"
Ε	ε	"e"
Ζ	ζ	"z"
Η	η	"ee"
Θ	θ	"th"
Ι	ι	"ee"
Κ	κ	"k"
Λ	λ	"l"
Μ	μ	"m"
Ν	ν	"n"
Ξ	ξ	"ks"
Ο	ο	"o"
Π	π	"p"
Ρ	ρ	"r"
Σ	σ, ς	"s"
Τ	τ	"t"
Υ	υ	"ee"
Φ	φ	"f"
Χ	χ	"kh"
Ψ	ψ	"ps"
Ω	ω	"o"

τοιχοκόλληση (η) bill posting
τοίχος (ο) wall
τόκος (ο) interest (*bank*) || **τόκος καταθέσεων** interest on deposits
τολμηρός/ή/ό daring
τόνικ (το) tonic
τόνος (ο) ton; tuna fish; tone of voice
τοξικομανής (ο/η) drug addict
τοπείο (το) landscape
τόπι (το) ball
τόπος (ο) place
τόσο so much
τοστ (το) toasted sandwich
τότε then
του his || **το σακκάκι του** his jacket
τουαλέτα (η) bathroom, toilet
τουρισμός (ο) tourism
τουρίστας/στρια tourist
τουριστικά: τουριστικά είδη souvenirs || **τουριστική αστυνομία** tourist police
Τουρκία (η) Turkey
τουρσί (το) pickle
τραγούδι (το) song
τραγωδία (η) tragedy
τραίνο (το) train
τρανζίστορ (το) portable radio
τράπεζα (η) bank
τραπεζαρία (η) dining room
τραπέζι (το) table
τραπεζομάντηλο (το) tablecloth
τραύμα (το) injury
τρεις three (*with masculine and feminine nouns*)
τρελός/ή/ό mad
τρέμω to tremble
τρέχω to run
τρία three (*with neuter nouns*)
τριάντα thirty
τριαντάφυλλο (το) rose
τρίβω to rub
τρίγωνο (το) triangle

A	α	"a"
B	β	"v"
Γ	γ	"gh" *or* "y"
Δ	δ	"dh"
E	ε	"e"
Z	ζ	"z"
H	η	"ee"
Θ	θ	"th"
I	ι	"ee"
K	κ	"k"
Λ	λ	"l"
M	μ	"m"
N	ν	"n"
Ξ	ξ	"ks"
O	ο	"o"
Π	π	"p"
P	ρ	"r"
Σ	σ, ς	"s"
T	τ	"t"
Y	υ	"ee"
Φ	φ	"f"
X	χ	"kh"
Ψ	ψ	"ps"
Ω	ω	"o"

Τρίπολη/ις (η) Tripoli
Τρίτη (η) Tuesday
τρίτος/η/ο third
τρίχα (η) hair
τρόλλεϋ (το) trolley bus
τρομάρα (η) fright
τρομερός/ή/ό terrible
τρομοκρατία (η) terrorism
τροφή (η) food
τροχαία (η) traffic police
τροχόσπιτο (το) caravan
τροχοφόρο (το) vehicle
τρύγος (ο) grape harvest
τρύπα (η) hole
τρώγω, τρώω to eat
τσαγιέρα (η) teapot
τσάι (το) tea
τσακίζω to smash
τσαλακώνω to crease
τσαμπί (το) bunch of grapes
τσάντα (η) bag
τσαντάκι (το) purse
τσέπη (η) pocket
τσιγάρο (το) cigarette
τσιμπώ to pinch
τσιρίζω to scream
τσίρκο (το) circus
τυπογραφείο (το) printer's
τύπος (ο) press, newspapers
τυρί (το) cheese
τυρόπιτες (οι) cheese pies || **τυρόπιτες σφολιάτα** flaky pastry cheese pies
τυφλός/ή/ό blind
τυχερός/ή/ό lucky
τύχη (η) luck
τώρα now

A	α	"a"
B	β	"v"
Γ	γ	"gh" or "y"
Δ	δ	"dh"
E	ε	"e"
Z	ζ	"z"
H	η	"ee"
Θ	θ	"th"
I	ι	"ee"
K	κ	"k"
Λ	λ	"l"
M	μ	"m"
N	ν	"n"
Ξ	ξ	"ks"
O	ο	"o"
Π	π	"p"
P	ρ	"r"
Σ	σ, ς	"s"
T	τ	"t"
Y	υ	"ee"
Φ	φ	"f"
X	χ	"kh"
Ψ	ψ	"ps"
Ω	ω	"o"

Υ, υ

υγεία (η) health || **στην υγειά σας** your health, cheers
υγειονομικός έλεγχος health inspection
Ύδρα (η) Hydra
υδραγωγείο (το) water reservoir
υιοθεσία (η) adoption
υλικό (το) material
Υμηττός (ο) Mount Hymettos; dry red or white table wine from Athens
ύμνος (ο) hymn, anthem || **εθνικός ύμνος** national anthem
υπερασπίζω to defend
υπεραστικό: υπεραστικό τηλεφώνημα long distance call || **υπεραστικό λεωφορείο** coach
υπερβάλλω to exaggerate
υπερήφανος/η/ο proud
υπερνικώ to overcome
υπέροχος/η/ο excellent
υπερφυσικός/ή/ό supernatural
υπερωκεάνειο (το) liner
υπερωρία (η) overtime
υπεύθυνος/η/ο responsible
υπήκοος (ο/η) citizen
υπηκοότης (η) nationality
υπηρεσία (η) service || **Υπηρεσία φορτώσεως εμπορευμάτων** cargo loading
υπηρέτης (ο) servant
υπηρέτρια (η) maid
ύπνος (ο) sleep
υπνωτικό sleeping pill
υπόγειος/α/ο underground || **υπόγεια διάβαση πεζών** underground pedestrian crossing || **υπόγειος σιδηρόδρομος** underground (*railway*)

A	α	"a"
B	β	"v"
Γ	γ	"gh" *or* "y"
Δ	δ	"dh"
E	ε	"e"
Z	ζ	"z"
H	η	"ee"
Θ	θ	"th"
I	ι	"ee"
K	κ	"k"
Λ	λ	"l"
M	μ	"m"
N	ν	"n"
Ξ	ξ	"ks"
O	ο	"o"
Π	π	"p"
P	ρ	"r"
Σ	σ, ς	"s"
T	τ	"t"
Y	υ	"ee"
Φ	φ	"f"
X	χ	"kh"
Ψ	ψ	"ps"
Ω	ω	"o"

υποδοχή (η) reception || **χώρος υποδοχής** reception (area)
υποθήκη (η) mortgage
υποκατάστημα (το) branch office
υποκρισία (η) hypocrisy
υπολογίζω to calculate
υπόλοιπο (το) remainder
υπομένω to tolerate
υπομονή (η) patience
ύποπτος/η/ο suspect, suspicious
υπόσχεση (η) promise
υπουργείο (το) ministry || **Υπουργείο Οικονομικών** Ministry of Finance || **Υπουργείο Πολιτισμού** Ministry of Culture
υπουργός (ο/η) minister
υποφέρω to suffer
υποχρέωση (η) obligation
υποχωρώ to give way
υποψήφιος/α candidate
ύστερα later
υστερία (η) hysteria
ύφασμα (το) fabric, cloth || **υφάσματα** textiles || **υφάσματα επιπλώσεων** upholstery fabrics
υψηλή τάση high voltage
ύψος (το) height || **ύψος περιορισμένο** height limit
υψώνω to raise

Φ, φ

φαγητό (το) food
φαγούρα (η) itching
φαΐ (το) food
φάκελλος (ο) envelope
φακός (ο) lens || **φακοί επαφής** contact lenses
φαλάκρα (η) baldness

A	α	"a"
B	β	"v"
Γ	γ	"gh" _or_ "y"
Δ	δ	"dh"
E	ε	"e"
Z	ζ	"z"
H	η	"ee"
Θ	θ	"th"
I	ι	"ee"
K	κ	"k"
Λ	λ	"l"
M	μ	"m"
N	ν	"n"
Ξ	ξ	"ks"
O	o	"o"
Π	π	"p"
P	ρ	"r"
Σ	σ, ς	"s"
T	τ	"t"
Y	υ	"ee"
Φ	φ	"f"
X	χ	"kh"
Ψ	ψ	"ps"
Ω	ω	"o"

φανέλλα (η) vest
φανερός/ή/ό evident
φανερώνω to reveal
φαντασία (η) imagination
φάντασμα (το) ghost
φαράγγι (το) gorge
φαρδύς/ιά/ύ broad
φαρμακείο (το) chemist's
φάρμακο (το) medicine
φάρος (ο) lighthouse
φασαρία (η) commotion
φασιανός (ο) pheasant
φασολάδα (η) boiled haricot beans
φασολάκι (το) green bean
φασόλι (το) haricot bean
Φεβρουάριος (ο) February
φεγγάρι (το) moon
φερμουάρ (το) zip
φέρνω to bring
φερρυ μπότ (το) ferry boat
φέτα (η) feta cheese
φεύγω to go away, leave
φθάνω to arrive
φθηνός/ή/ό cheap
φθινόπωρο (το) autumn
φθορά (η) deterioration
φιάλη (η) bottle
φίδι (το) snake
φιλενάδα (η) girlfriend
φιλέτο (το) fillet of meat
φιλί (το) kiss
φιλμ (το) film || εμφανίσεις φιλμ film developing
φιλοδώρημα (το) tip, service charge
φιλοξενία (η) hospitality
φίλος/η friend
φίλτρο (το) filter || φίλτρο αέρος air filter || φίλτρο βενζίνης petrol filter || φίλτρο λαδιού oil filter
φιλώ to kiss
φιστίκι (το) peanut || φιστίκια Αιγίνης

Α	α	"a"
Β	β	"v"
Γ	γ	"gh" or "y"
Δ	δ	"dh"
Ε	ε	"e"
Ζ	ζ	"z"
Η	η	"ee"
Θ	θ	"th"
Ι	ι	"ee"
Κ	κ	"k"
Λ	λ	"l"
Μ	μ	"m"
Ν	ν	"n"
Ξ	ξ	"ks"
Ο	ο	"o"
Π	π	"p"
Ρ	ρ	"r"
Σ	σ, ς	"s"
Τ	τ	"t"
Υ	υ	"ee"
Φ	φ	"f"
Χ	χ	"kh"
Ψ	ψ	"ps"
Ω	ω	"o"

pistachio nuts
φλας (το) flash (*camera*)
φλέβα (η) vein
φλόγα (η) flame
φλυτζάνι (το) cup
φοβάμαι I am afraid
φόβος (ο) fear
φοιτητής/φοιτήτρια student
φοιτητικό εισιτήριο student ticket *or* fare
φόρεμα (το) dress
φορητός/ή/ό portable
φόρος (ο) tax ‖ **συμπεριλαμβανομένων φόρων** including taxes
φορτηγό (το) lorry
φορώ to wear
φουντούκι (το) hazelnut
φούρνος (ο) oven
φουσκώνω to inflate ‖ **φουσκωτά σκάφη** inflatable boats
φούστα (η) skirt
φράουλα (η) strawberry
φράχτης (ο) fence
φρένα (τα) brakes (*in car*)
φρέσκος/ια/ο fresh
φρουρός (ο) guard
φρούτο (το) fruit
φρουτοσαλάτα (η) fruit salad
φρυγανιά (η) toast
φρύδι (το) eyebrow
φτερό (το) feather
φτωχός/ή/ό poor
φύκια (τα) seaweed
φύλακας (ο) guard
φυλακή (η) prison
φυλάκιση (η) imprisonment
φύλλο (το) leaf
φύση (η) nature
φυσικά naturally
φυσιοθεραπεία (η) physiotherapy
φυσώ to blow

A	α	"a"
B	β	"v"
Γ	γ	"gh" *or* "y"
Δ	δ	"dh"
E	ε	"e"
Z	ζ	"z"
H	η	"ee"
Θ	θ	"th"
I	ι	"ee"
K	κ	"k"
Λ	λ	"l"
M	μ	"m"
N	ν	"n"
Ξ	ξ	"ks"
O	o	"o"
Π	π	"p"
P	ρ	"r"
Σ	σ, ς	"s"
T	τ	"t"
Y	υ	"ee"
Φ	φ	"f"
X	χ	"kh"
Ψ	ψ	"ps"
Ω	ω	"o"

φυτό (το) plant
φυτώριο (το) nursery (*for plants*)
φωλιά (η) nest
φωνάζω to shout
φωνή (η) cry; voice
φως (το) light
φωτιά (η) fire
φωτογραφία (η) photograph
 || **έγχρωμες φωτογραφίες** colour
 photographs
φωτογραφίζω to take photographs || **μη**
 φωτογραφίζετε no photographs
φωτογραφική μηχανή camera
φωτόμετρο (το) light meter
φωτοτυπία (η) photocopy

Χ, χ

χαίρετε hello
χαίρομαι I am glad
χαλάζι (το) hail
Χαλκιδική (η) Halkidiki
χαλκός (ο) copper
χαμηλά low; down
χαμογελώ to smile
Χανιά (τα) Hania
χάνω to lose
χάπι (το) pill
χαρά (η) pleasure
χαρούμενος/η/ο pleased, glad
χάρτης (ο) map || **οδικός χάρτης** road
 map
χαρτί (το) paper
χαρτικά (τα) stationery
χαρτονόμισμα (το) note (*money*)
χαρτοπωλείο stationer's shop
χαρτόσημο (το) stamp tax
χασάπης (ο) butcher
χασάπικο (το) butcher's shop

A	α	"a"
B	β	"v"
Γ	γ	"gh" *or* "y"
Δ	δ	"dh"
E	ε	"e"
Z	ζ	"z"
H	η	"ee"
Θ	θ	"th"
I	ι	"ee"
K	κ	"k"
Λ	λ	"l"
M	μ	"m"
N	ν	"n"
Ξ	ξ	"ks"
O	ο	"o"
Π	π	"p"
P	ρ	"r"
Σ	σ, ς	"s"
T	τ	"t"
Y	υ	"ee"
Φ	φ	"f"
X	χ	"kh"
Ψ	ψ	"ps"
Ω	ω	"o"

χειμώνας (ο) winter
χειραψία (η) handshake
χειροκρότημα (το) applause
χειροποίητος/η/ο handmade
χειρούργος (ο) surgeon
χειρόφρενο (το) handbrake
χέλι (το) eel
χελιδόνι (το) swallow (*bird*)
χέρι (το) hand
χερσόνησος (η) peninsula
χήνα (η) goose
χήρα (η) widow
χήρος (ο) widower
χθες yesterday
χίλια one thousand || **δυο χιλιάδες** two thousand
χιλιόμετρο (το) kilometre
χιόνι (το) snow
Χίος (η) Chios
χιούμορ (το) humour
χοιρινό (το) pork
χονδρικός/ή/ό wholesale || **χονδρική πώληση** wholesale
χοντρός/ή/ό fat
χορεύω to dance
χορός (ο) dance
χόρτο (το) grass; green vegetable
χορτοφάγος (ο/η) vegetarian
χορωδία (η) choir
χουρμάς (ο) date (*fruit*)
χρειάζομαι I need
χρεώνω to charge
χρήματα (τα) money
χρηματοκιβώτιο (το) safe (*for valuables*)
χρήση (η) use || **άσκοπη χρήση διώκεται ποινικώς** anyone making improper use will be prosecuted || **οδηγίες χρήσεως** instructions for use
χρησιμοποιώ to use
χρήσιμος/η/ο useful

A	α	"a"
B	β	"v"
Γ	γ	"gh" *or* "y"
Δ	δ	"dh"
E	ε	"e"
Z	ζ	"z"
H	η	"ee"
Θ	θ	"th"
I	ι	"ee"
K	κ	"k"
Λ	λ	"l"
M	μ	"m"
N	ν	"n"
Ξ	ξ	"ks"
O	ο	"o"
Π	π	"p"
P	ρ	"r"
Σ	σ, ς	"s"
T	τ	"t"
Y	υ	"ee"
Φ	φ	"f"
X	χ	"kh"
Ψ	ψ	"ps"
Ω	ω	"o"

χριστιανός/ή Christian
Χριστούγεννα (τα) Christmas
χρόνος (ο) time; year
χρυσάφι (το) gold
χρυσαφικά (τα) jewellery
χρυσός/ή/ό (made of) gold || **Χρυσός Οδηγός** Yellow Pages
χρώμα (το) colour
χτένα (η) comb
χτες yesterday
χτυπώ to strike, knock
χύμα not bottled || **κρασί χύμα** house wine
χυμός (ο) juice || **χυμός λεμονιού** lemon juice || **χυμός πορτοκάλι** orange juice
χύνω to spill
χώμα (το) soil, earth
χώρα (η) country
χωράφι (το) field
χωριάτικη σαλάτα Greek salad
χωριάτικο ψωμί village bread
χωριό (το) village
χωρίς without || **χωρίς εισπράκτορα** exact fare, no change given
χωρισμένη (η) divorced woman
χωρισμένος (ο) divorced man
χωριστά separately
χώρος (ο) area, site || **αρχαιολογικός χώρος** archaeological site || **ιδιωτικός χώρος** private || **χώρος αλιευτικών σκαφών** for fishing boats only || **χώρος αποσκευών** car boot || **χώρος σταθμεύσεως** parking area || **χώρος υποδοχής** reception area

Α	α	"a"
Β	β	"v"
Γ	γ	"gh" *or* "y"
Δ	δ	"dh"
Ε	ε	"e"
Ζ	ζ	"z"
Η	η	"ee"
Θ	θ	"th"
Ι	ι	"ee"
Κ	κ	"k"
Λ	λ	"l"
Μ	μ	"m"
Ν	ν	"n"
Ξ	ξ	"ks"
Ο	ο	"o"
Π	π	"p"
Ρ	ρ	"r"
Σ	σ, ς	"s"
Τ	τ	"t"
Υ	υ	"ee"
Φ	φ	"f"
Χ	χ	"kh"
Ψ	ψ	"ps"
Ω	ω	"o"

Ψ, ψ

ψάθα (η) straw mat
ψάθινος/η/ο of straw
ψαλίδι (το) scissors
ψαράς (ο) fisherman
ψάρεμα (το) fishing
ψάρι (το) fish
ψαρόβαρκα (η) fishing boat
ψαρόσουπα (η) fish soup
ψαροταβέρνα (η) fish tavern
ψέμα (το) lie
ψηλά high up
ψηλός/ή/ό tall
ψημένος/η/ο cooked
ψήνω to cook
ψησταριά (η) rotisserie, shop selling
  spit-roasted poultry and meat
ψητός/ή/ό roast
ψιλά (τα) small change
ψιλικά (τα) haberdashery
ψυγείο (το) fridge
ψυγειοκαταψύκτης (ο) fridge-freezer
ψύλλος (ο) flea
ψύχρα (η) chilly weather
ψυχραιμία (η) self-control
ψωμάκι (το) bread roll
ψωμάς (ο) baker
ψωμί (το) bread || **ψωμί χωριάτικο**
  village bread
ψώνια (τα) shopping

A	α	"a"
B	β	"v"
Γ	γ	"gh" *or* "y"
Δ	δ	"dh"
E	ε	"e"
Z	ζ	"z"
H	η	"ee"
Θ	θ	"th"
I	ι	"ee"
K	κ	"k"
Λ	λ	"l"
M	μ	"m"
N	ν	"n"
Ξ	ξ	"ks"
O	o	"o"
Π	π	"p"
P	ρ	"r"
Σ	σ, ς	"s"
T	τ	"t"
Y	υ	"ee"
Φ	φ	"f"
X	χ	"kh"
Ψ	ψ	"ps"
Ω	ω	"o"

Ω, ω

ωδείο (το) music school
ωθήσατε push
ώμος (ο) shoulder
ωμός/ή/ό uncooked
ωραίος/α/ο beautiful, handsome
ώριμος/η/ο ripe, mature
ώσπου until
ωτοστόπ (το) hitch-hiking
ωφέλεια (η) benefit
ώρα (η) time ‖ **ώρες εισόδου του**
κοινού opening hours for the public
‖ **ώρες επισκέψεως** visiting hours
‖ **ώρες λειτουργίας** opening hours
‖ **ώρες συναλλαγής** banking hours
‖ **της ώρας** freshly cooked (*food*)

Α	α	"a"
Β	β	"v"
Γ	γ	"gh" *or* "y"
Δ	δ	"dh"
Ε	ε	"e"
Ζ	ζ	"z"
Η	η	"ee"
Θ	θ	"th"
Ι	ι	"ee"
Κ	κ	"k"
Λ	λ	"l"
Μ	μ	"m"
Ν	ν	"n"
Ξ	ξ	"ks"
Ο	ο	"o"
Π	π	"p"
Ρ	ρ	"r"
Σ	σ, ς	"s"
Τ	τ	"t"
Υ	υ	"ee"
Φ	φ	"f"
Χ	χ	"kh"
Ψ	ψ	"ps"
Ω	ω	"o"

The innovative colour layout of Collins bilingual Pocket Dictionaries leads you quickly and easily to the word you want to translate, while our user-friendly system of differentiating meanings ensures that you choose the most accurate translation.

Frequently-used words are given special treatment and the unique dictionary skills supplement helps you get the most out of your dictionary.

With over 40,000 references and 70,000 translations, the fully up-to-date wordlists cover all the vocabulary you will need for any everyday situation and more – and all this in a compact and practical format.